KINGS' MEN

For Barbara Penny, who died in Canberra on 30 June 1982; her example of grace, courage and scholarship remains

KINGS' MEN

*Australia's Governors-General
from Hopetoun to Isaacs*

CHRISTOPHER CUNNEEN

GEORGE ALLEN & UNWIN
SYDNEY LONDON BOSTON

First published in 1983 by
George Allen & Unwin Australia Pty Ltd
8 Napier Street, North Sydney, NSW 2060 Australia

George Allen & Unwin (Publishers) Ltd
Park Lane, Hemel Hempstead, Herts HP2 4TE,
England

Allen & Unwin Inc.
9 Winchester Terrace, Winchester, Mass 01890 USA

National Library of Australia
Cataloguing-in-Publication entry:

Cunneen, Christopher, 1940–
    King's men, Australia's Governors-General
    from Hopetoun to Isaacs.

    Bibliography.
    Includes index.
    ISBN 0 86861 238 3 hardback
    ISBN 0 86861 013 3 paperback

    1. Australia-Governors-General. 2.
    Australia-Governors-History. 3.
    Australia-Politics and government-
    1901–1945. I. Title.
354. 9403'12

Library of Congress Catalog Card Number: 83–71293

Set in 10/11.5 Plantin by
Graphicraft Typesetters Limited, Hong Kong
Printed in Hong Kong by
Bright Sun Printing Co. Ltd.

185—981 X

Contents

Chronology

	Governor-General	Prime Minister	Secretary of State
1901	Hopetoun, 1 Jan.	Barton, 1 Jan.	Joseph Chamberlain, (from 1895)
1902	Tennyson, 17 Jul. (acting)		
1903		Deakin, 24 Sep.	Alfred Lyttelton, 6 Oct.
1904	Northcote, 21 Jan.	Watson, 27 Apr.	
		Reid, 18 Aug.	
1905		Deakin, 5 Jul.	Earl of Elgin, 10 Dec.
1906			
1907			
1908	Dudley, 9 Sep.	Fisher, 13 Nov.	Earl of Crewe, 12 Apr.
1909		Deakin, 2 Jun.	
1910		Fisher, 29 Apr.	Lewis Harcourt, 3 Nov.
1911	Denman, 31 Jul.		
1912			
1913		Cook, 24 Jun.	
1914	Munro Ferguson, 18 May	Fisher, 17 Sep.	
1915		Hughes, 27 Oct.	Andrew Bonar Law, 25 May
1916			Walter Long, 10 Dec.
1917			
1918			
1919			Viscount Milner, 10 Jan.
1920	Forster, 6 Oct.		
1921			Winston Churchill, 13 Feb.
1922			Duke of Devonshire, 24 Oct.
1923		Bruce, 9 Feb.	
1924			J.H. Thomas, 24 Jan.
			L.S. Amery, 6 Nov.
1925	Stonehaven, 8 Oct.		
1926			
1927			
1928			
1929		Scullin, 22 Oct.	Lord Passfield 7 Jun.
1930			J.H. Thomas 5 Jun.
1931	Isaacs, 23 Jan.		
1932		Lyons, 6 Jan.	
1933			
1934			
1935			M. MacDonald 22 Nov.
1936	Gowrie, 23 Jan.		

Illustrations

Preface

When in 1970 I began to work on the history of Australian governors-general, I looked up the definitive work on *The Parliamentary Government of the Commonwealth of Australia* by Professor L.F. Crisp and found:

> The history of the Governor-Generalship of Australia . . . has been the history of sure and steady erosion of the small initial deposit of personal initiative and discretion vested in the holders of the office. In becoming, politically, ever more innocuous and unobtrusive — and provided it does not seek to become socially too pretentious — it constitutes an ever more satisfactory formal keystone to the constitutional arch.

The theory of sure and steady erosion was to colour my research until November 1975.

This book is based on a PhD thesis submitted at the Australian National University under a Commonwealth postgraduate scholarship in August 1973. I therefore had the opportunity of perceptively foreshadowing the political powers of governors-general. Unfortunately, the thesis reveals no such insight. But, being wise after the event, I can now present a book which, in surveying the history of the governor-generalship of Australia up to 1936, avoids the assumption that its political power gradually atrophied. On the contrary in the early decades of the Australian Commonwealth governors-general exercised their constitutional powers on several occasions. But rarely was this accompanied by controversy or even scrutiny. This was because the chief function of the office was its Imperial rather than its constitutional role.

I owe a great debt to my supervisor, Barbara Penny, for her suggestion that the topic would suit my interest in Australia's British connection and for her encouragement and advice. I thank Professor Manning Clark for giving me the opportunity to undertake full-time study; Dr J.J. Eddy, SJ, for wise counsel; Dr I.M. Cumpston for early guidance; Sir Zelman Cowen, Barry Smith, Gerry Walsh, Ian Marsh, Dick Hall, Heather Radi, George Winterton, John Iremonger and Warren Osmond for suggesting improvements to the manuscript; Allan Martin for help with the notes; John Poynter for generously sharing his research; Kerry Regan and Jim Davidson for proof-reading; Ivy Meere for typing and Bede Nairn, Geoffrey Serle and my colleagues at the *Australian Dictionary of Biography* for their friendship and support. I thank my parents and friends for their forbearance.

I have been helped by the librarians and staff of the National Library of Australia, and the Australian War Memorial, Canberra; the La Trobe Library, Melbourne; the Mitchell Library, Sydney; the Chifley and Menzies libraries at the Australian National University; and the Australian Archives offices in Canberra and Melbourne. I am grateful to the Marquis of Linlithgow for making available to me, through Mr Basil Skinner of the Department of Educational Studies, University of Edinburgh, papers of the first Marquis of Linlithgow. Miss V.J. Ledger undertook research on my behalf in London. Material was also provided by the Manuscript Division of the Public Archives of Canada, Ottawa, and by the Birmingham University Library, Birmingham.

In the course of a six-week research trip to Britain in 1981 I was helped by the Cambridge University Library; Churchill College Archives, Cambridge; the Bodleian Library, Oxford; the National Library of Scotland, Edinburgh; and the British Library and the Public Record Office, London. I am indebted to Lady Wardington, Lady Burrell, Lord Denman, the Earl of Dudley, the Earl of Iddesleigh, the Marquis of Linlithgow and Mr Tom Barlow for their generosity and interest in my work, and especially to Mr and Mrs A.B.L. Munro Ferguson for their friendly hospitality. Others to whom I owe warm thanks are Graeme Powell, Jill Waterhouse, Miles and Alison Hobart-Hampden, Patricia and John Dent and Meg and Jonathon Bell. I owe a great deal to Bill and Tricia Crowley.

For permission to reproduce illustrations I am grateful to: Parliament House, Canberra, for the front and back cover; the National Library of Australia for illustrations 1, 3, 4, 10, 11, 12, 13, 17, 20, 22, 23, 24a & 24b and 27, and for the front and back end papers; the Mitchell Library, Sydney, for 2, 8, 9, and 21; the State Library of South Australia for 6, 7 and 18; the Royal Military College Archives, Duntroon, for 15 and 26; the Archives Office, State Library of Tasmania for 19; and the Honourable Lady Burrell for 14. Illustrations 5 and 16 are from the *Bulletin*, Sydney, and 25 from the *Evening Standard*, London. I regret that the quality of some illustrations cannot be remedied in reproduction.

I am also grateful to Mrs J. Macgowen for permission to reproduce the letter on pages 179–81.

Canberra 1983

1 'Grand Seigneur to the tips of his fingers'

Sydney on the morning of Tuesday 1 January 1901 was wet and bedraggled. A heavy downpour the previous evening had dampened the New Years Eve celebrations. Showers continued into the morning, causing the flags and bunting with which the city was decked to droop soddenly from the standards and the paint on the newly erected triumphal arches to run on to the pavement. But by 9 o'clock the weather had cleared. A strong north-easterly breeze dried out the banners while workmen repaired the damage to the decorations, and the citizens of Sydney, armed with umbrellas and mackintoshes, began to gather in the city streets.

It was the start of a week-long festival of celebration. Visitors had booked out all hotels. The crowds which began to take up vantage points in the city from the early hours of New Years Day settled down to wait for the parade. At Centennial Park others were assembling to witness the formal ceremony of Australia's accession to nationhood: the swearing in of the governor-general and his ministers.

The spectacle commenced in the city at 10.30 a.m. Two hundred mounted policemen trotted into Macquarie Street to commence the five-mile parade through the packed streets. The cavalcade was a representative selection of colonial society. Early in the ranks came the railway band leading the Trades Union representatives. Overalled silver miners from Broken Hill, oil lamps in their hats and carrying picks, marched with bakers, who wore their white caps. Fire-brigademen, university officials and judges took part and Commandant Booth led the Salvation Army delegation. Politicians were prominent. While most of the federal leaders from the other colonies passed unrecognised by the Sydney crowd, George Reid, recently premier of the colony of New South Wales, was favoured with especially noisy acclamation.

According to Labor politician William Morris Hughes, 'the outstanding feature of the procession' was the trades section. But that was the portion he had organised. The *Sydney Morning Herald* reported, on the contrary, that 'certain grumblers amongst the crowds complained of the length of the trades part of the procession', while the major attraction was the military contingent. Despite the presence of colonial and federal organisations and individuals, it was predominantly an Imperial occasion. A thousand Imperial troops from a variety of famous regiments had been sent out by the British government to 'give éclat to the historical spectacle' and their vivid display was greeted enthusiastically. Interspersed with the Household Cavalry, in scarlet and steel, and the Indian troops, in spectacular red and emerald green regimentals, were the 'khaki clad centaurs of the Australian contingents', while occasional shafts of sunlight lit the flashing breast-plates and pinions of the Lancers. To one reporter the visiting troops seemed, 'as they were intended to do, to embody our unity with the mother country and identification with its Indian and colonial empire'.

The highest embodiment of this Imperial patriotism was the governor-general, who rode in an open carriage attended by richly dressed postilions and grooms in gold embroidered livery. In full court dress, bowing, and doffing his plumed hat, the Earl of Hopetoun acknowledged the enthusiastic cheers of the crowd. Representative of Queen, Empire and federated Australia, he was the central point of the inaugural ceremonies. The crowd's acclamation for him was a celebration both of Australian nationhood and Imperial patriotism — a dual loyalty represented by the Imperial officer who was to be sworn in as Australian governor-general. Patriotic zeal was augmented by enjoyment of the occasion's colourful theatricality. A wave of enthusiasm and affection had swept Sydney. 'Hopetoun colours were adapted in every possible way ingenuity ... could think of. Corsets (in shopwindows) were laced with them, so were "Hopetoun shoes" displayed in bootmakers shops. Cakes were quartered with the buff and blue. Horses wore rosettes, dogs' tails flaunted them.'

The climax of the day's activities was reached when Hopetoun was sworn in — 'first Governor-General of the newest born of nations'. The ceremony took place at Centennial Park, echoing the centenary celebrations of 1888. At 1 o'clock the great crowd (more than 100 000, according to the *Herald*) saw the governor-general mount the steps of an ornate, open pavilion. Its platform was a huge block of granite, six-sided to represent the number of original States, embedded into the earth to remain a permanent indication of the exact spot (now commemorated by a monument) on which the Commonwealth came into being. The archbishop of Sydney offered a prayer composed for the occasion by the absent governor of South Australia, Lord Tennyson, son of the late poet laureate. Then Hopetoun stepped to the table in the pavilion and took the oaths of office. The unfurling of the Royal Standard at the dome and a volley of cannonfire signified the assumption of office of the governor-general and the inauguration of the Commonwealth. This was followed by the swearing in of Prime Minister Edmund Barton and the first cabinet. A chorus of 10 000 children voiced the hopes of all for the future in a song for 'Federated Australia', and the choirs and bands filled the air with 'O God our help in ages past'.

At the week-long celebrations which followed, the governor-general was as prominent as his health would allow. He visited Sydney Cricket Ground and saw Victor Trumper bat. He inspected a grand military review of all the Imperial troops assembled in Sydney. On Monday, 7 January, there was a re-enactment of Captain Cook's landing at Kurnell, featuring 25 Aborigines, all over six feet two inches in height, specially sent from Queensland to participate.

In an editorial on 27 December 1900 the Melbourne *Age* described Sydney as 'full of symbols of the Imperial grandeur of which Federated Australia forms only a part'. The celebrations had a meaning beyond 'simple parade and spectacle', speaking 'in eloquent language of the vast strength of that Empire

The inauguration of the Commonwealth. Lord Hopetoun is sworn in as governor-general at Centennial Park, Sydney, on 1 January 1901.

which an ignorant Boer autocracy recently threatened and attempted to overthrow'. Newspaper reports of the inauguration ceremony spoke proudly of nationhood achieved without the spilling of blood. But behind the glitter of the Household Cavalry was the reality of the war in South Africa. Australian lives were being lost on the Veldt as the Australian Commonwealth 'emerged from the dim shades of the upbuilding to take its bright place in the world of free-born British men'.

John Adrian Louis Hope, seventh Earl of Hopetoun, was a young-looking man, clean shaven (though later in his term he grew a moustache) with a broad, high brow and deep set eyes. Slightly built, he was described by the Sydney *Bulletin* as having a 'willowy stoop and a cat like, Lord Chamberlain's tread'. He was born on 25 September 1860 at Hopetoun House, Queensferry, Scotland, first son of the sixth real. His mother was Etheldred Anne, née Reynardson. After education at Eton, where he was very happy, rowed (but not in a big race) and debated a little, he went to the Royal Military College, Sandhurst, passing in 1879. But he did not enter the army. He later explained: 'the affairs of the family estate, to which I had succeeded at 13, seemed to call for my personal attention'. His one hobby was hunting and he was a fearless rider — 'Probably he had more of his bones broken in the hunting field than any man of his time in England'.

Lord Hopetoun, 1902. Photograph by J.H. Newman Studios, Sydney.

His estate was very large — over forty two and a half thousand acres (17,199 ha) on both sides of the Firth of Forth — and his home, Hopetoun House, near Edinburgh, was a palace. In 1883 he was appointed Conservative whip in the House of Lords, in 1885 lord in waiting to Queen Victoria, and in 1889 lord high commissioner to the general assembly of the Church of Scotland. He had married in 1886 the third daughter of the fourth Baron Ventry, Hersey Alice Eveleigh-de-Moleyns, whom he had known since childhood.

Hopetoun was appointed governor of Victoria in 1889, at a time when, reflecting Britain's more flamboyant pride in Empire, Australian colonial governors began to display a new colour and ostentation. The increased splendour of vice-regal functions was enhanced by a change in the backgrounds of the men selected. Increased interest in Empire had resulted in the appearance of young and wealthy aristocrats in place of the previous career administrators. One observer described them as 'untried and juvenile noblemen'. Sir John

Lady Hopetoun

Robertson, the New South Wales politician, commented: 'they send out boys now'.

In New South Wales the first of the new breed of governor was Lord Carrington, who arrived in December 1885. A close friend of the Prince of Wales, he brought wealth and regal glamour to Sydney society. Government House banquets became lavish and ostentatious affairs. Carrington boasted to the artist, Julian Ashton: 'We've opened enough champagne since I've been here to float a man-of-war in Farm Cove'. Once he had a salmon sent out on ice from England.

Hopetoun's term was the height of the new era in colonial governorships in Victoria. He entered Melbourne in November 1889 in a blue and yellow state carriage, attended by bewigged postilions, footmen and outriders dressed in liveries and knee britches. He entertained extravagantly, treating Melbourne to several spectacular vice-regal galas. For some of the more popular public celebrations, usually during the Melbourne Cup racing season each November, there were often suites of three or more colonial governors ensconced in Melbourne's Government House. Despite colonial astonishment at his habit of using hair-powder, Hopetoun won friends by his fondness for informal horse-back tours of the outback, and youthful enthusiasm for even routine duties.

Hopetoun handled the administration of the colony of Victoria ably during a difficult period of strikes, bank failures, depression and political instability. He stayed longer than the usual term. In contrast, his Sydney contemporary, Lord Jersey, returned early — partly 'influenced by finding that there is less individual power to his office than he had imagined'. Increasingly, the role had become that of local constitutional sovereign, rather than administrator. This reflected developments in the British monarchy during Queen Victoria's reign, as well as the evolving independence of the colonies. Though they may have possessed little individual power, during the 1890s governors retained significant responsibilities.

The powers of Australian governors, and those to be exercised by the governor-general in the new Commonwealth, had been discussed at the constitutional conventions during the 1890s. Objections were sometimes raised to the governor-general's excessive powers. But there were no express safeguards against a governor-general who interpreted his powers undemocratically. This was partly because the relationship of the Australian colonies with Britain was involved. Most Australians accepted that their status was less than full independence and that the Imperial government, acting through its official representative, had to protect Imperial interests. Also the role of the Crown in Britain was itself far from clearly worked out. During Victoria's long reign development towards a constitutional monarchy had taken place, but the reduction of the powers of the Crown had not been enunciated, an uncertainty echoed in the conventions which established the constitution of the Commonwealth of Australia. So far as the role of governor-general was concerned, the result was, as the Hobart *Mercury* remarked in 1891, 'nobody knows what they can and what they cannot do'.

Hopetoun's term in Victoria coincided with important years of the federation movement, and he seized upon the topic of federation as a suitable non-political subject for vice-regal speeches. He was present at the famous banquet in Melbourne in 1890 when Parkes invoked the 'crimson thread of kinship' in support of federation. At a later banquet Hopetoun went so far as to offer to return to Australia as first governor-general. He left Victoria in March 1895 universally liked, even in Sydney where he was afforded an official farewell dinner, unusual for a governor from Melbourne. In 1898 he was offered the post of governor-general of Canada, but declined.

When the time came to select a governor-general to inaugurate the Commonwealth of Australia, Hopetoun's was one of the names most prominent in speculation. By May 1900 no announcement had been made. Barton, leader of the Australian delegation which was in England to pilot the Commonwealth Bill through the Imperial parliament, asked that the appointment be made as soon as possible after the proclamation of the Commonwealth by the Queen. On 13 July 1900, the Colonial Office announced that Her Majesty had graciously approved Hopetoun's appointment. In his submission to the Queen on 10 July the secretary of state for colonies, Joseph Chamberlain, had described Hopetoun as 'exceptionally qualified to discharge the duties of this important position with ability and efficiency', and informed her that the appointment would be 'heartily welcomed' in Australia. There is no direct evidence that Chamberlain consulted the Australian delegation, but Barton was informed of the selection several weeks before the name was submitted to the Queen.

Titled, wealthy, amiable and experienced, Hopetoun was an excellent choice. The one cloud was his poor health. The Australian climate suited him during his Victorian posting, but on his return to Britain he had fallen ill. He told Barton in London in 1900 that he had seen a physician, who had said 'there is nothing to prevent my going out and that I need not fear breaking down'. But he was not altogether frank, for he arranged privately with the secretary of state not to remain in Australia for a full term.

As Chamberlain had anticipated, the appointment of an 'old friend' was generally welcomed in Australia. Some intercolonial jealousy obtruded. The Melbourne press was smugly satisfied that a former governor of Victoria had been selected. In Sydney a few editorialists expressed the parochial sentiment that the appointment was a victory for 'Victorian intrigues in London' and evidence of the 'undue, predominant influence of Melbourne in Federal affairs'. William John Lyne, premier of the mother colony, thought it a mistake that 'a statesman of Cabinet rank' had not been selected. The *Sydney Morning Herald* would have preferred the appointment of a stranger, free of any suspicion of political or colonial bias, to begin a new era. If experience of Australian conditions were a required precondition, the Sydney paper continued, then Hopetoun was the best choice available and New South Wales would have to swallow its intercolonial envy.

In London the most important consideration was Hopetoun's acceptability to the Colonial Office. In his letter of recommendation to the Queen the secretary of state commented that, as governor of Victoria, Hopetoun had 'acquitted himself to the entire satisfaction of Lord Knutsford and Lord Ripon'. He was also a good Tory. After returning from Melbourne he had been paymaster-general in Salisbury's government from 1895 to 1898 and lord chamberlain from 1898 to 1900. His close association with Queen Victoria's court ceremonial augmented his natural tendency to play the *'Grand Seigneur* to the tips of his fingers', as Paul Blouet described him in 1898.

Before leaving London Hopetoun prepared for his assumption of office. A list of questions which he submitted to the Colonial Office revealed some awareness of the problems he would face in Australia. He asked what arrangements were proposed during a governor-general's illness or absence. The reply was that the senior State governor should receive the Dormant Commission. In answer to a request for advice as to the conduct of Executive Council meetings, he was informed that this, and the difficult question of precedence, were matters to be worked out with his ministers. He also requested, and received, instructions as to the formal steps taken in inaugurating the Confederation of Canada in 1867.

Hopetoun also arranged for his suite to proceed to Melbourne. His staff comprised a private secretary, assistant private secretary, military secretary, aide-de-camp, house steward and twenty house servants. In addition there were seventeen horses, thirteen stablemen and his carriages. He later admitted that the whole of his yearly income was expended in paying off the cost of his outfit and the expenses connected with bringing out his establishment. These preparations reveal him to have been seriously out of touch with the predominant desire in the Australian colonies that federation should be cheap.

Hopetoun left England on 4 October. His itinerary showed some of the early difficulties of the post he was taking up, in particular the problem of inter-colonial jealousy. The New South Wales ministry desired that the governor-general disembark at Sydney before setting foot in Melbourne. Pending establishment of a new capital, the senior colony had been forced to recognize Melbourne as the seat of government. Premier Lyne, wishing Sydney to have its share of Imperial pageantry, contemplated 'great public rejoicings' to welcome the governor-general. At the urging of the Colonial Office he agreed that the welcoming ceremony should be incorporated in an inauguration festivity for the Commonwealth. The governor of New South Wales, Lord Beauchamp, vacated Government House and conveniently returned to England to assist Lyne's arrangements.

Careful plans had been laid for the governor-general's arrival in Australian waters. He would land in Fremantle in early December after a short holiday in India. He and Lady Hopetoun would leave the mail vessel for a one day visit to Perth and then embark on the flagship of the Australian Squadron, the 'Royal Arthur', for conveyance direct to Sydney. The object was to avoid going ashore at Adelaide or Melbourne, the normal ports of call for the mail steamer, to allow the New South Wales government to have its welcoming ceremony.

Petty manoeuvring over where they should first set foot on eastern Australian soil was made even more unseemly by Hopetoun catching typhoid fever in India. Though he began to recover in time to leave Colombo on 25 November, Lady Hopetoun, who had been stricken with a severe attack of malaria, was too ill to accompany him. The visit to Perth had to be cancelled. Forbidden by his medical advisers to leave his cabin when he reached Fremantle, the governor-general was forced to arrange that the 'Royal Arthur' precede the mail steamer to Adelaide before he transhipped. Although he did not land there he received official visitors and spoke briefly to reporters who noted his 'sallow face and bent attitude'. From Adelaide the flagship sailed direct to Sydney, landing on schedule at Farm Cove on the morning of 15 December 1900.

Despite Colonial Office advice to the contrary and the physical weakness of the star attraction, the New South Wales government had arranged a public welcoming ceremony. John Norton's *Truth*, in a page otherwise taken up with the sensational Coningham divorce scandal (in which a Catholic priest was co-respondent), devoted half a column to an attack on the 'gross and atrocious cruelty' of the government's exploitation of the 'care-worn cadaverous Earl'. Norton conceded that the governor-general had performed his first public duty in Australia heroically.

The *Sydney Mail* did not allow Hopetoun's frailty to distract it from the symbolic significance of the occasion:

> Isolated as we are here in the Southern Hemisphere, with common interests to defend, and a common destiny to work out, the federal idea was nothing more than the instinct of common protection and development. For Australians last Saturday all this received personal expression and embodiment in the Governor-General. He is the figurehead of the Commonwealth, the personal symbol of the union itself, and, as the direct representative of Her Majesty, of union under the Crown. In applauding him we were applauding the realisation of our federal hopes, and that imperial tie which makes and keeps us part of the great British Empire, which the Commonwealth will worthily represent in this quarter of the globe.

Barely recovered from his illness and anxious about the condition of his wife, who had suffered a relapse on her journey across Australia, Hopetoun's first two weeks were made even more uncomfortable by a pressing, constitutional task. It was necessary to choose a prime minister, since the cabinet had to be approved and ready to be sworn in by 1 January 1901 in accordance with the planned ceremonial for the inauguration. This would be the only time that the representative of the Crown would not have an existing parliament from which to choose his government. On 19 December Hopetoun ended the speculation by asking the New South Wales premier, Lyne, to form a ministry. Stipulating that he did not consider himself bound to 'accept *any* list' the governor-general required Lyne to satisfy him that 'the proposed government contained nothing but first-class names from each of the colonies and that above all Victoria should have had proper share in quality and quantity of representation'.

The choice of Lyne has achieved notoriety in historical accounts of the early Commonwealth as 'The Hopetoun blunder'. There is no doubt that it caused surprise. In Australia it had been generally anticipated that Barton, the acknowledged leader of the federal movement, would be offered the post. London opinion agreed. When told of the choice of Lyne, one senior Colonial Office official commented: 'It is a false step on Ld Hopetoun's part and probably will give him a good deal of trouble'. Cabling on 22 December that the choice of Lyne had caused 'great surprise', Chamberlain asked Hopetoun to 'please give reasons'.

Several explanations have been advanced for Hopetoun's action. The most likely solution is that he simply followed the Canadian precedent. In 1867 John A. Macdonald had been chosen because he was prime minister of the senior of the confederating provinces. Most later commentators agree that if Reid had still been premier of New South Wales he would rightly have been chosen. Reid had been replaced by Lyne. Barton was not even a member of parliament. It seems logical that Hopetoun believed Lyne should be given the opportunity which would in other circumstances have belonged to Reid.

Possibly the governor-general was also impressed by the undoubted political toughness of the New South Wales premier. In contrast, Barton was politically inept and inexperienced, qualities which were to have disastrous consequences for Hopetoun within eighteen months. While federalists might argue that Lyne's previous anti-federalism disqualified him from the post of first prime minister, the selection of such a man can also be seen as a sensible and statesmanlike effort to bind an influential and potentially dangerous opponent to the federation. But, as the days passed, it began to be clear that he would be unable to fulfil the conditions imposed on him by the governor-general. Leading Victorian politicians, encouraged by the influential Alfred Deakin, declined his offers of portfolios. In these circumstances Lyne had no choice but to admit failure. At 10 p.m. on 24 December he abandoned his commission and advised Hopetoun to send for Barton.

There is a sad irony in the fact that accounts of this episode disparage the name of the man whose motives were the most disinterested. Lyne's attempt to form a broadly based Commonwealth ministry failed largely because of intrigues by Deakin. The result of these political manoeuvres should not be blamed upon the action of the representative of the Crown. One conclusion to be drawn from the events in Sydney during late December 1900 was that the office of governor-general in Australia promised to be a post of considerable difficulty. A man of the lofty character and political inexperience of Hopetoun was not likely to be successful in dealing with Australian politicians.

Hopetoun delayed answering Chamberlain's cable for several, no doubt anxious, days. But by Christmas Day he was able to advise London that though he had found the New South Wales premier in a very strong position in his own State, Lyne had failed to form a representative ministry. He reported that Barton had therefore been commissioned and that it seemed likely that he would be successful in forming a government. 'All's well that ends well', was the reaction at the Colonial Office. A federal cabinet, including both Barton and Lyne, was ready to be sworn in after the governor-general at the inauguration of the Commonwealth on New Years Day 1901.

The governor-general was the focal point for Australian Imperial patriotism at the inauguration ceremony. No other representative of the Queen was present. In order to avoid problems of precedence and residence during the early period of the governor-generalship, and because of uncertainty about the continued status of future State governors, the Colonial Office had delayed making appointments in New South Wales and Victoria. Lieutenant-governors also administered the governments in Tasmania and Western Australia. But the governors of South Australia and Queensland and even Sir John Madden, lieutenant-governor of Victoria, were conspicuously absent from Sydney's festivities. The *Age* reported that this was due to Chamberlain's suggestion that it would be wiser if they presided over local celebrations in their own capitals. On the contrary, the initiative for this early display of State jealousy of the federal authority had come from the South Australian governor, Lord Tennyson, who had telegraphed in August to Chamberlain: 'It is felt that politically it would be a mistake for Governors to attend arrival or swearing in of Governor-General at Sydney . . . The States would resent any appearance of subordination of Governors of States to Governor-General.'

Shortly before 4.30 p.m., following the ceremonies on inauguration day, the men who were to guide the Commonwealth's first months as a federated nation assembled at Sydney Government House for the first meeting of the Federal Executive Council, under the chairmanship of the governor-general. Hopetoun was conscious that his term of office would be important in establishing precedents and breathing life into the Australian Constitution. Under Section 61 the executive power of the Commonwealth was vested in the Queen to be exercised by the governor-general as her representative. Section 62 provided for a Federal Executive Council to advise His Excellency. Scattered throughout the Constitution were numerous references to the power of 'the Governor-general in Council'. There was no mention of a 'cabinet' in the Constitution. The gathering of the first Executive Council therefore echoed the ancient ritual of a Privy Council meeting, and was the formal assumption of executive authority by Barton's ministry.

The Federal Executive Council was not intended by the makers of the Constitution to be a policy-making body. Twenty-five years earlier its colonial counterparts had possessed some life. But by the end of the nineteenth century, as the political role of governor declined, colonial Executive Councils had become mere formalities. Cabinets formulated policy and made administrative decisions and the Executive Council recorded and confirmed these resolutions. In Canada a similar process had been carried a stage further; after Confederation the Queen's representative no longer even attended the formal meetings. Hopetoun was aware of this development for in August 1900 he had asked the Colonial Office whether he should attend meetings of the Executive Council, as he had in Victoria, or follow the practice of Canada 'where matters are settled beforehand and two members attend to advise him afterwards'. The matter was left to be decided after the Commonwealth was constituted, but the Colonial Office expected the Canadian example to be followed, particularly because the governor-general would often be away from headquarters.

No Commonwealth public service yet existed, so clerks were borrowed from the New South Wales government for the inaugural gathering of the Federal Executive Council. Seven of the nine politicians at the meeting were appointed to administer the Departments of State specified in the Constitution, the other two were designated 'honorary ministers'. Considering that the meeting lasted for an hour and a half, remarkably little formal business was transacted.

Most members of the first Commonwealth Executive were already well-known to the governor-general. All had been involved in the public and political life of their respective colonies for more than a decade. Hopetoun's experience, personal charm and the authority of the British government gave him considerable personal influence, especially in the early days. In a farewell speech in London to the Institute of Naval Architects, of which he was president, Hopetoun had anticipated that his role would be like that of a captain taking command of a new steam ship: 'He would be privileged to . . . endeavour to discourage any tendency to strain the engines, to utter a word of caution here, to apply a little lubricant there until all danger of heated bearings . . . was a thing of the past . . . and the great ship of state was fairly and fully started on her voyage.' Lubrication was certainly needed in the first Australian cabinet. On one occasion Lyne came to Hopetoun complaining that the 'Victorian combination' in the cabinet 'disregard[ed] him and treat[ed] him with contempt'. The governor-general listened sympathetically to his problem, and later informed Barton: 'I smoothed him over'.

If the governor-general were to exercise any personal influence it was important that the relationship with his Executive Council be close and co-operative. Even more crucial was the association of governor-general with his prime minister. Barton was not only his chief adviser but also minister for External Affairs, and all relations with the mother country were conducted through the office of governor-general. Though I have found no evidence that there was coolness between them, it is likely that in the beginning Barton's dignity would be injured by the false start with Lyne. But Hopetoun's personal charm and urbanity were more than adequate for dealing with someone with the temperament and fondness for high living of 'Toby Tosspot', as the *Bulletin* had dubbed Barton. The governor-general's attentiveness and the prime minister's natural respect for a British nobleman soon established a confident working relationship, and eventually a close personal friendship.

A banquet in Sydney Town Hall was planned to complete the inauguration day ceremonies but Hopetoun was too exhausted to attend. He later wrote: 'My job may not require extreme cleverness but it does want a reasonably sound stomach and lots of energy'. Banquets and public functions enabled the governor-general to meet and converse casually with prominent people in Australia, and small private dinners at Government House provided opportunities for more serious conversation. Hopetoun made use of these avenues of contact early in his tenure of office. Reid, effectively leader of the opposition, was, like Barton, a frequent visitor to Government House while Hopetoun stayed in Sydney. The prime minister held office only until the election in April and there was every possibility that the Australian public might prefer someone else.

In the first weeks of the Commonwealth Hopetoun came almost daily to the closed-in verandah of one of the State government departments in Sydney where the prime minister had his office. In this informal atmosphere they discussed affairs. Hopetoun was a sympathetic counsellor removed from the strains of party and personal allegiances, while Barton had many problems in handling a cabinet of colleagues who were used to exacting obedience rather than offering it.

The weeks after the inaugural festivities were occupied with establishing the departmental machinery of the new Commonwealth. One department not mentioned in the Constitution, though its existence was assumed, that is the office of the governor-general, had already been set up. This was to be the Australian government's channel of communication with Britain and, conse-

Lord Hopetoun's staff, 1901. Photograph taken at Government House, Melbourne, by the Crown Studio. (Back row: Mr Gillington, Lord Victor Hope, C. Saville Gore. Front row: Hon. Charles Melbourne Hope, Captain B. Corbet, Major C.S. Philson, Major the Hon. Claude Willoughby, Captain E.W. Wallington.)

quently, with other nations. Ultimate responsibility for all external correspondence was the governor-general's, but the man with direct control was his private secretary, Captain Edward Walter Wallington.

Wallington was an Englishman who had hovered on the periphery of public affairs in Australia for fifteen years. As private secretary to governors Carrington and Jersey in New South Wales, Hopetoun and Brassey in Victoria and Tennyson in South Australia, 'Wal' had acquired an invaluable acquaintance with most of the public men in Australia and one of Hopetoun's earliest actions as governor-general had been to secure his services. Experienced, deferential and tactful, Wallington had earned the nickname 'Mr Better-Not' for his tendency to dissuade newly arrived governors from engaging in over-ambitious schemes. On being told how 'a certain Australian Governor had run amok' Carrington was said to have commented: 'He wouldn't have run off the track if Wallington had been driving'. His knowledge of the conduct of correspondence with the Colonial Office was expert. As Hopetoun's secretary he was responsible for both private correspondence and the drafting, decoding and encoding of official despatches. He was thus responsible for all the government's external correspondence. When, after a few weeks, the temporary clerk to the Federal Executive Council returned to his position in New South Wales, Wallington took over his duties as acting secretary.

The situation posed problems for the future. It was inappropriate that an officer with no responsibility to the Australian parliament should be in charge of the public business of the Commonwealth, despite Wallington's quiet efficiency and the graceful condescension of Hopetoun in sparing his secretary. Another problem was payment. Primarily Wallington was employed by Hopetoun, who paid him a salary in that capacity; but he was also carrying out governmental duties. The question of an official allowance for the governor-general was still not settled. Wallington's salary became involved in the difficult problem of providing for the expenses of the representative of the Crown in the Commonwealth. For the time being an allowance of £150 per annum was provided to pay for his duties as secretary to the Federal Executive Council.

In early February Hopetoun's attention was drawn to a matter which was disturbing the smooth efficiency of Wallington's unofficial department. In the Draft Constitution of 1891 there had been a clause providing that the governor-general should be the sole channel of communication between the States and the Imperial government. Although both Deakin and Barton urged its retention, the clause was omitted from the Constitution. Nevertheless, Chamberlain decided in September 1900 that, for the governor-general to be in a position to discharge his duties satisfactorily, he should be aware of correspondence passing between the State governors and the Colonial Office. An instruction was drafted requiring governors to supply the governor-general with copies of all dispatches addressed to the secretary of state. This direction was conveyed to Hopetoun before he left London, and forwarded to all Australian colonies on 2 November 1900. On 9 February Hopetoun wrote to the governors of South Australia and Queensland requesting that they comply with Chamberlain's instruction.

Tennyson's reply was abrupt. He rejected the governor-general's right to see his dispatches and indicated that his government objected to the interference of the Commonwealth in State affairs. While prepared to forward copies of purely formal covering dispatches and acknowledgments, he strongly opposed the suggestion that more important correspondence should be made available to the governor-general. He especially denied Hopetoun's right to see communications relating to disputes between the Commonwealth and the States and recommendations for honours.

The governor-general was taken aback by the vehemence of Tennyson's reaction. He referred the matter to Chamberlain with the comment that he envisaged great difficulty in administering the government of the Commonwealth 'unless fully informed as to what is the substance of communication' between State governors and the secretary of state. While acknowledging the necessity of preserving the positions, prerogatives and dignity of the governors he specifically disagreed with the examples specified by Tennyson as communications which the governor-general should not see. On the contrary he thought that these were two subjects upon which 'above all others' he ought to be kept fully informed. Finally, he protested at Tennyson's threat to flood his office with endless documents of a purely formal nature. This, he thought, would reduce the secretary of state's instruction to something approaching a farce.

Hopetoun interpreted Tennyson's stubbornness as fear for the loss of dignity and prerogatives of State governor. He and the Colonial Office deprecated such an attitude. But the position of State governors after federation was a difficult one. At the first Sydney convention of 1891 there had been considerable support for the proposition that States be enabled to elect their governors. But this was not followed by the later convention. Late in 1899 Chamberlain asked for the views of colonial ministers on the continuance of the practice of appointing governors from Britain. He suggested that the federating colonies would 'still wish to secure the advantage of having at the head of affairs Governors who have had no association with local party politics and will be above suspicion of partiality, and who by their presence in the capitals of the States will emphasize and promote the close connection of the States with the Mother Country'. However, he stressed that it would be difficult to find suitable governors willing to accept posts which would 'naturally be overshadowed by the great office of Governor General'; and he warned that the task would be even more difficult if the colonies persisted in moves to reduce vice-regal salaries. He was correct in assuming that Australian governments wished to continue the system of appointing British governors, but his hopes concerning salaries proved less apt. The immediate result of this exchange was another change in the type of State governors in Australia. The young, rich peers who had held those positions since 1885 gave way to older public servants, often naval or military officers.

The question of State independence within the federation was more important than that of the remaining prerogatives of the various Queen's representatives. Soon the channel of communication dispute broadened, with the Commonwealth government entering the controversy. By June 1901 a compromise had been reached: copies of dispatches of general interest had to be forwarded to the governor-general, while those dealing with 'local affairs' need not. The discretion as to what constituted matters of general interest was left to the State governor rather than to the governor-general. It was evident that any attempt of the latter to supervise the former was doomed to fail.

The dispute over State governors' correspondence was an early blow to the dignity of the office of governor-general. In 1891 Deakin had forecast that unless the principal representative of the Crown in the Commonwealth had access to State governors' dispatches he would cease to be a governor-general: 'He will become one governor among many, and he will lose the dignified position in which this constitution proposes to place him'. Even allowing for Deakin's enthusiasm for a strong central authority, the institution of the governor-generalship had suffered a considerable setback over channels of communication.

This dispute over correspondence had revealed to Hopetoun the jealousies and tensions between Commonwealth and States. An opportunity to recover some of the initiative presented itself in mid-1901, during the visit of the Duke of York. The royal tour was an opportunity to submerge parochialism in ceremony, and to emphasise Australia's membership of the larger community of the British Empire, rather than its divergent parts. The tour also promised to enhance the prestige of the governor-general, for he was formal host to the royal visitors. Furthermore, the absence of governors in Sydney, Melbourne and Hobart gave Hopetoun an opportunity to take their place. In this way he hoped to soothe the States' resentments towards the Commonwealth. By accompanying the Duke of York on his tour His Excellency would also be able to renew old acquaintances and establish new relationships with State leaders and politicians.

Hopetoun's prior experience as lord chamberlain was particularly appropriate for the task of supervising the visit of the Duke of York, since close attention to protocol and precedence was required to avoid unpleasantness or offence during the tour. He had become well-known to the royal family through his previous court appointments and was familiarly addressed as 'Hopie' by the royal visitor, his 'sincere friend George'. He was solely responsible for the overall planning of the tour, since his ministers were increasingly preoccupied with other political and administrative matters. He complained to Tennyson in March 1901 that it was difficult to distract his advisers from their election campaigning.

Royalty had toured the Australian continent on only two previous occasions. In 1867 the Duke of Edinburgh had visited all the colonies, and had survived an assassination attempt in Sydney. Fourteen years later the Duke of York, as a boy midshipman, had visited parts of Australia with his elder brother in the course of the cruise of HMS 'Bacchante'.

The origins of the 1901 tour lay in suggestions during the 1890s and earlier that Australia might have as first governor-general a member of the royal family or, if not, that a royal duke would open the first session of parliament. In 1893, after the federal movement had received a temporary setback, the prime ministers of the Australian colonies had officially invited the Duke of York to tour Australia. But none of these initiatives received encouragement from Britain. It therefore came as a surprise to the Australian public when, in September 1900, the Queen announced her assent to the British government's suggestion that her grandson open the first session of the parliament of the Australian Commonwealth, to signify her 'sense of the loyalty and the devotion which prompted the spontaneous aid so liberally offered by all the colonies in the South African war'. The tour also reflected Chamberlain's probing of ideas of Imperial federation after the notable display of unity in the Boer War. The reaction in Australia was general surprise and delight, though the *Bulletin* winced in anticipation of 'the coming crawl'.

The practical organisation of the visit was made more difficult by the news received on 22 January that the monarch who had ruled Britain for 60 years was dead. For a few days the tour seemed in doubt. Indeed, the new King did cancel it, but at his ministers' urging reviewed his decision. With much emotional publicity it was announced that, since the tour had been 'the Queen's wish', it would proceed, and that Canada and the Cape Colony were to be included in the itinerary.

The death of the Queen and the planned tour of the heir apparent focused the attention of a large section of Australia upon the institution of monarchy and on its representation in Australia. Messages and loyal addresses inspired by devotion to the late Queen flooded into the office of the governor-general. One Australian Imperialist commented: 'the most wonderful, the most beloved, the wisest and best, of all the monarchs of the world known to history, after a reign of unparalleled length and brilliancy, has been laid to rest with a sob of heart-break girdling the whole world round'. The royal visitor was now direct heir to the throne and Australian newspapers seemed to consider this a particular honour. The result was that the real purpose for the visit, namely the opening of the first federal parliament, tended to be obscured by pageantry, Imperial patriotism and enthusiasm for monarchy.

Balls and lavish public entertainments could not be indulged because the Empire was in mourning, but Hopetoun obtained confirmation that dinner parties and levees were considered suitable in the circumstances, and in the itinerary which he planned he mixed dutiful solemnity with public demonstrations of loyalty. Australia's loyal participation in the South African war had been specifically mentioned by the Queen in announcing the visit of her grandson. Military ceremonies for the presentation of South African war medals and reviews of colonial troops, therefore, were particularly appropriate occasions, combining sombre gravity with enthusiastic and colourful Imperial patriotism.

There were sticky problems of precedent and precedence raised by the presence of the Duke of York at the first meeting of Australia's parliament. The only appropriate precedent was the opening of the first Dominion parliament in Canada, which had been performed by the governor-general. In Britain parliament was traditionally opened by a speech from the throne read by the sovereign. In the colonies this function had belonged to the governor. Although Hopetoun agreed to allow the Duke of York precedence over himself in Australia, he baulked at allowing him to usurp the function of reading the speech from the throne. Upon receiving Chamberlain's dispatch announcing that the Duke of York would perform the act which legally opened parliament, the governor-general wrote to his prime minister. The result was a dispatch in March from Hopetoun: 'Prime Minister feels clear ... that it is the Governor-General and none other who should declare the causes of the summons ...'. Chamberlain and the King acquiesced. The governor-general thus retained a central function in the planned ceremonial for the official opening of parliament.

The Duke and Duchess of York arrived in Australian waters on 3 May 1901 when their ship, the 'Ophir', anchored off Albany in Western Australia. Again, careful arrangements ensured that the visitors did not set foot on Australian soil before landing in the city where the major ceremony was planned. A suggestion that they land at Sydney before proceeding to Melbourne had caused an immediate, indignant objection from the Victorian government. Consequently, the royal visitors first set foot upon Australian soil at St Kilda Pier in Port Phillip Bay on 6 May 1901 to a tumultuous welcome.

In the following eleven weeks the party travelled through Australia and New Zealand. The planned itinerary was much the same in each State. Hopetoun had scheduled a round of Government House dinner parties, foundation stone laying, military reviews, levees and assemblies of school-children. At the specific request of the Duke of York shooting expeditions were arranged for relaxation in most States. On 9 May, in a scene recorded by the painter, Tom Roberts, he performed his primary task by declaring open the first session of the

Australian parliament and directing members to retire, appoint their president
and Speaker and reassemble on the following day when the governor-general
would state the causes for which the parliament was assembled. After eleven
days in Victoria the royal tourists spent a week in Queensland to allow
Hopetoun time to rush to Sydney, where there was still no governor, and
prepare for his official duties as host there. From Sydney the 'Ophir' sailed to
New Zealand, returning to Australia early in July for a short visit to Tasmania.
On 20 July, after visiting South Australia and Western Australia the royal party
sailed from Fremantle.

The tour of the Duke of York in 1901 rededicated Australia to the institution
of monarchy. It emphasised the Commonwealth's membership of the Empire
and the personal allegiance of her citizens to the British Crown. The Australian
press was effusively patriotic. The *Sydney Morning Herald* was confident that
'the acclamation of the thousands who thronged the line of the procession's
march ... showed their recognition of the Imperial tie that binds us, and their
loyalty to the person of the Sovereign and his heir'. The visit illustrated
Australia's refusal to seize the occasion of federation to assert a claim for
independence. The earliest public act of the Commonwealth was 'to acclaim
with loyal enthusiasm the landing of the Heir Apparent'. The *Sydney Morning
Herald* saw good reason for this, reflecting that, 'In times like these, when the
rumours of wars fill all ears, and when the Empire has two serious engagements
actually on hand, every additional evidence to the solidarity of Empire is of
value.' Like the inauguration ceremony, the opening of the Commonwealth's
first parliament was a striking manifestation of the spirit of anxious militarism in
Australia. In an editorial commenting on a review of Imperial troops at
Flemington, the *Argus* referred to 'possible menaces' confronting the Commonwealth and declared 'Federated Australia does not want to become a warlike
nation, but it must essentially be a virile one'. The constant message in this and
other comments at the time was that the Imperial connection was necessary to
combat external menace.

Opposition to the tour expressed itself chiefly in the scorn and disgust of the
radical press. The *Bulletin's* principal form of attack was sarcasm. It invented
various nicknames for the royal visitor, such as 'The Mighty Atom' or, more
often, 'the Jookoyork', and beseeched Australians to recognise that the visitor
was obscuring the really significant aspect of the events in May, namely the
opening of Australia's first national parliament. The Victorian socialist journal
Tocsin also railed against the toadying engendered by the tour, and carried
opposition to the institution of monarchy so far as to publish a 'foul libel on the
king'. It reprinted an article from *Irish People* which had been suppressed in
Britain, including a virulent attack on 'Edward Rex ... the old and bald-headed
roué — the "lover" of every woman of fair features who has appeared in English
"Society" for forty years'. An immediate public outcry, fanned by the *Argus*, led
both to an unprecedented demand for this issue of *Tocsin* and to the expulsion
of its manager, Edward Findley, a Labor parliamentarian, from the Victorian
Legislative Assembly. But more significant than these isolated examples of
anti-monarchic sentiment was the awareness expressed in them that the general

Australian attitude was quite different. The *Bulletin* conceded, exasperatedly, that in the public eye the Duke of York was 'apparently three fourths of the pageant'. Commenting, sadly, that the Trades Hall Council had allowed itself to be bribed into taking part in the grovel, *Tocsin* reproached the young Commonwealth for starting 'its infant life with the polluting finger-marks of old-world royalty smeared over it'.

There was an air of equivocation even in the *Tocsin*'s attitude towards the Empire. In the 'foul libel issue' it specifically repudiated republicanism, seeing 'advantages in the English limited monarchy system' not evident in any republic. Nor did it object to imported nominee governors or the British connection. The institution it seemed to find most objectionable was 'Government House'. In May 1901 the *Age* had devoted several columns to a description of the royal levee held at Melbourne Government House for the Duke of York. Though its mild comment fell far short of the fatuity of *Argus* or *Sydney Morning Herald* editorials on the subject, *Tocsin* was stirred to issue a vigorous reply, denouncing levees as exalting and glamorising the office of governor. It categorised those who attended at Government House as

> the most notorious sweaters, the bank disaster magnates, the rank and file of the Imperial Federation Scheme, the class-conscious legislative councillors almost to a man, every Assembly 'smoodger', turncoat, and traitor to democracy and Australia, the unspeakable justices of the peace in shoals, and the Troglodyte shire councillors in crawling droves, the sad catspaws of ambitious title-hunting women, lickspittle junior officials, developing fungi from the University, and all the Procrustes who would confine the giant limbs of free Australia in the limited bedsteads of English art, religion, literature, philosophy, and polity.

To a certain extent such an outburst was merely sniping at an obvious target. But objections to the undemocratic nature of the institution of Government House and the toadying of those who patronised it was to remain a persistent feature of Australian society during the early part of the twentieth century. Moreover, in the newly elected Australian parliament the strength of the Labor Party indicated that the attitudes of the more democratic elements in the Commonwealth would need to be considered.

Much of the credit for the success of the royal visit was rightly attributed to Hopetoun as official host. Though careful not to upstage his royal guest in public processions, he was usually prominent at the Duke's side on other occasions. When the visitors sailed from Hobart to South Australia the governor-general's direct supervision of the tour ceased. There had already been comment on his drawn and exhausted appearance during the latter part of the royal progress. In July his health gave way and it was announced that all official functions were cancelled. Next month Hopetoun obtained some relief from the Melbourne winter climate by visiting north Queensland, where a relation had property.

The visit of the Duke of York had enabled Hopetoun to fulfil a function which he regarded as of great importance, namely the encouragement of

Commonwealth rather than provincial patriotism. The transition from colonies to Commonwealth had already provided pitfalls for the governor-general. In the early encounter with State governors over the channel of communication problem there were obvious lessons to be drawn concerning the need for caution and tact in the difficult early years of federation. Hopetoun was confident that he could, to some extent, mediate between the Commonwealth and the States. The charisma imparted to his office by the visit of the heir apparent added to his already high prestige and popularity in Australia. The visit to Queensland was in part an attempt to wield that reputation in the State most uneasy in the federation.

Until the federal capital was built there was very little apart from the governor-general to remind Australians of their new unified nationhood. The task of travelling constantly around the continent promoting the unity of Australia was to remain an important function of the principal representative of the Crown in the Commonwealth. Hopetoun commented upon this aspect of his role at a banquet given in his honour in Brisbane after his return from Cairns. Pledging that he would avoid parochialism, he vowed not to rest until he had shown himself 'to the people of his great proconsulate' and proved 'to the many that a governor-general really exists and that they are living under one central Government'.

His undertaking to travel was carried out zealously. In eighteen months of office he travelled 14 000 miles. Aware of the jealousies of Sydney and Melbourne concerning the possession of the governor-general's residence he journeyed frequently between those cities. In addition he visited each of the other States. On these official and formal tours he was usually accompanied by most of his staff.

It was becoming increasingly clear after six months of the Commonwealth that the office of governor-general was involving Australia in considerable expense. At first the States were disposed to be generous in meeting his travelling expenses. New South Wales, in particular, treated him with munificence. A luxurious carriage was constructed to carry the vice-regal suite upon the New South Wales railways. But other States were less enthusiastic. Both the Queensland and South Australian governors complained of the outlay in entertaining the governor-general during his official visits, especially in view of the imminent reduction in State governors' salaries. General disillusionment with the Commonwealth government had led State premiers to insist that costs incurred by the vice-regal suite be borne by the central authority. This became one of several contentious matters in relations between the Commonwealth and the States which lasted beyond Hopetoun's tenure of office. Not until 1905, when the Commonwealth agreed to reimburse the States for costs of the railway travel of the governor-general and his entourage, was the dispute settled.

A major responsibility of representatives of the Crown in Australia was the making of public speeches. Nervous and often ill, Hopetoun disliked this duty. But quite apart from his personal aversion to speech-making, public pronouncements had always been fraught with danger for Australian governors. Colonial newspapers and politicians tended to be excessively critical, quick to take

THE SPECIAL CREATION.

"They would end by making him feel that either he had been specially created to occupy the position of Governor-General of Australia, or that the position of Governor-General of Australia had been specially created to be occupied by him."

AUSTRALIA: "*Great Scott! has it come to this?*"

Bulletin cartoon by Ambrose Dyson, 14 December 1901

offence at any imagined slight or indiscretion, and critical when a speech referred to a politically contentious topic.

As governor of Victoria Hopetoun had been successfully uncontroversial, and he began his term as governor-general in similar vein. During his official visit to Queensland he was careful to avoid too specific references to political questions. Barton's policy prohibiting Melanesian labour had led to considerable hostility throughout the northern State. Hopetoun feared that 'the feeling of unrest' would make speeches on his part rather difficult. He promised the prime minister that he would 'put a very sharp guard on my tongue and try not to put you into the cart'. He succeeded by an emotional style of oratory and simple metaphors. The difficulties of 'fitting into new shoes', 'running a new ship' or 'driving a state coach' were employed with unvarying success.

The constant search for topical but non-polemic subjects took its toll. By the end of his first year of office vague admonitions to unity in the Commonwealth became *passé*. Perhaps the eulogistic reception generally accorded his public utterances overcame his previous caution. During a visit to Western Australia in December 1901 he allowed himself the risk of referring to the need for the construction of a trans-continental railway, and there were some rumblings from the opposition over this reference to an 'active political subject'. But in Melbourne he made a political mistake.

Hopetoun had to address the annual luncheon of the Australian Natives' Association in January 1902, a patriotic gathering which included most of Australia's prominent public figures. The topic he chose was the government's policy towards the Boer War. Referring to accusations of backwardness which had been levelled at Barton, he assured the guests at the luncheon that the position taken up by the cabinet had been freely approved of by himself. After asserting that Barton and he had for many months discussed the question of the propriety of offering, unasked, a further supply of troops for South Africa, the governor-general stated: 'we were not of the opinion that the moment was a favourable one to ask the Australian people to make further sacrifices unless we had the assurance of the Imperial Government that such sacrifices were necessary and desirable.' Whatever the measure of blame or praise, His Excellency stated that it was his duty to share it.

The oration was loudly applauded, and the prime minister thanked the governor-general for his 'manly and generous references'. But among those present at the banquet was the leader of the opposition, George Reid, who took prompt action at the next available meeting of the House of Representatives to submit a motion disapproving of the governor-general's speech. In the words of Melbourne's *Punch* Reid 'reproved all concerned like a cooing dove and gently belaboured the governor-general with a feather'. Whilst appreciating the motives which prompted the speech, the leader of the opposition urged the House to declare its earnest hope that the course would not be regarded as a precedent. Other speakers agreed on the impropriety of such remarks by the representative of the Crown. Like Reid, most were personally complimentary to Hopetoun, but adamant that he had exceeded the proper limits of responsible government. With obvious chivalry Barton attempted to defend the governor-general, contending that the matter had passed out of political controversy. But his argument lacked conviction.

The debate was a revealing early insight into attitudes of Australian politicians towards the role of a governor-general. Higgins felt that 'the most excellent governors are always governors who express the least opinions'. The ablest speech was made by Isaac Isaacs, later to be the first Australian occupant of the post. He stressed that in all Australian governmental action the governor-general must assume no responsibility but stand clear of the whole region of debate and controversy. He must be particularly careful that he did not, even by accident, intervene between ministers and their responsibility to parliament and the nation. Another member, Joseph Cook, asserted that the duty of the governor-general was to 'guard Imperial interests, and to leave his Ministers to guard the interests of the Commonwealth at large'. As might be expected the Labor Party was strongly represented in the debate, and critical of the speech.

Isaacs' conclusion that 'the observations of Lord Hopetoun were unfortunate' was a fair summary of the opinion of non-Labor parliamentarians. Reid withdrew the motion in order to avoid a division which might be regarded as a censure of the King's representative. But the implications of the debate were clear. In his somewhat embarrassed report of the affair to the secretary of state Hopetoun commented, 'I am bound to consider that I have been guilty of an error of judgment'. He hoped that no serious harm had been done to the position he occupied though he placed himself in Chamberlain's hands as to whether he ought to be relieved of his post. At the Colonial Office the general opinion was that His Excellency's minor indiscretion threatened no permanent ill-effects and a soothing reply urged him to remain at his post.

Though the references made by Hopetoun to the delayed contingent were reported in most newspapers, no adverse editorial comment appeared until after the parliamentary debate. Then there was general agreement with Reid's action. The *Brisbane Courier*'s reaction was typical. It felt that Hopetoun's 'manly and good-natured utterances were unconsciously a violation of the principles of responsible government'. Most newspapers agreed that the fabric of self-government had suffered no lasting damage.

Predictably, the *Bulletin* was more critical: 'Since the day of the Governor-General's arrival he has shown a disposition to assert, and Mr Barton to allow, powers utterly at variance with the rights of a self-governing people.' It attacked Hopetoun's ingenuous confession during his speech that he was 'a real good old-fashioned Tory of the old school'. Certainly his private political views were conservative. After leaving Australia he was to comment that 'the jealousy and infernal wrong headedness of the labour party' there strangled private enterprise. The *Bulletin* perceived something sinister in Hopetoun's admission of 'constant and anxious consultation' on the subject of Australian troops for the war in South Africa. But the Sydney journal was one of the few public organs to oppose Australian participation in the war, and its opinions on Hopetoun's influence on government policy were not typical of the general Australian attitude.

The controversy re-emphasised the need for the representative of the Crown in Australia to refrain from public comment on political policy. Although the significance of this was not fully recognised at the time, the role of the governor-general as diplomat was becoming separated from his function as head of State. However there was less clarity about the extent to which the governor-general ought to be able to influence policy in private. It was this aspect of his position to which the *Bulletin* objected.

In defending the propriety of the governor-general's speech, Barton specifically denied that Hopetoun had 'intended to convey the impression that the policy of the Government was carried out in conjunction and in equal terms by him and myself'. He claimed that no one who understood the principles of constitutional government would read His Excellency's words as meaning that he was a participant in the policy of the government. But, as J.C. Watson, the leader of the parliamentary Labor Party, interjected, 'that is the only inference'. The prime minister did admit that 'a policy was mentioned to His Excellency by myself on behalf of the Ministry . . . and that being mentioned it happened to have his approval'. He also conceded that in private conversations he had intimated what he intended to propose to the cabinet, arguing that it was a 'courteous and beneficent practice' to consult with the governor-general, 'an officer with whom it is of the essence of success of Government that we should maintain confidential relations'.

These admissions raise the question: did Hopetoun's 'close and confidential' relationship with the Australian prime minister influence government policy? An examination of his confidential dispatches suggests that he did. In December 1901 Chamberlain had asked whether the Commonwealth would be prepared to receive an official request for additional troops. Barton's apparent reluctance to commit such a Commonwealth force had already led to considerable criticism from jingoistic elements. On 15 December he instructed Hopetoun to inform Chamberlain that an official request should not be made by the British government until the new year. This cable was sent. But two days later the governor-general sent the following message to the secretary of state: 'I have . . . again conferred with Prime Minister and pointed out urgency of matter with regard to suggested contingent and with his approval I am now able to say that whenever you deem it advisable to despatch an official request for reinforcements he is prepared to receive it.' Clearly, Barton's mind had been changed, perhaps by a visiting British member of parliament and Imperial busy-body, Henniker Heaton, but most likely by Hopetoun himself.

In this affair can be found an example of the dual role of the representative of the Crown in the Commonwealth. As channel of communication between Australia and the British government he was aware of the negotiations. As representative of the British government it was his duty to urge upon his local ministers the view of the Colonial Office. Some Australians, such as Cook in the House of Representatives, and the *Daily Telegraph* recognised that it was a valid part of the governor-general's function to make representations on behalf of the home government, but Hopetoun's mistake lay in making those representations public. His successors learned from his misjudgement. Thenceforth normal diplomatic secrecy surrounded the governor-general's interventions on behalf of the British government.

One subject in which the governor-general might be expected to have exercised some personal influence was the selection of a commandant for the newly amalgamated Australian Defence Forces. Hopetoun's Sandhurst education, his acquaintance with others of the British ruling class, as well as his position as representative of the British government in Australia qualified him to assist Barton in the choice. Yet he exercised only marginal influence. Barton's correspondence reveals that Hopetoun freely offered advice, encouraged action of which he approved and discouraged if he disapproved. Hopetoun urged the Australian government to provide a generous salary for the position; he endorsed the selection of one candidate and advised against the appointment of another; and he urged that the matter be settled as quickly as possible. Though the pressure he exercised was neither blatant nor decisive it was constant. No longer able to command, a governor-general retained opportunities to persuade.

Hopetoun's representations on behalf of the British government were more fruitful on other occasions. In April 1901 the Australian government decided not to send a delegate to a proposed conference on the question of establishing a Court of Appeal for the Empire. To Chamberlain the governor-general expressed regret at the decision arrived at by his ministers despite his 'utmost endeavours to secure a compliance with the wishes of H.M.G.'. Nor did he allow the matter to rest. A few days later he pressed cabinet to reconsider its decision, and the government did, eventually, decide to send a representative to the conference.

In one important policy decision during the first year of the Commonwealth Hopetoun was able to persuade Barton to amend proposed legislation in order to accommodate the views of the British government. This was the Immigration Restriction Bill of 1901. Its introduction also raised the question of the remaining discretionary powers of the governor-general. One of the last vestiges of Imperial control over colonial legislation was the power of the representative of the Crown to reserve legislation for the Royal Assent and the power of the British government to advise the Crown to disallow such legislation. This was one instance where gubernatorial authority exceeded that of the British monarch, for in Britain the royal power of veto had not been used since the reign of Queen Anne. During the nineteenth century there had been a number of occasions when governors had suspended the operation of colonial legislation by reserving bills for the Royal Assent. One advantage of this suspensory power was that time was gained during which amendments could be suggested which might bring the legislation within the scope of Imperial political policy. As a final recourse the bill might be disallowed. But there were dangers in refusing assent to such legislation. Chamberlain considered that the extreme step of disallowance should be employed only to protect Imperial interests as a whole and not in local matters.

The matter of alien immigration posed a conflict between these two spheres of interest. In the Australian colonies discriminatory legislation against Asian settlers had resulted from fear of the racial and economic consequences of such migration. Anxiety about the offence which such legislation might arouse, both within the Empire and outside it, led the British government to retain ultimate authority over this subject. Governors were instructed to reserve such bills for the Royal Assent. As late as January 1901 Governor Lamington of Queensland had reserved the Sugar Works (Amendment) Bill since it referred to the employment of immigrant labour. On the grounds that it 'may disturb the good relations existing between' Britain and Japan, the British government objected to this bill and declined to advise His Majesty to give Royal Assent.

In August 1901 Barton introduced the Immigration Restriction Bill into federal parliament. Hopetoun immediately checked his Instructions for advice as to his action if the legislation were passed. He found that, contrary to the position when he had been governor of Victoria, there were no specific classes of legislation upon which he was required to reserve the Royal Assent. On 19 August he cabled for advice from the secretary of state: 'my Instructions seem to contemplate the possibility of my reserving Royal Assent to Bills: but they contain no categorical list of subjects to be so dealt with ...' He informed Chamberlain that a bill had been introduced to restrict immigration by a 'somewhat severe education test viz. that any person who fails to write and sign a passage of 5 words dictated in English is prohibited', and asked whether under any circumstances a bill of this kind should be reserved.

The secretary of state replied that in exercising his discretion, the governor-general should consider the broad principles governing reservation elsewhere. In cases of doubt he was instructed to communicate by telegraph with the Colonial Office. In the immediate circumstances Chamberlain advised that the bill should be reserved 'if it passes in its present form ... You should therefore press for substitution of European for English language'.

On 12 November Hopetoun forwarded to Chamberlain a copy of the bill as it then stood in the Senate. In a long covering dispatch, he drew attention to one section which 'May possibly lead to friction in the immediate future with the Government of nations with whom it is essential that His Majesty's Government should maintain relations of a cordial character'. The governor-general pointed out that, in deference to Chamberlain's suggestion, the education test had been amended. He continued:

> I am aware that legislation of the character contained in this Bill, is hardly likely to commend itself to His Majesty's Government, but the feeling in Australia against the unrestricted entry into the Commonwealth of large numbers of Foreigners, and more especially of large numbers of Asiatics, is so intense that I cannot blame my Government for having introduced a measure of this kind.

He requested special instructions in respect to clause 4, and undertook that if the bill passed in its existing form he would communicate immediately, hoping to receive by telegram the decision of the British government as to whether the bill should be reserved or not.

This dispatch was sent by sea and did not reach London until 19 December. In the meantime the bill had been swiftly passed by both Houses of the

Commonwealth parliament. Accordingly Hopetoun cabled on 12 December: 'Immigration Restriction bill has passed through both Houses of Parliament. In accordance with your suggestion word European has been substituted for English in clause 4(a) and in view of your despatch ... of 18 October I do not see any reason for withholding royal assent.' Deliberating on this cable, officials at the Colonial Office felt that little would be gained by instructing the governor-general to reserve the bill, but they failed to reply immediately. Instead, a copy of the cable was forwarded to the Foreign Office for its consideration.

During this correspondence with the secretary of state, Hopetoun had been carrying on a parallel exchange with his chief Australian adviser over the issue. In August he had commented that there were no specific classes of legislation upon which he was instructed to reserve the Royal Assent and asked the prime minister to consider 'whether there is the shadow of a reason for my reserving the aliens immigration Bill'. Barton had not needed to be told about the provisions of the governor-general's Instructions. During his stay in Britain in 1900, the Colonial Office had consulted him about their form, and copies were later sent to him. To Deakin he had then expressed satisfaction that 'they are as wide as we could possibly have wished. Absolutely no stated restriction on the power to sign the Royal Assent on the spot.'

Labor's power in federal parliament in 1901 made Barton anxious to avoid Hopetoun's reservation of the Royal Assent. In July 1901 a radical MHR, R.A. Crouch, had tabled a question which objected to the Instructions of the governor-general as 'subversive to responsible government'. Representations on behalf of the secretary of state pressing for the substitution of a test in any European language rather than in the English language were probably decisive in Barton's acceptance of the amendment, to avoid an excuse for Hopetoun to reserve the bill. He had, perforce, to keep secret His Excellency's role in suggesting the alteration, to avoid the accusation of Downing Street control.

Even after the dictation test provision was altered, Hopetoun was careful to retain the option of reserving the bill. On 11 November he wrote to Barton: 'The question as to whether or not this Bill will have to be reserved will have to be considered and I shall be gratified if you will ... make known to me your opinions on this point'. At the same time he informed Barton of his intention to send a copy of the bill as it then stood to the secretary of state. A month later he would still not commit himself. When the Speaker signified his intention to present both the Pacific Island Labourers Bill and the Immigration Restriction Bill for the Royal Assent, Hopetoun informed Barton that he would receive both bills but did not propose to assent to them immediately. He wanted an opportunity to consult the prime minister about them. In particular he felt that the Immigration Restriction Bill required 'careful and earnest consideration'. He assured Barton that he was 'most anxious to do whatever is right'.

Rejecting a last-minute appeal from the Queensland premier to reserve the Pacific Island Labourers Bill Hopetoun assented formally to that bill on 19 December. However he did not assent to the Immigration Restriction Bill, probably waiting for definite instructions from the Colonial Office. To further complicate the situation he was due to leave Melbourne for a four weeks tour of Western Australia on 21 December. By the time he left no reply had been received from the Colonial Office, and the governor-general had still not signed the Royal Assent. As the delay could not continue much further without becoming public, and Barton was obviously concerned that His Excellency deal with the matter himself, Hopetoun eventually gave way. On 23 December in the train at Adelaide en route to Perth the governor-general signed the necessary documents.

While His Excellency was still absent from the seat of government a protest by the Japanese acting consul-general in Australia reached Melbourne, belatedly drawing attention to a serious conflict between the Immigration Restriction Bill and a protocol adhered to by the Queensland government in October 1900. The governor-general cabled the substance of the Japanese protest to Chamberlain on 18 January 1902 and was surprised to receive in reply an instruction to defer assent to the bill until he had received advice from the British law officers of the crown. As it was over a month after assent had been granted, the objection had come too late. Writing to Chamberlain in February 1902 Hopetoun explained that the bill had given him 'much anxiety. But after a great deal of thought I gave my assent to it as in my opinion the least evil course to follow. I felt that if I reserved it there would be a violent agitation against what still remains of Imperial control.' Hopetoun's action confirmed Australia's larger independence within the Empire. In the absence of specific instructions from Chamberlain he had decided, on his own discretion, that reservation might encourage a reaction against the powers of the King's representative. By avoiding a confrontation on this issue he hoped to retain sufficient influence to be able to present the point of view of the British government in private with reasonable anticipation of success. Although it took a further six years for this procedure to become regularised, the power of the governor-general to reserve legislation for the Royal Assent when his local ministers did not advise him to do so was to fade altogether.

Hopetoun's handling of this difficult issue showed an appreciation of local attitudes and a concern for constitutional propriety fully in keeping with his deserved popularity. Yet, despite his sympathy with Australian views, he failed to recognise that Australian politicians were unwilling to allow the office of governor-general to be one of expensive pomp and ostentation. His career in Australia came to an end humiliatingly, in a dispute over money.

The Constitutional Conventions of the 1890s had eventually settled, though not without dissension, that the salary of the governor-general should be £10 000 per year. This was generous by ordinary Australian standards, equalling the salary paid to the governor-general of Canada, and far exceeding the salary of the chief justice in New South Wales (£3500). But in Canada substantial travelling and entertainment allowances were also provided; in 1901–02 these amounted to £17 137. Although it had been generally assumed that some payment would be made by the Commonwealth for His Excellency's expenses of office no provision for this appeared in the Constitution.

In August 1899, recognising that the question of the governor-general's allowances needed clarification, the Colonial Office had asked governors of the federating colonies to draw their ministers' attention to the matter. Presuming that the governor-general would 'mainly reside at Melbourne' until the establishment of the federal capital, Chamberlain asked colonial ministers what provision should be made for his residence.

The responses of the two rival colonies were predictable. In Victoria, Premier George Turner informed Chamberlain that Government House, Melbourne, would be made available for the governor-general. Though undertaking to provide another residence for the governor of Victoria, he urged that a combined appointment would have 'obvious advantages'. But in New South Wales Lyne argued that His Excellency should stay in Melbourne only during the sessions of the federal parliament. Ample provision would be made for his residence in Sydney at other times. Later, Lyne unsuccessfully urged that the posts of governor-general and governor of New South Wales be held jointly.

For the next twelve months Lyne continued to urge that, except during sessions of federal parliament, the governor-general's proper place was in Sydney. Melbourne had acquired the parliament, Sydney should at least have the viceroy. At the Colonial Office these endeavours were seen as showing a 'great lack of consideration and decency'.

While the Australian delegates were in London during mid-1900 further correspondence about the residence question passed between Sydney and London, and Lyne, like Turner, offered to find another residence for the State governor. While willing to meet the wishes of New South Wales, the Colonial Office insisted that the decision 'must be subject to provision being made to meet the extra expenditure involved by the maintenance of two, and at no very distant date three, Government Houses'. In addition the matter also involved the future Commonwealth government, and Chamberlain insisted that it would be impossible to maintain two establishments unless either the States or the Commonwealth provided for upkeep, travelling expenses and entertainment. Chamberlain's personal opinion was that no governor-general could perform the duties of the office and exercise hospitality in a fitting manner, residing in two or more cities and visiting other states, for less than £25 000 per year. He therefore suggested that either the States or the Commonwealth guarantee an additional annual allowance of £10 000.

At Lyne's behest, the New South Wales parliament quickly passed a measure providing for the contribution of approximately £3000 towards the governor-general's allowance. In Victoria, Turner introduced a similar bill into the Legislative Assembly, where it met with determined opposition. Victorian parliamentarians accused the secretary of state of trying to raise the governor-general's salary to £20 000. Provincial jealousy also intruded. A significant number of politicians agreed with Thomas Bent: 'If the people of New South Wales want him in Sydney, let them pay for it'. Others agreed with Lieutenant-colonel Reay, who argued that the federal government ought to take the responsibility of paying whatever charges were incidental to the working of the Commonwealth. In the face of this opposition the bill was rejected by the Assembly, leaving a confused and troublesome question entirely unresolved.

Hopetoun had been shown copies of correspondence about this matter before he left London, and in November 1900 he was instructed by Chamberlain to call the attention of his ministers to the problem of an allowance at an early date. Commonwealth ministers should be asked to consider 'what provisions shall be made for the governor-general's establishment and for the expenses of entertainment. So far as your personal staff is concerned I trust that your Ministers will readily agree that it is impossible to provide for them out of the salary fixed by the Act.' This instruction was followed by a reminder in January 1901 and Hopetoun again drew Barton's attention to the matter. The prime minister agreed to submit a measure to the Commonwealth parliament which would meet the situation. Privately he informed Hopetoun that an allowance of £8000 per year would be provided. No further action could be taken until the first Commonwealth parliament met in May.

In his dispatch of November 1900 Chamberlain had warned that hospitality in capitals other than Sydney should be limited to such official entertainment as was 'necessarily demanded, unless and until some fair and suitable provision be made by the States or by the Commonwealth for the expenses involved'. But frugality was not one of Hopetoun's virtues. In March the Colonial Office suggested that he ask for a special grant from the Commonwealth parliament to cover the exceptional expenses during the royal tour. But he replied that since his advisers intended to grant a generous entertaining allowance of £8000 per year and make it retrospective to 1 January 1901 he did not feel justified in asking for extra money.

Foolishly, Barton neglected to act while the royal visitors were touring Australia and when the euphoria associated with the inauguration of the Commonwealth was still in the public mind. Though the subject was occasionally raised in the House of Representatives, the prime minister evaded the issue, perhaps through fear of Labor Party opposition in a parliament where the government's position was extremely insecure. Fifteen months passed before Barton acted. Larger political issues preoccupied him: the administrative difficulties of establishing various departments, setting the machinery of state in motion, differences in his cabinet, and the long, slow conflict over the tariff took up most of an extended parliamentary session.

Barton's dilatoriness was careless and inefficient, however, for he knew from the debates during the conventions that the matter was likely to be contentious. Had he introduced the measure earlier, and allowed judicious consideration of his proposals, it is possible that the result might have been more favourable. Instead, he rushed the matter through at a most disadvantageous time. Australia was in the middle of the most severe drought in its history (1895–1903) and the resulting recession stimulated a rather hysterical campaign for retrenchment, particularly in Victoria. With this clamour for economy as a background and on the last day of the parliamentary session before a brief adjournment during which members were to inspect the federal capital site and the prime minister was to leave for England, Barton moved the second reading of a bill to provide an allowance of £8000 per annum for the governor-general's establishment.

Barton's speech in support of the bill was half-hearted. Perhaps he had already learned that the government whips had failed to find one supporter of the bill outside the ministry. Avoiding any reference to Chamberlain's dispatches to Hopetoun, he reminded the House that before federation the figure of £5000 had been suggested as being necessary to cover the governor-general's allowances. To justify the increase to £8000 he pointed out that the expenses of carrying on the establishments in Sydney and Melbourne had been larger than anyone had anticipated. Items such as fuel, gas, salaries to staff, breakages and printing were estimated as amounting to £4250. The balance, £3750, was intended as partial reimbursement for expenditure upon entertainment and other matters which the prime minister was unable to define. However, he assured parliament that even if this measure were passed the governor-general would still be at a considerable loss, indicating that on the royal visit alone the governor-general had spent £10 000 'seeing that the position of Australia was properly and worthily maintained'.

The House of Representatives was not persuaded. Every speaker after Barton opposed the proposal. Consequently, with rather more discretion than valour, the prime minister weakly claimed that 'in a measure of this kind no one can say that the fate of the ministry is involved' and indicated his readiness to accept an amendment converting the bill into one to recoup the £10 000 expended by the governor-general during the visit of the Duke of York. Leadership of the committee stages was taken over by H.B. Higgins who skilfully manoeuvred the amended measure to its third reading.

The governor-general could be forgiven if he regarded Barton's performance as at the best inept, at the worst devious. He had allowed the bill, which he had presented in fulfilment of an undertaking made in February 1901, to be amended beyond recognition. As the *Daily Telegraph* later succinctly commented, the ministry had 'left His Excellency in the lurch'.

Two days after the debate Barton and Turner conferred with the governor-general and informed him that no allowance of any kind would be approved by parliament. Hopetoun was horrified. He had spent generously in spite of warnings from the Colonial Office. In addition he was concerned that future occupants of the office would find that they could not manage without a large private fortune such as his. On 5 May 1902, while on an official visit to Adelaide, he cabled to the secretary of state: 'No allowance whatever will be given. On a salary of £10 000 per annum I am expected to pay a staff, visit various states, paying all travelling expenses excepting railway, occupy two great Government Houses, paying lights, fuel, stationery, telegrams, postage other than official, dispense hospitality, maintain dignity of the office.' He assured Chamberlain that he had no cause of complaint for himself, but he anticipated grave difficulties as to the future for himself and for his successors. He had already strained his private resources. In these circumstances he concluded: 'The position is impossible. After grave consideration I think you had better recall me after the Coronation.' Meanwhile, in a belated, symbolic gesture, 'all the gas lamps in the Government House drive were at once extinguished', leaving the approaches to Hopetoun's official Melbourne residence in darkness.

In London, the official response was sympathy for the governor-general and resentment at the action of Barton's government. A senior civil servant at the Colonial Office exasperatedly minuted: 'It must be brought home somehow to the Australian mind that all the peers of the realm are not dying with anxiety to take the post of Governor-General in order to provide him with lavish entertainment.' No effort was made to dissuade Hopetoun from the course of action he proposed, partly because he had originally asked to be allowed to return prematurely should his health deteriorate or his financial situation be disadvantaged. It was also felt that the loss of so popular and successful a man might persuade the Commonwealth government to treat his successor more generously.

It was not until 14 May, when Hopetoun returned to Melbourne, that the acting prime minister, Deakin, was informed of the governor-general's decision. As the Senate was still in session, the public announcement was made immediately in that House and Hopetoun's cable of resignation was tabled, together with Chamberlain's reply. The government braced itself to withstand, in Deakin's words, 'a veritable cyclone'.

Barton bore the brunt of the blame. His departmental head, Atlee Hunt, remarked in a letter to the prime minister: 'The public regret is sincere and there is of course a tendency to blame somebody, that somebody is for the present yourself, "les absents ont toujours tort".' The *Daily Telegraph* regarded the ministry's action as 'weakly maladroit'. *Truth*, unrestrained as usual by the normal courtesies of respectability, blamed both Hopetoun's 'own love of lucre and the cowardly unconstitutional conduct of . . . [his] chief constitutional counsellor, Boozer Barton'. The more circumspect *Argus* considered that ministers had 'incurred a great responsibility in first allowing affairs in connection with the pecuniary position of the governor-general to drift'. The *Brisbane Courier* accused Barton's cabinet of 'conspicuous supineness'.

But the prime minister was not the only public scapegoat. The *Sydney Morning Herald* reminded its readers that New South Wales had been willing to shoulder its share of the cost of His Excellency's establishment, but that the other States had refused to follow the mother colony's lead. On the other hand Melbourne's *Punch* thought that as Sydney was so anxious to be the seat of government it ought to vote the necessary money for the upkeep of the governor-general's establishment while he resided there. In Perth, distance lent a wider perspective. The *West Australian* blamed both Sydney and Melbourne. The 'lamentable lack of a federal spirit' in these two cities had, in its opinion, been primarily responsible for the quarrel over who was to house the representative of the Crown.

The *Bulletin* seized the opportunity to castigate those colonial politicians and others who demanded that the governor-general should be 'a circus and a travelling show, humping at enormous expense the pomp and glory of his establishment round the continent and entertaining at various cities'. It identified the primary cause of the quarrel as 'a haughty clique which dines and dances at Government House . . . and is mad in its paltry little soul because one city sees more of a certain ordinary looking man than another'.

Some, like the Hobart *Mercury*, felt that the governor-general himself was primarily at fault. The Tasmanian newspaper believed that his appointment had been 'a mistake' and that Hopetoun had been a 'show Governor-General' when 'what really was wanted was a plain strong capable man, one who would have set an example of that rare but valuable thing, republican simplicity'. Though some Labor members also criticised Hopetoun, these attacks were unrepresentative of the general press and parliamentary opinion. Most newspapers expressed perturbation at the retirement of 'so able and excellent a vice-regent'. Even the *Bulletin* felt that there would be 'disappointment at losing the services of a gentleman who, as a figurehead, was always amiable and dignified'.

Throughout this furore Hopetoun himself maintained a dignified reticence. 'He is as courteous as ever to all of us' Deakin informed Barton, '& makes not a word of complaint'. But Deakin felt that, underneath, Hopetoun blamed the ministry and especially Barton for the fiasco. The inner strain showed a little in a letter to Tennyson in which Hopetoun suggested that 'the two Govt Houses had better be turned into lunatic asylums'. 'I am on terms of affectionate friendship with [Mr Barton]' he told Chamberlain, '. . . but I do think I have a distinct cause of complaint against the government for their procrastination and delay in this matter'.

Hopetoun went to pains to assure Barton that he born no ill will. In addition to friendly letters to the prime minister en route to Britain, he asked Chamberlain, privately, to ensure that Barton was not made to feel that he was 'in any way responsible for my debacle'. When informed of a comment in *The Times* which reported dissension between him and his ministers he cabled to Barton, authorising publication of an unqualified denial. Whatever His Excellency's private feelings may have been, in public he condemned only himself. Writing to Deakin, he singled out his own ambition for the office as the prime cause of his error. He explained that he had placed the office

> on a pedestal . . . not for my own sake but because I believed it to be the best way to make it an office of real usefulness to the Empire and one acceptable to the people of this country . . . I set to work to overbuild myself, and . . . if one day, I found myself sitting on the ground surrounded by the ruins of my own ideal, I have no reason to complain, for I have myself alone to blame.

This emotional farewell address — 'a love letter from a disappointed suitor' — was published in the press.

Despite differing explanations for Hopetoun's unhappy fall from the 'pedestal', an almost unanimous conclusion emerged. Tennyson, who held the Dormant Commission and therefore seemed likely to succeed Hopetoun, at least temporarily, noted: 'The Commonwealth do not want their Governor-General to keep up a great deal of State'. Not everyone approved of this. The *Argus* was forced to conclude that the representative of the Crown 'must be simply a Government administrative officer' confined to one residence, compelled to exercise the strictest economy and unable to travel about the Commonwealth. It was 'not an agreeable outlook for a great and loyal community'.

But this assessment was too alarmist. On 3 June 1902 Senator O'Connor, leader of the government in the Senate, announced that agreement had been reached with the New South Wales government concerning the upkeep of Government House in Sydney. When the House of Representatives resumed, the treasurer, George Turner, persuaded the House to authorise the expenditure of £5000 for the governor-general's past official expenses. Although ostentation must be avoided in future, certain official expenses would be met by the Australian parliament. Government Houses at Sydney and Melbourne continued to be maintained for another decade and vice-regal tours continued to be a vital element in the role of the representative of the Crown in the Commonwealth. Hopetoun's resignation was probably crucial in the resolution of the question.

The whole allowance affair had undoubtedly been grossly mismanaged. But the confusion was itself partly due to uncertainty in Australia over the role to be played by the governor-general. In the absence of clear guide-lines Hopetoun had allowed his naturally extravagant personality to influence his concept of the office. He came to the post with visions of it as being analogous to that of viceroy of India. Barton, his chief adviser, was not the man to disabuse him of these erroneous preconceptions. The first prime minister was himself unsure of the proper role of the governor-general in Australia.

Since 1885 wealthy peers had endowed colonial capitals with an aura of Victorian magnificence. Hopetoun's appointment extended this to the Commonwealth sphere. But his rebuff temporarily checked any grandiose concept of the office. Neither of his two immediate successors had the manner of courtiers. The shearing away of the trappings with which Hopetoun had attempted to deck the post allowed those of his successors who were astute enough to understand the position to operate more efficiently and with less friction than might otherwise have been the case.

In the debate over the governor-general's resignation some more radical members revived earlier suggestions that future occupants be elected. But most politicians expressed satisfaction with the system of British appointments. A classical statement of the conservative point of view was provided by Sir William McMillan. He stressed that as the representative of the Crown was the one visible link remaining between Australia and the Empire, he ought to be given the facilities to visit various States and come into contact with the people as much as possible. He continued: 'Brilliant young men belonging to the upper classes in England, and, as a rule, taken from the House of Lords, are appointed to these posts ... because their position as the apex of our political and social system will be beyond cavil.' The argument that the governor-general, as apex of the political system, ought to be impartial, and that this was best secured by continuing with British appointments, was to persist for 30 years and in some circles for long after that. McMillan also raised another abiding concern of Australian politicians, the need for sympathetic consideration of an Australian point of view in London. In McMillan's opinion, men who had become acquainted with Australian conditions were added, year after year, to the political life in England. These showed themselves 'the friends of Australia whenever political discussions regarding us arise there ... we should give them every facility to make themselves acquainted with the conditions of Australia and so help to remove the false impression which so often prevails in regard to this country on the other side of the world'. He, and others in Australia, were concerned at the adverse publicity created in Britain by the undignified retreat of the Commonwealth's first governor-general.

Many pressed him to reconsider his decision, but Hopetoun was determined to return to England. His departure was a sad affair. The popular and emotional viceroy was reduced to tears at farewell ceremonies in Melbourne. There and in Sydney sympathetic crowds witnessed his final processions through the streets. Always generous to the poor, as a farewell gift he had provided £100 to Melbourne's unemployed for champagne. In the early morning of 17 July, on board a mail steamer bound for Canada, he sailed from Brisbane. Though honoured by the King, and elevated in the peerage as Marquis of Linlithgow, there was little doubt that he had been less than successful in the great test of his public career. As he sailed for home it was clear that his concept of the vice-regal office in Australia had been rejected by the people he had hoped to serve.

Political developments in England and continual ill health prevented Linlithgow from attaining what would have been the supremely satisfying post for him, viceroy of India. He was secretary for Scotland during the last months of Balfour's struggling ministry in 1905. He died of pernicious anaemia at Pau in France on 29 February 1908. In June 1911 an equestrian statue of him by Birnie Rhind was erected in St Kilda Road, Melbourne, near Government House gates. Present at the unveiling was his eldest son, the second Marquis, who in 1935 declined the post of governor-general of Australia and was viceroy of India from 1936 to 1943.

Contemporary sympathy for the first governor-general has only partly been echoed in subsequent accounts of the early years of the Commonwealth. Historians have preserved his name, humiliatingly, in connection with his selection of Lyne as prime minister. The conventional explanation for his discomfiture has been ill health. It is true that he was unwell for much of his term of office and never regained complete health after his return. But there were other reasons for the unfortunate conclusion to what had seemed a promising gubernatorial career. In some senses his failure was personal, in others it was related to the ambivalent nature of the role of governor-general in the early years of federation.

Hopetoun had attempted to use his personal popularity to make his position that of an active, ostentatious viceroy. The presence at the Colonial Office of the great Imperialist, Chamberlain, had supported these ambitions and Barton did not discourage him. His recall ended the period of charisma for the office of governor-general and provided a frame of reference, albeit a negative one, for his successors. Deakin, writing anonymously in the *Morning Post* for an English audience, drew the lesson from Hopetoun's experience:

Our first Governor-General may be said to have taken with him all the decorations and display and some of the anticipations that splendidly surrounded the inauguration of our national existence . . . we have . . . revised our estimate of his high office, stripping it too hastily, but not unkindly, of its festal trappings. The stately ceremonial was fitting, but it has been completed.

Writing to Barton, Deakin abandoned the rhetoric. In future, he thought, Australia wanted a governor-general who would be 'purely a political officer & not a social functionary except within narrow official limits'.

2 Sons of eminent Victorians

The man who was to replace Hopetoun in somewhat confused and difficult circumstances was the governor of South Australia, Hallam, Lord Tennyson. Physically and temperamentally they were markedly dissimilar. A sober, stolid man, Tennyson lacked Hopetoun's elegance and aristocratic confidence. Photographs emphasise his sterner aspects — burly figure, dark beard, heavy browed forehead and features which seem naturally set in a scowl. But his delicate, spidery handwriting reveals another, softer side to his nature — he had published a volume of children's poetry. His public character seems generally to have been gruff and abrupt, perhaps because he, too, was unwell during his term as governor-general. But, in contrast to the nervous disability which upset Hopetoun, Tennyson's affliction was gout.

In his antecedents he also differed from his aristocratic predecessor. Tennyson's mother Emily, née Sellwood, was no noblewoman. His paternal grandfather was a drunken rector from Lincolnshire. The Marlborough College education Hallam had obtained, and the Eton training he was concerned to provide for his three sons, had been won by the literary abilities of his father, Alfred, first Lord Tennyson, the most popular poet in English history who, during his own life time, had become a symbol of the Victorian age.

Hallam Tennyson lived more than half his life in his father's shadow. Born on 11 August 1852 and named after Arthur Hallam, the poet's brilliant friend whose early death had been commemorated by the poem 'In Memoriam', he passed through Marlborough, Trinity College, Cambridge, and the Inner Temple. In 1874 he abandoned his own career to become his father's reader, secretary and constant companion. After the poet's death in 1892, the son devoted himself to the task of writing an official, two-volume biography, published in 1897. His memoir of the first Lord Tennyson is a careful but unrevealing account of the poet's life. But it does show the son's reverence for the patriotic values of his father's later years.

In the 1880s the poet had become converted to the Imperial Idea. One of his verses became an anthem for the Imperial Federation League. Its oracular, declamatory style is a reminder of the peculiar fervour of late Victorian Imperialism — a fervour with which the second Lord Tennyson was deeply imbued.

> Sharers of our glorious past
> Shall we not through good and ill

Cleave to one another still?
Britain's myriad voices call
'Sons, be welded, each and all
Into one Imperial whole
One with Britain, heart and Soul!
One life, one flag, one fleet, one throne!'
Britons, hold your own!

In 1883 Hallam Tennyson had become a member of the Council of the Imperial Federation League and he remained interested in the British colonies. It was because his father would have approved, duty called and he had nothing else to do that in January 1899 he accepted when Chamberlain offered him the governorship of South Australia.

His appointment to Adelaide was Tennyson's first experience of public office. He did not possess the great wealth which had previously been regarded as a prerequisite, but the imminence of federation seemed to foreshadow a change in the type of colonial governor sent to Australia. Representatives of the Crown in the States were expected to be overshadowed by the governor-general.

Tennyson and his family took up residence at Government House, Adelaide, in April 1899. A governor's home life in 1900 was an extension of his public life. He was required to entertain the colony's public men, their ladies and visiting celebrities. His wife was also expected to be prominent — opening bazaars, visiting hospitals and chairing worthy causes. Tennyson had, in 1884, married Audrey Boyle, the niece of a family friend. By the time they arrived in Australia they had three young sons. One of these boys, Lionel, became an English test cricketer.

Lady Tennyson, an intelligent, active woman, enjoyed her public work as governor's lady. But she regarded her stay in Australia as an exile and she had an abiding horror that her three boys would develop the local schoolboys' 'terrible twang'. Her long, weekly letters home provide an engaging account of family routine and public duties in the rarefied atmosphere of an Australian Government House.

Some doubted Tennyson's suitability for the post of acting governor-general. Centralists in Barton's cabinet suspected him of a too vigorous provincialism. As governor of South Australia he had boycotted the inauguration ceremonies and refused to forward copies of his correspondence to the governor-general. Liberals and nationalists also suspected his close involvement with Chief Justice Sir Samuel Way. He had been associated with the latter's campaign against the Privy Council appeal clauses in the Commonwealth Constitution and in so doing earned the disapproval of his premier, Frederick Holder. Deakin told Barton he feared that they would 'have trouble with Tennyson'.

In Britain, too, there were misgivings about his fitness to act as representative of the Crown in the Commonwealth. Twelve months earlier Colonial Office officials had been chary of issuing the Dormant Commission to so inexperienced a governor — only doing so to forestall any Australian proposal that the chief justice of the Commonwealth High Court should exercise that office. Upon Hopetoun's resignation, Chamberlain delayed confirming that the Dormant

Lord Tennyson and Lady Tennyson in the grounds of Government House, Adelaide, 1899.

Commission should come into effect for several weeks. But no permanent appointment could be made while the problem of an allowance was still unsolved. So on 4 July the secretary of state authorised the South Australian governor to assume, temporarily, the administration of the Commonwealth government. Tennyson remained as acting governor-general until the following January, when, with the agreement of Australian ministers, he was confirmed in the post. At his own wish the appointment was for one year only.

Though Deakin and others feared problems, the Australian press applauded the choice. Melbourne's *Punch* considered him 'a gubernator of the rare, common-sense order, one who can be absolutely relied upon never to say a foolish thing or to do the wrong thing'. His rule in Adelaide had possessed 'an easy home-like quality' which *Punch* found at once 'piquant and comfortable'. Other newspapers were just as complimentary. Even the *Bulletin*, never one to congratulate governors, had in the past expressed sarcastic approval of 'the persistency with which ... Lord Tennyson dodges public functions' and commended his frugality. It was confidently felt that these characteristics were appropriate after Hopetoun's ostentation.

The first problem facing the acting governor-general was the allowance question. His predecessor had hoped that resignation would shame parliament into making generous provision for entertainment and other official expenses. There was certainly some shame in the political furore which had followed Hopetoun's recall. But public opinion eventually resolved that both Hopetoun and Barton had been at fault. In both press and parliament the opinion was expressed that Hopetoun had been far too extravagant but shamefully treated by Barton. The conveniently absent prime minister was universally criticised for undertaking to provide for the governor-general a yearly allowance of £8000 in addition to the £10 000 salary provided by the Constitution. However only the extremists opposed *any* allowance for the governor-general. The problem was to reach an acceptable compromise.

Tennyson, frugal and unostentatious by nature, agreed that Hopetoun's immoderate display was unnecessary. But there was no doubt that the maintenance of two Government Houses was an expensive business. He, Deakin and Turner examined the public functions of the governor-general in detail. They arrived at a figure of £5500 per year for the costs of maintaining Government Houses at Melbourne and Sydney. In addition, an 'official Secretary to the Governor-General and the Executive Council' would be appointed and paid by the Commonwealth.

Deakin presented this proposition to parliament in August 1902. Despite objections from the Labor Party, the new arrangement, phrased as 'an expenditure upon Government House of £5500 a year ... during the term of office of the next Governor-General', obtained parliament's approval. Several politicians who had voted against an allowance for Hopetoun supported Deakin's measure. Some claimed that their earlier stand had been due to the insufficient time for consideration allowed by Barton and inadequate information as to the details of the proposed expenditure. But Hopetoun's resignation had evidently been a contributing factor in their reappraisal.

Some difficulty arose over the position of official secretary. Deakin explained that this appointment was intended 'to take out of the hands of the Governor-General's staff all the public duties connected with the office of Secretary to the Executive Council'. He proposed that this officer also take charge of 'the whole of the correspondence which is transmitted from the Commonwealth through the Governor-General to the Secretary of State for Colonies, to foreign powers and to the Governments of the States'. The man selected to carry out these

duties was His Excellency's private secretary, Wallington. Labor parliamentarians objected to the appointment as providing a sinecure for a 'society
favourite'. But Deakin was insistent that he was establishing an important
matter of principle. He explained that for some time he had felt that an official
who was responsible to the Commonwealth should be in control of the public
business associated with the office of governor-general. In particular he
considered that the bureaucrat who handled the Australian government's
correspondence with Great Britain should be paid by and therefore accountable
to the Commonwealth.

Though this aspect of Deakin's proposal may have been misunderstood by
the Labor Party its implications were clear enough in Downing Street. Sir John
Anderson minuted that Wallington was, no doubt, an excellent person for the
post, but if he were replaced by 'an Australian nominee of Ministers', it would
be 'impossible for the Gov.-Gen. to use him for the personal and confidential
purposes for which a Gov. requires a Private Secretary'. Sir Montagu Ommanney agreed that the proposed arrangement was impossible. He considered that
Australian officials, from ministers downward, 'had exceedingly lax ideas on the
subject of secret and confidential communications'. Several dispatches were
addressed to Tennyson requesting clarification of the position of official
secretary. But the acting governor-general apparently failed to grasp the
situation. He seemed too concerned to congratulate himself on the settlement of
the allowance question and on the Australian satisfaction with his thriftiness.

In December 1902 the difficulty foreseen by the Colonial Office came to a
head when Wallington resigned, to take up a position on the staff of the Prince
of Wales. Tennyson and his family were spending the hot summer months in
the familiar comfort of Marble Hill, the South Australian governor's country
residence. On Christmas Day the man chosen by cabinet to replace Wallington
as official secretary began duty in Melbourne.

At the time of his appointment George Steward was chief clerk in the
Department of External Affairs. Born in Scotland in 1866, Steward had joined
the Commonwealth civil service early in 1901 after ten years experience in the
Tasmanian public service. Barton had evidently regarded him as reliable, for in
January 1902 Steward had been entrusted with the delicate task of conveying to
Brisbane's customs inspector secret and incriminating instructions under the
Immigration Restriction Act. Though he was trustworthy and had considerable
administrative and secretarial experience, his chief drawbacks were an unfortunately brusque manner and an over-developed concern for his own dignity. He
worked comfortably with later governors-general, but with Tennyson relations
were sometimes strained. In a letter to Barton shortly after Steward had taken
up his appointment His Excellency complained that the new official secretary
was 'too big for his boots'.

The trouble arose partly from Steward's agitation. During Tennyson's
absence in South Australia a list of 'Rules of Procedure' drawn up by Wallington
was left for Steward in Melbourne. Steward complained to Atlee Hunt,
secretary of Barton's Department of External Affairs, that these rules subordinated him to the governor-general's private secretary, Lord Richard Nevill. Hunt

must have informed the prime minister, for three weeks later Barton wrote to Tennyson asking that Steward's instructions be amended. He suggested that as they stood the 'Rules of Procedure' conflicted with parliament's intention that the official secretary 'was to have charge of all communications which pass between the Commonwealth and the Imperial or State Governments'. In the meantime, Hunt refused to supply postage stamps at Commonwealth expense to anyone on the governor-general's staff apart from Steward.

Barton's letter was stiffly polite but firm. So was Tennyson's reply. He quoted a communication from the Imperial government instructing the official secretary to take charge of all public dispatches but requiring that all secret and confidential communications be dealt with by the private secretary. The prime minister reacted indignantly, interpreting Tennyson's proposal as an attempt to set up his office as an intervening authority between the Commonwealth and United Kingdom governments. He feared that the governor-general would be able to withhold some possibly vital correspondence from his Australian advisers or otherwise interfere in the rights of the Commonwealth as a sovereign state. In a long-winded memorandum Barton reminded the governor-general of the monarch's constitutional duty to accept the advice of his ministers.

Tennyson was not prepared to accept this admonition quietly. The correspondence increased in vehemence until, eventually, Deakin's mediation was sought. He advised them to stop writing sharp letters to each other and find a compromise at a private meeting. On 5 February such a confrontation took place and the misunderstanding was smoothed over. Barton agreed that some of the governor-general's correspondence with the Imperial government was necessarily private. Tennyson had received from the Colonial Office a concession that their earlier instruction had been too wide. The governor-general suggested that the use of two cyphers would provide a way out of the difficulty. One code would apply to His Excellency's private correspondence, a second, kept by the official secretary, would be used for official communications between the Commonwealth and Imperial governments.

The effect of this dispute was to separate more clearly than before the two functions of the King's representative — constitutional head of state and agent of the British government. From March 1903 a Commonwealth public servant, responsible to the Department of External Affairs, was in charge of correspondence between the Australian and British governments.

In these circumstances it was becoming increasingly clear that diplomatic abilities rather than administrative efficiency or social leadership were the qualities most necessary in a governor-general if he were to exercise his role to the satisfaction of both Australia and Britain. Unfortunately Tennyson, fired with ideas of Imperial federation and lacking the unction of an ambassador, was not able to recognise this. Stirred by Barton's assertion of the principles of responsible government, he sought from the professor of law at Adelaide University, J.W. Salmond, a definition of the governor's powers in a self-governing colony. The predictably legalistic reply was seized upon by Tennyson as justification for a wide interpretation of those powers, and he secretly circulated the memorandum to all Australian State governors. In a covering letter he deprecated any suggestion that a governor was merely an agent of the Imperial government and denied that his position was analogous with that of a minister resident at a foreign court. A copy of the correspondence was sent to the secretary of state.

By this time the Colonial Office was irritated with the meddlesome governor-general. Anderson minuted acidly: 'Lord Tennyson and his constitutional pedagogue should really try and mind their own business'. The memorandum was, in his opinion, 'misleading and mischievous'. The Australian governor-general did not seem to appreciate that

> the day of personal governorship has gone and that the one cardinal fact for a Governor to bear in mind that [sic] for every official act a minister must be responsible ... Where Imperial interests are concerned, if a Governor differs from his Ministers and cannot bring them round to his view, he should apply to his chief — the S[ecretary] of S[tate] — for instructions.

From the point of view of the Colonial Office, the representative of the Crown was to avoid unnecessary interference in local affairs. Too rigorous an interpretation of his powers in these matters might hinder his efficacy as an advocate for Imperial concerns. Chamberlain sent Tennyson a stiff dispatch which specifically rebutted Salmond's interpretation of the governor's role.

In his capacity as representative of the British government, Tennyson was still expected to provide the secretary of state with strictly confidential reports independent of his ministers. This had been the basis of the difficulties surrounding Steward's appointment. Tennyson interpreted this responsibility widely. In his reports to the Colonial Office he commented freely on Australian affairs and frequently offered his own suggestions. He was, for example, genuinely interested in the Australian Aborigines and their welfare. In Adelaide he had spoken publicly for a more humane treatment and he corresponded privately with administrators and anthropologists. He was convinced that control over Aborigines ought to be a Commonwealth responsibility.

In April 1903 the governor-general informed the secretary of state that a great deal of dissatisfaction was being caused by the 'disloyal attitude' of Cardinal Moran, Roman Catholic archbishop of Sydney, who, he charged, was continually 'stirring up ... sectarian strife'. His Excellency praised the Roman Catholic archbishops of Adelaide and Melbourne as 'excellent leaders of men and thoroughly good citizens' but he felt that it would be greatly to the advantage of Australia if the Cardinal were 'removed from the Commonwealth', and he suggested that the authorities in Rome be approached to this effect. Though in Anderson's opinion there was no doubt that Moran was 'a mischievous ill-affected fellow' the Colonial Office was understandably unwilling to interfere in what was patently an internal matter for the Commonwealth government. Fortunately perhaps for Tennyson's public image, the quite improper suggestion remained undiscovered.

On one occasion His Excellency was embarrassed when a comment which he had made in what was intended to be a confidential dispatch was made public by the British government. In the course of transmitting a letter from the acting prime minister concerning a petition from natives of the Pacific Islands residing in Queensland, the governor-general questioned the consistency of Deakin's stated policy. Nine months later the dispatch was published by the Colonial Office. Deakin immediately wrote to Tennyson denying that he had contradicted himself. He remarked pointedly that he had seen no portion of the dispatch and had been unaware that Tennyson purposed to make the representations he had made. He warned, indirectly, that if the correspondence were referred to in parliament he would not support the governor-general. Though a short item referring to this disagreement did appear in the press and the Labor Party raised the matter in the House of Representatives Barton was able to deflect most of the criticism.

If immigration policy were one sphere in which the governor-general was entitled to ensure that Imperial interests were protected, an even more significant responsibility was defence policy. Tennyson's term of office was during an important period in Australian and Imperial defence planning. During 1902 and 1903 tentative signs of a national defence policy within the aegis of Empire began to emerge in the Commonwealth. Tennyson felt himself to be a vital link between the Australian and Imperial governments in these negotiations.

A month before he had taken office the Treaty of Vereeniging had finally brought to a close the war in South Africa. To those who were clear-sighted enough to see it, this war had revealed serious deficiencies in British and Imperial defence strategy. At the same time, the loyal and generous participation of the British self-governing colonies had led Chamberlain and others to hope for that closer union which Imperial federationists had preached for twenty years. This hope was to be shattered on the rocks of colonial nationalism and British liberalism. In the process the Australian insistence that its own priorities might conflict with those of Great Britain was to prove an early indication of Dominion autonomy within the Empire, especially in the sphere of naval defence.

Under the Naval Defence Agreement of 1887, negotiated at the first Colonial Conference, Australian colonies contributed towards the maintenance of a squadron of the Royal Navy stationed at Sydney. The development of colonial sea-going forces was discouraged but the British squadron was tied to Australia's neighbouring seas. During the following decade this stipulation came under attack in Britain in the course of a controversy over the relative merits of naval dispersal or fleet concentration. By 1902 the latter point of view had begun to prevail. At the Colonial Conference of that year it was expounded by the first lord of the admiralty, Lord Selborne, to the assembled colonial ministers.

The 1902 conference was destined to be a disappointment to those who hoped that an Imperial council might develop from the colonial unity displayed in the Boer War. Moreover, Canada obdurately refused to contribute towards naval defence of the Empire. For imperialists the only light seemed to be provided by Australia and New Zealand. Both agreed to renew the 1887 naval agreement. Both agreed to scrap the earlier condition that the royal naval squadron remain permanently in Australasian waters, a provision which was anathema to fleet concentration theorists like Selborne.

In acceding to Admiralty pressure Barton was probably influenced by the conviction that Australia could not at that stage afford the expense of establishing a naval nucleus of her own. But there were others in Australia who disapproved strongly of the terms negotiated in London. To many, a straightout subsidy to the Royal Navy smacked of vassalage and guaranteed no definite local protection. For a time the passage of the new naval agreement through the Commonwealth parliament remained in doubt.

The governor-general was one of the avenues of influence which Selborne used in an attempt to persuade Australian politicians to ratify the agreement. A correspondence arguing the merits of the naval proposals passed between Tennyson and the first lord of the Admiralty. At the same time Tennyson discussed this vital aspect of policy with the prime minister, the minister of defence, Sir John Forrest, and the leader of the opposition, Reid, who promised support for the agreement but asked Tennyson 'not to inform Cabinet of this'. When the agreement was finally ratified by the Commonwealth parliament, Selborne wrote to thank the governor-general for his assistance. He complimented Tennyson on his influence upon the Australian politicians, without which, he suggested, it was doubtful if the agreement would have passed.

This was merely formal courtesy on Selborne's part; Tennyson's lack of expert status minimised his effectiveness. But the passage of the naval agreement did illustrate the opportunities available to a governor-general. Not only was he a useful advanced listening-post for the British government, he also had special means of persuasion and influence. Tennyson's inexperience and obvious lack of prestige in Imperial circles made it unlikely that his personal views were very significant to Australian politicians. Had he been more of an expert, such as the Victorian governor, Sir George Clarke, his opinion could have carried more weight. In 1904 Reid asked the British government whether there were objections if the Australian ministry consulted State governors, 'gentlemen of high Naval and Military experience', upon matters pertaining to the defence of Australia. Had Hopetoun remained until 1903 he may have been a more influential advocate. In 1902 he had prepared a memorandum for Barton urging the advantages of continuing to contribute to the Imperial navy. As it was, Tennyson was only one of a circle of Imperial officials, such as Clarke and the admirals of the Australasian station, who urged the Commonwealth to agree with Admiralty doctrine.

In a typical piece of self-aggrandisement, Tennyson allowed himself to claim, in 1914, that he had 'worked hard that Australia should have a fleet of her own'. In fact his counsel was in the opposite direction. But his governorship in Adelaide had brought him into contact with the most voluble exponent of a local navy, Captain W.R. Creswell, and they continued to correspond after Tennyson had become governor-general. Tennyson's correspondence reveals that the representative of the Crown had unique access to a whole range of opinions and attitudes. Barton, Forrest, Reid, Creswell, Clarke, Selborne and Chamberlain received the benefit of Tennyson's opinions on the question of renegotiation of the naval agreement. His influence was probably marginal. But an abler, subtler, more diplomatic governor-general would have utilised the opportunities to greater effect.

In the sphere of military defence the governor-general was no less active in making known his views. Tennyson quickly became close to the commandant of the federal forces, Hutton, who was a constant visitor to Government House. But the general could be an embarrassing associate. Tennyson soon became embroiled in the conflict over military reorganisation between the single-minded soldier and the economy-minded Australian government. Tennyson's letters and conversations with his ministers, especially with Forrest, urging compliance with Hutton's plans for a field force, were well-meant but ineffective.

It was not only in Australia that the defence reorganisation planned by Hutton encountered opposition. In February 1903 a Colonial Defence Committee memorandum criticising Hutton's field-force scheme was forwarded through the office of governor-general for the information of the Commonwealth government. Tennyson, probably at the instigation of Hutton, withheld this document from his ministers. Explaining his action to the secretary of state, he argued that the general's plans were already encountering sufficient opposition within the Commonwealth, and that if the committee's memorandum were transmitted to the cabinet, Imperial interests would be harmed.

This was a serious intervention by the representative of the Crown in a matter of vital concern to the Commonwealth government. Tennyson was mistaken in attempting to withhold from his advisers the views of British experts on Hutton's schemes. Fortunately a more realistic view of the situation was taken by the Colonial Office. The governor-general's caution was brushed aside and he was instructed to forward the memorandum in question to his ministers. Though he did show it to Barton and Forrest, His Excellency did not retreat from his position and in a personal letter to Chamberlain expressed his disapproval of any action which tended to make the commandant's position more difficult than it already was.

Though the contretemps over the Colonial Defence Committee memorandum was an indiscretion on the part of the governor-general, some of his reasoning was realistic. He pointed out with admirable insight that Australia regarded herself as an ally of Great Britain, but as a self-governing community she refused to bind herself. Britain must be content to trust to Australian loyalty. Tennyson assured the British government that if the mother country became involved in any grave national crisis, Australian support would be unstinting. In these assertions his judgement was sound. Yet he badly misread Australian opinion regarding Imperial federation. He remained convinced that Australian leaders were becoming more favourably inclined towards closer union, and in a speech on the eve of his departure he expressed the hope that this would soon be achieved. The *Daily Telegraph* chided the governor-general for his remarks, asserting that 'Representation in the Imperial Parliament or in any Imperial council with power to do anything, would deprive us of a corresponding amount of our existing autonomous rights, and would therefore be a backward step on the road of British destiny'.

Tennyson was more scrupulous than his predecessor in the conduct of Executive Council meetings. In August 1901 Hopetoun had delegated to the vice-president of the council authority to conduct business during the governor-general's temporary absence. Tennyson renewed this practice but he secured from the prime minister an undertaking that he would be given advance notice when important business was to be discussed. His Excellency made a point of being present on such occasions. His written delegation of authority stipulated that only business of a formal or routine character was to be dealt with in his absence. These arrangements remained the basis of the Executive Council machinery for at least the next quarter of a century.

Tennyson left Australia in January 1904. In contrast to the departure of his predecessor, press opinion concerning his term of office was universally enthusiastic and complimentary. His occasional indiscretions had been kept remarkably quiet, while his frequent assertions that a governor-general need not entertain extravagantly seemed to provide what most Australians required of him. One magazine commented that 'Lord Tennyson departed almost as unobtrusively from the Commonwealth as he had come'.

In several respects the end of Tennyson's career in the Commonwealth coincided with significant developments in Australia's relationship with Britain. The departure of Chamberlain from the Colonial Office in October 1903 and his replacement by Alfred Lyttelton signified the end of that department's most energetic phase of existence. In local political affairs, Barton had, in September, been replaced by the more decisive Deakin. But prospects for political stability were poor. The December elections had returned a parliament with three parties evenly divided. In such a situation the governor-general needed qualities of judgement and experience which Tennyson clearly did not possess.

But there had been some resolution of the ambiguities of his office during Tennyson's term. Control of the public correspondence of the Commonwealth had been transferred to a public servant responsible to the Department of External Affairs where it remained for a further 25 years. Though Tennyson himself failed to recognise the development, both the Colonial Office and the Australian government had clarified their concept of the role of governor-general. In matters of domestic concern he was to act as impartial constitutional sovereign, independent of any British suzerainty. In matters which affected Imperial interests he was to act on the instructions of the Imperial government. The extent to which he was successful in these two capacities depended upon tact, prestige and diplomatic skills. Tennyson's tour of duty had seen the consolidation of the office of governor-general as an institutional framework which assisted in maintaining the Imperial connection.

Though he lived until 1928 Tennyson never again held any public office. In November 1905 he was offered the governorship of Madras but refused. On his return to England he took up residence in his father's house, Farringford on the Isle of Wight, which he preserved as it had been when the poet lived there: 'To cross the threshold ... was ... like returning as if by some magic into that Victorian Age which now seems so remote. Time in that house in the hollow seemed to have stood still'. Two of his three sons were killed in World War I and Lady Tennyson died on 7 December 1916. Two years later Tennyson married a widow, Mary Emily Hickens, née Prinsep. He died at Farringford on 2 December 1928.

Though in the exercise of his role of governor-general the second Lord Tennyson was pompous and inflexible it was perhaps to have been expected. He was an ordinary man of no particular talent, thrust by his father's eminence and the accident of Hopetoun's resignation into higher public prominence than his capacities warranted. The delicate relationship of a colony to its Empire, developing towards 'Dominion Status', was too subtle for his imagination, which had remained rooted in the high Victorian ideas of his father. But he had enjoyed his life as governor-general, and in his subsequent, long, empty career looked back with affection and self-satisfaction to those few years in his life in which he was Lord Tennyson and not 'the son of Lord Tennyson'.

Lord Tennyson's successor, the third Australian governor-general, was sworn in on 21 January 1904 in the Queen's Hall of the Federal Parliament House in Melbourne in the presence of leading politicians, judges and other public figures. To many in Australia the swift succession of representatives of the Crown in the Commonwealth had been an unsatisfactory feature of the early years of federation. The *Australasian* recalled earlier expectations that 'the Office would be coveted as one of comfort as well as high honour and that the term of five years at least would be ... regularly served by its occupants'. Instead, as the *West Australian* pointed out, they had so far averaged one a year. It was hoped that the coming of Sir Henry Stafford Northcote, first Baron Northcote, would be 'the commencement of a stable era'.

In the choice of a successor to Tennyson the Commonwealth government had exercised only nominal influence. Barton had requested in October 1902 that the names under consideration be made known to the Australian cabinet before an appointment was made, but the Colonial Office had been unsympathetic to the suggestion. In July 1903 the secretary of state cabled to ascertain whether Northcote's appointment 'would be acceptable'. The matter was considered in cabinet a few days later and the selection was approved.

The new governor-general was 'a spare little man with a dark weather beaten face' and a bushy moustache. He had been born in London on 18 November 1846, second son of Sir Stafford Northcote and his wife Cecilia Frances, née Farrer. His father, later the first Earl of Iddesleigh, was Disraeli's second in command, and Northcote inherited his conscientious, virtuous but dull character. Northcote had a great deal of practical experience in the workings of British bureaucracy and politics. Following an Eton and Oxford education he was forced, as a second son, to make his own way and had entered by examination the Foreign Office as a clerk in 1868. He accompanied a mission to the United States of America to arrange the Alabama Treaty in 1871 and in 1873 had married Alice, the wealthy adopted daughter of Lord Mount Stephen, a Canadian railroad tycoon. In 1876 he was private secretary to Lord Salisbury in Constantinople. Like Tennyson, Northcote was for a time his father's private secretary. In 1880 he entered politics in the Conservative interest as representative for Exeter, remaining in the Commons until 1899. This experience gave

Lord Northcote and Lady Northcote

him an understanding of parliamentary forms and political conventions which neither his two predecessors nor his two successors possessed and which was to be invaluable during his term in Australia. He gained some experience of minor office in Britain as financial secretary to the War Office and surveyor-general of ordnance. In 1899 he accepted the post of governor of Bombay, largely because his wife wished to be out of England. Her father had married again, and in Northcote's words it was impossible 'for Alice and the present lady of Brocket to stable their horses together'. The same circumstances meant that, upon leaving Bombay in 1903, he was prepared to accept Chamberlain's offer of the Australian post.

By 1904 the quasi-ambassadorial nature of the office of governor-general of Australia was becoming clearer. A few years earlier the *Age* had described a constitutional governor as 'an English official at the other end of the wire . . . an intermediary between his constitutional advisers on the spot and his official employers at home'. Even the *Argus*, whose attitude towards the British Empire was more often emotional than dispassionate, compared the governor-general to 'the head of a diplomatic mission'. In addition to this role, as the *Age* pointed out, a colonial governor had a 'considerable amount of routine work of the goose step order to get through . . . and much of his popularity will depend upon his capacity for looking cheerful upon an unsucculent diet of official addresses and municipal congratulations'. Northcote proved conscientious in fulfilling these mundane duties as official apex of society.

During the first four months of office, Lord and Lady Northcote acquainted themselves with the social functions of governor-general in Melbourne. For most of this time Victoria was without a State governor, so he was able to undertake a constant round of vice-regal activities without fear of offending or slighting the incumbent at State Government House. Their Excellencies visited hospitals, held small dinner parties and presented trophies at a polo gymkhana in Kooyong. Northcote lacked the seigneurial charm of Hopetoun and the pomposity of Tennyson, having a reserved, punctilious manner which did not always impress. To Forrest he seemed 'slow'. But Chief Justice Way of Adelaide felt that while he was 'not showy, everybody recognizes that he is safe, sincere, and honest' and on occasion he had exhibited a 'pleasant flavour of dry humour in his speeches'. He was not a music lover, for in July 1904 he wrote to his close friend 'Willy' (Lord Selborne), 'I survived two solid hours of listening to Paderewski last night'.

To Deakin, however, there was no question of Northcote's personal qualities. The prime minister appreciated Northcote's restrained public manner and inner shrewdness. Moreover, the governor-general was a representative of that world of Imperial politics in which Deakin was so interested. They became close personal friends, and remained so, whether Deakin was in or out of office. Ten years later Deakin still thought of Northcote in terms of affection and respect, observing that Northcote's 'tactful, patient friendliness and modesty had given him not only knowledge but power among politicians and over the much wider area in which he was trusted and warmly liked'.

Northcote's contacts with British society and his connections with British

Lord Northcote on a tour of New South Wales. Much of a governor-general's popularity depended upon 'his capacity for looking cheerful upon an unsucculent diet of official addresses'.

politicians provided an opportunity for Deakin's own views, and Australia's, to be conveyed through a persuasive confidante. Deakin had always considered that an Australian viewpoint was too often unavailable in London. This had been one reason which led him to write, from 1900 to 1914, anonymous articles for the *Morning Post*. He explained to Richard Jebb in May 1907 that his first aim was 'to inform English readers of the inner meaning of Australian politics'. He realised that if Australia were to have a voice in international affairs, it must be raised in London. Australian governors who returned to England provided a circle of men there with first-hand knowledge of Australia and, presumably, sympathy for its special problems and needs. The *Sydney Morning Herald* expressed this opinion in a leading article on the day Northcote was sworn in. His predecessor, Tennyson, would, it hoped, become 'one of that growing number of ex-Australians, if the term may be used, who represent Australian feeling with understanding as well as sympathy at the centre of the Empire'. Deakin carefully maintained contact with ex-governors. Through Northcote many of his ambitions and hopes for Australia reached Balfour and the British cabinet.

In turn, Northcote regarded Deakin as 'a chivalrous gentleman' and 'a very nice fellow'. On occasion there were differences of opinion, but these were always accompanied with respect and restraint on both sides. Compared with the sometimes strained relations between Tennyson and his prime minister, the affectionate but independent mutual admiration between Deakin and Northcote was both positive and fruitful.

While privately on the closest terms with Deakin, in public Northcote was strictly impartial. Reid, the Labor leader J.C. Watson and other politicians were frequent guests at Government House. Because of the political instability which existed for much of his term of office it was vital that Northcote keep abreast of the political situation. He was a shrewd observer of events and trends, and a conscientious examiner of parliamentary debates and official papers, 'with the English trained official's respect for blue books'. His own parliamentary experience made Australian political developments particularly absorbing for him, and in both official and private communications with the British government he transmitted his assessments of events and personalities.

The governor-general was only a few days in Australia when he heard, at a luncheon of the Australian Natives' Association, the prime minister liken the state of parties in the Commonwealth parliament after the 1903 election to 'three elevens in the field'. To act as umpire in this field was no easy task. Three months after he arrived, the defeat of the Deakin government over an amendment to a clause in the Arbitration Bill, bringing State public servants within the scope of the legislation, placed the governor-general, *prima facie*, in a difficult position. Normally when a government was defeated the leader of the opposition could be expected to be called on to form a ministry. But in this case Reid had voted with the government in the vital division. Moreover the motion had been moved, not by Watson, but by Andrew Fisher, his deputy. Though the *Argus* continued to scout the possibility that Reid would be asked to form a government, most Australian newspapers agreed that the governor-general ought to call on the leader of the Labor Party. It was generally known that if Deakin's advice were requested, he would suggest that Watson be invited to be prime minister. Even the *Argus* commented that 'as a general rule, if the leader of a government on leaving office is consulted [as to his successor] his opinion carries considerable weight'.

The political crisis came to a head during the fourth week in April 1904. Melbourne was agog with rumours. The chief protagonists were the guests of the governor-general at a Government House luncheon on the day that Deakin submitted his ministry's resignation. In the midst of all the public fuss, with perfect constitutional propriety, Northcote asked Deakin for his advice. Acting upon it, he commissioned Watson to form a government.

Though much of the credit for this action, which gave the Labor Party its first experience of Commonwealth office, must go to Deakin, a certain amount of recognition ought to be accorded the governor-general. In March he had written to Lyttelton that though it would be 'disagreeable' to him personally 'the best thing for Australia would be to have a Labour Ministry in office'. He believed that experience of office would teach Labor responsibility: 'If they can govern wisely & successfully, so much the better; if not there will be a popular rally of moderate forces, & socialism will receive a great setback'. It would have been natural enough for one of the governor-general's class and status to have been hostile to Labor. Tennyson, in contrast, had constantly denigrated the Labor Party and criticised Barton's dependence upon its support in the first Commonwealth parliament. Reid's comments after Watson was commissioned suggest that had he been offered the opportunity he would have accepted. However consideration of other courses open to the governor-general merely emphasises the constitutional propriety of Northcote's action in asking Deakin's advice. It seems that he also required to be satisfied by Deakin that a Labor government would not be immediately defeated. Writing to the secretary of state he explained 'Mr Deakin ... will certainly wish to give the new Ministry a fair trial'.

Relations between the new prime minister and the governor-general were cordial and seemed to indicate mutual respect. Two weeks after Watson had taken office Northcote wrote to Balfour in amused but commendatory fashion, describing the new regime: 'The situation has a distinctly comical side. The Labour Ministers words are a mixture of honey & butter — no extreme measures — bow to the will of the House — take into consideration, etc. — in short all of the orthodox phrases of the most respectable of Administrations.' Though patronising, Northcote's comment was accurate and indicated his goodwill towards the Labor government.

Northcote continued to regard Deakin as unofficial adviser. One subject about which he asked Deakin's opinion was his touring itinerary. During his four-and-a-half years of office he visited every State and also visited the Northern Territory, besides travelling regularly between Melbourne and Sydney. At first there were objections from the States at the cost of this use of their services, but eventually the Commonwealth government agreed to meet His Excellency's travelling expenses. To some extent climate, and a concern for his own comfort, influenced Northcote's enthusiasm for this aspect of his role. He did not like Melbourne winters. Consequently he moved his residence to Sydney in May 1904 and on 30 June set off on a three-week tour of Queensland.

It was while he was on his tour of Queensland that Northcote discovered the hidden dangers in apparently inoffensive public remarks made by the representatives of the Crown in Australia. In his public speeches since he had arrived he had been judiciously non-committal. He had discerned that it was better for a governor-general to be uncontroversial, even dull, in his speechmaking, than to risk commenting on current affairs. Avoiding the emotional oratorical style of Hopetoun and the self-assurance of Tennyson, Northcote was cautious to the point of being trite. He tended to urge conventional Victorian virtues, such as thrift and self-sufficiency, and later was a fervent advocate of immigration. One journalist recalled that, as a speaker, he had 'that ponderous style which seems ingrained in Englishmen. He was not eloquent. But he had a sustained consecutiveness of expression which made him exceedingly easy to follow ... There were no fine periods, no striving after phrase making. But he talked pleasantly and with fine diplomacy of whatever was uppermost in his mind.'

During his tour of Queensland in 1904, confronted with a deputation of Melanesians who presented a petition protesting against their prospective deportation, Northcote expressed sympathy for their plight. There were murmurs from some Labor parliamentarians, though W.M. Hughes, then minister for external affairs, stated publicly that the government took no exception to the governor-general's remarks. As the *Argus* pointed out, 'words of sympathy convey no expression of opinion as to the justice or policies of the law under which the deportation may take place'.

A more controversial case occurred in September the following year. Against a background of debate over the possible introduction of a citizen military force along Swiss lines, in a speech to army officers in Perth Northcote warned that Switzerland's situation was not entirely parallel with Australia's.

On the surface it was hardly a profound remark, but Labor Senator William Higgs moved that: 'it is contrary to the established principles of constitutional and parliamentary government that the head of the Executive should in public express himself on matters of public policy unless advised to do so by his responsible Ministers'.

Replying on behalf of the government, Senator Playford, minister for defence, agreed with Higgs that it was the duty of the governor-general 'to hold the balance evenly'. But he denied that Northcote had exceeded the proper bounds of action for a constitutional monarch. Among the other speakers opinion was divided. Some disapproved of the governor-general's remarks. Others, such as the Labor leader in the Senate, George Pearce, could not see that His Excellency 'in this or any other speech had transgressed the liberty that should be accorded to him'. On the contrary, Pearce considered that the governor-general had 'rendered Australia a service in directing public attention to an important question, without involving himself in party politics'. As a result of the attitude taken by Pearce and two other Labor senators, the Senate rejected Higgs' motion by a narrow majority.

Though precluded from replying in public to the implied censure involved in Higgs' motion, the governor-general vehemently justified the propriety of his speech in a private letter to Deakin. To deny to the representative of the Crown a right 'to express himself on matters of public policy', Northcote felt, was far too sweeping. But he was careful in speeches thereafter never to sail so close to the wind. His reputation emerged relatively unscathed. Even Higgs, on occasion an outspoken republican, conceded that the governor-general, as a man, had impressed him favourably and he believed that 'no Vice-regal couple . . . have been more anxious, and more successful, in placing people whom they have met at their ease and un-embarrassed'. (He was not to be so complimentary to Northcote's successor.)

Northcote's high esteem among politicians by October 1905 reflected his notably successful exercise of constitutional functions. On several occasions during the previous eighteen months he had been required to play an active role in Australian political affairs and thus risk controversy. It is a tribute to his tact and good sense that not even among Labor members of parliament was any rancour expressed, and this despite his refusal to follow the advice of the first Commonwealth Labor government.

During the winter of 1904 the political situation had gradually worsened for the minority Watson ministry. From the day that he had become prime minister, the press had constantly reported rumours of a coalition between elements of Deakin's Protectionists and Reid's Free Traders. Eventually an unofficial combination of these elements succeeded in narrowly defeating the Labor government over a clause in the Conciliation and Arbitration Bill. Northcote hurried to Melbourne from his winter residence in Sydney's Government House. On 13 August Watson called on the governor-general and requested him to exercise his constitutional power to dissolve the parliament. Northcote promised that he would consider this advice. For 48 hours those Australians who followed the manoeuvrings of the Commonwealth parliament awaited his decision.

The right to dissolve parliament was the most powerful prerogative of the Crown remaining to colonial governors in 1904. In normal cases where the parliamentary term had expired, dissolution was a formal step in which the representative of the Crown acted upon the advice of his cabinet. But, in the British parliamentary system, the Crown was not obliged to act upon the advice of ministers where the life of the parliament had not expired.

Though Watson's request in 1904 was the first occasion on which an Australian governor-general had been faced with this problem, it had been a regular occurrence in the various self-governing colonies prior to federation and in Canada. At the 1887 Colonial Conference an attempt by New Zealand to restrict the governor's power in this sphere had received little support. Indeed, Samuel Griffith, representing Queensland, had asserted that there was a need for 'some superior and calmer authority to determine whether a dissolution is necessary or not'. The representative of the Crown thus retained his unfettered discretion to refuse or accept such advice. But there were no clear rules governing the situation. Only fifteen years earlier, an Australian governor had granted a dissolution, although the life of parliament had not expired and it was probable that an alternative government would be found. Lord Carrington dissolved the New South Wales parliament at Sir George Dibbs' request in January 1889 only two years after the previous election and despite the possibility of another leader being able to carry on the government.

But Carrington's action in 1889 had been strongly criticised at the time. It was more commonly thought that, unless there were a vital question of public policy at issue upon which the electors ought to be given the opportunity to express an opinion, all reasonable combinations of parliament ought to be attempted before a dissolution were granted. In 1899 governors in three of the Australian colonies had refused requests for dissolutions. The grounds upon which such decisions should be reached remained vague. Northcote did consult the leading text book in 1904, Alpheus Todd's *Parliamentary government in the British Colonies*, which stipulated that 'the Governor must be himself the judge of the necessity for a dissolution'.

In the Australian press only the *Age* advocated that on this occasion parliament ought to be dissolved. But its ardent Protectionist bias precluded support of any action which allowed the arch-Free Trader, Reid, to form a government. The *Age* commented: 'If Mr Watson asks for a dissolution it should not be refused ... Mr Reid does not and cannot represent the Commonwealth. He does not even represent the Opposition. The House has exhausted itself and ought to be dissolved.' The *Argus*, on the other hand, was of the opinion that Reid ought to be called for by the governor-general, who would thus have to refuse Watson's request for a dissolution. Other leading Sydney and Adelaide newspapers also supported Reid. There was, therefore, general newspaper acclamation of Northcote's action when on 15 August he notified Watson that 'a General election at the present moment does not appear to ... be essential in the public interest'. On the same day he commissioned Reid to form a government.

In a private letter to Balfour a week after the crisis had been resolved, Northcote praised Watson's behaviour and conceded that:

> He had considerable Constitutional claims to a Dissolution, viz. that he was only beaten by 2 in a full House, & that a House not elected under his party's regime. Also that the whole trend of elections throughout Australia during the past eight months go to show that he would have come back strong enough to carry his arbitration Bill as it stood.

Northcote was sympathetic to the main arguments pleaded by the Labor cabinet, but he had warned Watson 'when he came in that he must not count on a Dissolution if a stable Government could be formed without one'. Watson accepted Northcote's decision without demur. Though Hughes and others said harsh things about their political opponents, they were not aggrieved with the governor-general.

Nor have subsequent commentators considered this decision as remarkable.

A. Berriedale Keith in his *Responsible government in the Dominions* (1912) commented that 'the possibilities of carrying on the Parliament were not exhausted'. H.V. Evatt, in his standard work on the reserve powers of the Crown, *The King and his Dominion governors*, published in 1936, considered that Reid's success in forming an alternative ministry justified the governor-general's action. E.A. Forsey notes in *The royal power of dissolution of parliament in the British Commonwealth* (1943) that 'Supply had not been voted'.

Within seven months of assuming the office of governor-general, Northcote had no less than three prime ministers. Whether it was this experience of the instability of Australian politics and the relative permanence of his own tenure of office, or the natural result of his native self-assurance, he showed himself more determined to press the independence of his functions as governor-general during Reid's term of office than he had been with either Deakin or Watson.

The chief cause of concern during the brief Free Trade-Protectionist coalition was the Arbitration Bill. Exhibiting his usual political nimbleness, Reid himself secured the final passage of this bill through parliament. But, after the measure had finally received parliamentary approval, sudden and unexpected opposition was raised by the governor-general. A few days before the Arbitration Bill passed the Senate, Northcote telegraphed to the Colonial Office his disquiet at the publicly expressed opinion of his attorney-general, Sir Josiah Symon, that the inclusion of State public servants in its scope was unconstitutional. He informed the secretary of state that, as the usual certificate from the attorney-general advising that he might constitutionally accept the measure would be inconsistent with this public statement, he proposed 'to require [a] special and satisfactory certificate from him' before he assented. He asked if the law officers of the Crown would suggest an appropriate form upon which he should insist. He also suggested that another possibility would be for him to reserve the bill.

Colonial Office officials were in no doubt that it would be highly impolitic to advise His Majesty to refuse assent on a matter in which no Imperial interest was involved. Though in the past the Colonial Office had taken on the mantle of advisers to colonial governments, and encouraged amendment to measures which might be later declared to be unconstitutional, the practice had long since ceased. Moreover the Colonial Office had always been reluctant to use this power of administrative review of colonial legislation when Imperial interests were not directly affected.

Secretary of state Lyttelton's reply to Northcote's telegram pointed out that 'no imperial interest appeared to be involved'. Consequently, if the attorney-general were able and willing to advise Northcote to assent, this advice should be acted upon. Any question as to constitutionality could be subsequently decided by the High Court. The secretary of state also commented that there seemed no reason for obtaining any special form of certificate from the attorney-general, or for consulting the law officers of the Crown in Britain.

Northcote proceeded to ignore this dispatch. Three days after it arrived he wrote to Symon indicating that he was reluctant to assent to the measure. He specifically referred to 'one very important provision . . . which two Attorneys-

General believe to be outside the Constitution which the Governor-General has sworn to maintain'. Symon responded with a long memorandum. He claimed that while he still regarded the provision to which Northcote referred as beyond the scope of the legislative power conferred upon the Commonwealth, no legislation was unconstitutional until the High Court had so decided. Nor did he think that Northcote was justified in withholding assent because part or all of a bill appeared to the governor-general to exceed the powers of the Common-wealth. In all the circumstances, the attorney-general was not prepared to advise His Excellency to withhold assent. Yet the receipt of this clear communication still did not persuade the governor-general. He transmitted copies of his correspondence with Symon to the prime minister, asking whether 'Ministers are prepared to advise him to give his assent'. It was only after he received a terse reply from Reid that the governor-general finally gave way.

Throughout this curious correspondence it appears that Deakin was privy to the governor-general's actions. The day before he first communicated his doubts about the Arbitration Act to Lyttelton, Northcote wrote to Deakin: 'Assuming that I find Sir J.S. to have expressed these views would you favour me with your opinion confidentially as to whether inclosed telegram is sufficiently clear & comprehensive.' It seems probable that the telegram referred to was his cable to the secretary of state, and that 'Sir J.S.' was Sir Josiah Symon. Deakin's reply is not known. Properly, he ought to have counselled the governor-general to follow the opinion of his constitutional advisers. However three months later Northcote was still consulting him about the matter. At the governor-general's request Deakin composed a series of questions which Northcote intended to have asked in the House of Lords concerning the assent to the Commonwealth Conciliation and Arbitration Act.

It seems extraordinary that Northcote, previously so constitutionally correct in his relations with his Australian governments, should have allowed himself, not only to interfere in a matter of purely domestic politics, but to consult Deakin about one of his opponent's measures. Both actions were ill-advised; yet they reflect the concern Northcote felt that the office of governor-general should be more than a rubber-stamp. In justifying his actions to the secretary of state he disagreed with the assertion by Symon that the governor-general's discretion to interfere in the passage of a legislative measure should be limited to cases in which Imperial interests alone were concerned. He agreed that in practice this would 'almost invariably' be the case, but he did not think that it 'should be laid down as a principle'. To do so would, in his opinion, further restrict the governor-general's already limited constitutional powers. As his action would be a precedent for future holders of his office, and in view of his opinion that the constitutional question was a serious one, he asked to be favoured with the views of His Majesty's government on the position he had adopted.

But the British government was reluctant to engage in any dispute with the Commonwealth over Northcote's concern for the narrowing role of the governor-general in domestic affairs. Lyttelton's reply was concise. He ex-pressed entire agreement 'with the views of the Attorney-General of the Commonwealth'. A few months later unofficial advice from Sir R. Findley, law officer of the Crown, agreed with the Colonial Office instruction. Northcote's attempt to establish the office of governor-general as a constitutional board of review for Commonwealth legislation was against the current of colonial development. Indeed it was exceedingly out of place in the wider sphere of self-government achieved long before federation in the Australian continent. The extraordinary thing is that Deakin did not point out to Northcote the anachronistic nature of his views. The comment by a Colonial Office official that Lord Northcote was 'taking too much upon himself' neatly summarised his unsuccessful but persistent action over the Arbitration Bill.

Yet Northcote proved anxious to take upon himself much more, as shown by his action in December 1904 over the procedure for recommending honours for Australian citizens. Many colonials, no less than Englishmen, had a weakness for titles and ardently sought them, but the system by which they were awarded was somewhat different. From about the middle of the nineteenth century colonial governments submitted to the Crown recommendations of local citizens for British honours. But these lists had to pass through two intermediate authorities. The first was the local governor, who could make additional suggestions of his own or subtract from the list names which he considered undesirable. The second was the secretary of state for colonies, who was hampered by restrictions on the number of honours available for colonial citizens. In these intermediate stages the lists of recommendations could be altered considerably or ignored completely.

The establishment of the Commonwealth of Australia introduced a further complicating factor. After 1901 there was a seventh Australian government hoping for the patronage which the conferring of honours provided. Chamberlain's inclination, strongly supported by Hopetoun, was to centralise the system for recommending honours for Australian citizens, just as he had hoped to make the office of governor-general sole channel of communication in other matters. State governors were instructed to forward such recommendations through the governor-general.

Though convenient for the Colonial Office, this suggested procedure immediately encountered opposition from the governors and the governments of all Australian States. It was Tennyson, when still governor of South Australia, who in 1902 led the opposition to this new attempt to whittle away the prerogatives of the State governors, and to threaten State 'sovereignty'. As a compromise, he suggested that though recommendations for the bestowal of honours for purely State services should continue to be sent directly to London by State governors, copies could be sent simultaneously to the governor-general for his information. Chamberlain accepted this solution, consoling Hopetoun with the assurance that he would still wish to have the advantage of the governor-general's observations, and would defer acting upon State recommendations until he had received an expression of the governor-general's views. By thus establishing the governor-general as an advisory authority Chamberlain was sowing seeds of discord for the future.

So long as Hopetoun and Tennyson were in office the compromise functioned fairly smoothly. But Northcote's pedantic mind found the procedure unsatisfactory. State governors were not complying with instructions to forward copies of their lists to the governor-general. In addition he felt that there was a disconcerting vagueness about the respective responsibilities of premier, prime minister, governor and governor-general.

In 1904 Northcote was correctly reproved by Lyttelton for submitting a Queensland honours list to his prime minister, Deakin. Such lists, he was told, were forwarded for His Excellency's personal observations, not for those of his ministers. The governor-general was stirred to take action on his own initiative to clarify the procedure. In December 1904 he wrote to all State governors urging the adoption of a uniform system for honours recommendations, and submitting for their consideration a plan which he had discussed with the prime minister. He and Reid had agreed that State and Commonwealth premiers should submit names to the governor or governor-general, who should send the entire list, without deletions, to the Colonial Office. In so doing the representatives of the Crown should communicate their own views of the recommendations made by ministers. As this was an Imperial and not a local obligation, the governor-general was of the opinion that a governor was not obliged to reveal to his ministers the advice he had tendered to the secretary of state.

All except the Victorian governor replied favourably to the governor-general's suggestions, and he then forwarded the correspondence to the Colonial Office. A few months later the Colonial Office circulated a set of rules which specified that recommendations for 'Imperial or Municipal services or public services of a charitable, literary or scientific character' could be initiated by a governor-general or governor as well as by his prime minister. By also following Northcote's proposed procedure for awarding such honours, this dispatch clarified what had been a confusing situation.

Though some order had been achieved, the dissent of the Victorian governor, Sir Reginald Talbot, initiated another long controversy over States' rights. At first the dispute centred on whether it was proper for the governor-general to comment upon recommendations for State honours, without providing his State counterparts with his reasons. Then the area of contention widened to include the whole question of the governor-general's competence to comment on States' honours lists. Lyttelton had instructed governors to ensure that the governor-general was afforded 'an adequate opportunity of expressing his views in regard to State honours'. Talbot objected to this as an interference in State concerns.

Behind his stand on this issue there was a practical cause for complaint. Talbot's recommendation of a knighthood for Victoria's self-seeking premier, Thomas Bent, was blocked by Northcote, who stressed Bent's 'grossly offensive language' and 'disreputable past'. Early in their term the premier, when dining at Government House, had 'scandalized' Lady Northcote by 'blowing his nose on the table napkin ... then tucking it under his chin'.

Talbot, like other State governors before and after him, was concerned that if the governor-general could review and practically neutralize his recommendations where no question of national interests were involved, the position and privilege of the governor, as direct representative of His Majesty, would be seriously affected. Acquiescence on his part 'would be tantamount to the abandonment of certain principles for which Victoria as well as other States have strenuously contended, namely, that they are independent Governments with the Governor as representative of the Crown at their head, and that they are not subordinate in any way to the Commonwealth Government'. He hastened to assure the secretary of state that relations between himself and Northcote were, despite the 'peculiar position', most cordial.

The Colonial Office was in the invidious position of being unable to please either governor-general or governor. In May 1906 Northcote was so frustrated by the situation as to consider resigning.

Though he was an inveterate seeker after honours himself, and pompously critical of Australians who presumed to similar aspirations, behind Northcote's stand on the question of honours there was more than just a desire for personal aggrandisement. Throughout his letters runs a fundamentally centralist attitude to Australian federation. One dispatch exhorted the British government to do all it could 'to make Australians realize what Federal citizenship means; and to induce them to feel that they are Australians first, and New South Welshmen, Victorians, & c, only in the second place'. This was a logical position for an Imperial officer sent to supervise a growing nation. Consistently, he held that the post of governor-general should be maintained as a superior authority in the Commonwealth. It seemed to Northcote to be against the 'best interests of Australia' for the British government 'to issue instructions which would be taken as lowering the position of the Head of the Federal Government in deference to the susceptibilities of State Ministries'.

Though the governors agreed, in May 1906, that no objection could be taken to the procedure, provided that the governor-general refrained from communicating States' lists to Commonwealth ministers, the State governments remained dissatisfied with the situation. In 1908 Victoria took the dispute to the Premiers' Conference, which resolved to object to the practice of passing recommendations for honours through the governor-general. But the new secretary of state, Lord Crewe, declined to disturb the compromise reached earlier. He informed the States that the governor-general's views would continue to be sought on all Australian honours, but he rejected Northcote's claim to a right of absolute veto.

The dispute over honours had been a problem for Hopetoun and was to be so for Northcote's successors. Tennyson reconciled differences only by conceding that the governor-general was 'primus inter pares'. Northcote felt that as federal figurehead he was obliged to assist in making federalism work — to promote nationalism as opposed to provincialism. In the process he asserted the superior function of the governor-general, and aroused the defensive reaction of State governors.

Once again political instability publicised Northcote's constitutional responsibility as head of state. Reid's fall from office in 1905 was swift and controversial. Interpreting a speech by Deakin in June as a 'notice to quit' he threw the newly reassembled parliament into confusion by omitting from the governor-general's speech any policy proposals for the session. Behind this manoeuvre lay a determination to force a vote of confidence leading to a dissolution of parliament. Reid hoped to convince Northcote that, as all party combinations had been exhausted, a new House of Representatives should be elected. But Deakin's political skill was equal to these tactics. His expected censure motion, carried by a large majority, was worded so as to indicate parliament's intention to proceed with the business of the session. Consequently, when Reid called to see the governor-general and requested a dissolution, it was clear that an alternative government could be found.

Nevertheless the first weekend in July was an anxious time for some parliamentarians. The press was evenly divided, albeit along partly lines, as to whether the governor-general should grant the dissolution. The *Sydney Morning Herald, Daily Telegraph* and *Argus* all emphasised that the House had exhausted its usefulness and ought to be dissolved. On the other hand the *Age*, with characteristic vigour, warned the governor-general that 'a dissolution would be such an outrage as would probably lead to an almost instant reform of the constitution'. As usual, less prejudice was evident in the Adelaide press. Both the *Advertiser* and *Register* agreed that after Deakin's successful censure motion, His Excellency would be unlikely to sanction an early election, so long as there was a reasonable prospect of the House proceeding with the dispatch of business. The *West Australian* was 'fairly certain' that Reid's request would be refused.

Knowing Northcote's high opinion of Deakin's qualities, it is not surprising that he declined Reid's advice and sent for the former prime minister. However, as on earlier occasions, the governor-general acted throughout this crisis with cautious good judgement. Before reaching a decision on whether to grant a dissolution, he asked Deakin how the situation differed from that of 1903. The Protectionist leader was able to assure Northcote that Watson had pledged the support of the Labor Party for the remainder of the session. With this written submission in his possession, Northcote then proceded to set out his reasons for refusing Reid's advice in a courteous memorandum of impeccable constitutional propriety. He was unwilling to put the country to the 'trouble and expense of a General election' when the House of Representatives had indicated 'its readiness to go on with public business'. Reid immediately resigned and Deakin was commissioned to form a government. Throughout these events Northcote had maintained a calm and confident demeanour, and acted with admirable discernment. His decision was accepted with good grace even by those newspapers which had counselled an opposite course. Reid made no public sign of displeasure though privately he criticised Northcote's action.

By twice refusing to follow his ministers' advice to dissolve parliament, Northcote drew attention to the important powers of the governor-general in the machinery of the Commonwealth government. A pseudonymous letter to the *Advertiser* compared the function of governor-general to a mechanical governor in a steamship's engine; 'ornamental in fine weather, but necessary to control and regulate the engines in a heavy sea'. It was a strained metaphor but it did express an essential truth. During its early years the Commonwealth seemed to require a constitutional monarch to act with decision in times of political crisis.

In 1904 the rules by which the governor-general was guided on such occasions still allowed him considerable discretion.

Not only had the governor-general acted throughout the recent political crisis with formal correctness, but he had also adhered closely to Deakin's advice. Their close and productive relationship was to continue for almost the whole of Deakin's second, most successful administration. There was a unity of purpose on most issues and a trust in each other's integrity.

One important issue on which the prime minister and governor-general were in accord was the persistent dispute with the States over the channel of communication with Great Britain. As early as two weeks after he assumed office, Northcote had complained that State governors were not forwarding to him copies of their correspondence with the Colonial Office. On that occasion the secretary of state had declined to interfere and risk contention. In June 1905 Northcote repeated his complaint, observing that the time had arrived 'when the instruction should either be repeated or cancelled'. In pressing his point of view he emphasised that in this function the governor-general was independent of the Commonwealth executive.

If, as seems likely, Northcote showed Deakin this dispatch, the prime minister must have been delighted by the centralist position proposed by the governor-general. Compared with Tennyson's cautious federalism, this bold assertion of Commonwealth ascendancy over States encouraged Deakin to revive his aim of achieving Commonwealth supervision of State correspondence with the Colonial Office on matters of Commonwealth interest.

After consulting the State governors, Lord Elgin, who had replaced Lyttelton in December 1905, decided not to disturb the existing compromise, leaving it to the State governors to judge which correspondence concerned Commonwealth affairs. This was still unpalatable to Northcote, so he enlisted Deakin's support for his earlier request. In a long memorandum urging a reappraisal of the decision, the prime minister advanced an extraordinary and unprecedented interpretation of the independent role of the governor-general.

Elgin had admitted that to enable the governor-general to discharge the duties of his office properly, he should be made aware of the contents of all dispatches which bore in any way on federal interests. Deakin agreed, but objected that, under the system as it had operated since 1901, the authority to decide whether or not a dispatch was one concerning federal interests belonged to the governors of the States. He pointed out that they had not proved capable of judging correctly in the few cases of the kind which had arisen during the first years of the Commonwealth. To Deakin it was essential for the smooth working of the federal Constitution that there should be an authority in Australia capable of deciding whether State dispatches affected federal interests or not. In his opinion, 'the only person at once capable and impartial who can discharge that duty is the Governor-General'.

Deakin listed the qualifications of the governor-general to act in this capacity:

> By virtue of his office as leader of society, he comes into contact with men representing every class and is in a position to understand public opinion in all its shades. His jurisdiction extends over the whole of Australia, he pays

periodical visits to every important centre of the Commonwealth, and thus acquires a wide and intimate knowledge of Australian affairs, including State politics and parties in their larger aspects as well as those of the Commonwealth. No-one else has so many and so various sources of information.

In view of these considerations, he asked the secretary of state to vary the then existing practice so as to enable the governor-general to exercise the role of 'arbiter with a right to receive all State communications to the Colonial Office, and decide in the first place which of them require to be classed as having a federal bearing, and further which despatches included in such category he will communicate for the information of his Ministers'. In so acting, Deakin considered that the governor-general would be 'entirely independent of Government, Ministers and parties'.

At first sight this was a bold attempt to establish the governor-general's office as an independent authority in the federation. There is no doubt that the prime minister wished to promote the superiority of the governor-general over State governors. In the *Morning Post*, 8 January 1908, Deakin wrote, 'As our sense of Australian unity grows the influence of the Governor-General grows too, while that of his associates diminishes'. From later actions, however, it is clear that Deakin only intended the governor-general to exercise such an independent authority in the narrow field of Commonwealth-State relations.

In the event, the attempt to set up the office of governor-general as a superior functionary was destined to fail. The States were too jealous of their sovereignty to allow any interference in their right to communicate with Great Britain. Elgin did not reject Deakin's ambitious proposal, but his suggestion that the governor-general should himself consult the State governors effectively ended the dispute. It was clear that the States would never voluntarily retreat from their firm line on the subject and Deakin advised Northcote to allow the matter to rest.

Though Deakin was in favour of strengthening the role of the representative of the Crown as the channel of communication, in other respects he was zealous in preventing any regression in the independent status of the Commonwealth within the Empire. The vague but still current power of the governor-general to reserve the Royal Assent to Commonwealth legislation seemed to him an anachronism which needed elimination. Hopetoun had considered invoking the powers under Section 58 of the Commonwealth Constitution in connection with the Immigration Restriction Act, but eventually decided to assent to the controversial legislation himself, rather than reserve it for the King. It was the last real opportunity a governor-general had to exercise this discretion. During Northcote's term of office, the discretionary powers of the governor-general to reserve such legislation in Australia, or indeed in any self-governing colony, finally became obsolete. In this constitutional development Northcote allied himself with his Australian advisers and against the Colonial Office.

Once again it was in connection with legislation discriminating against Asians that the issue of Royal Assent was raised. By November 1905 the British government was becoming disturbed at racially discriminatory legislation in various parts of the Empire. In September 1905 the secretary of state for India had drawn Lyttelton's attention to Section 46 of the Western Australian Factories Act, which prohibited a person of 'Chinese or other Asiatic race from registering as the owner or occupier of a factory unless he had carried on such business or was employed in such a factory before November 1903'.

The secretary of state's response to this representation was a confidential dispatch, circularised to all self-governing colonies in November 1905, advising that if a measure imposing disabilities upon Asians were passed by the colonial parliament, it should be reserved for the signification of His Majesty's pleasure. Early in the following year Northcote learned that Richard John Seddon, prime minister of New Zealand, planned to enter a public protest against the circular on the grounds that it was an unacceptable limitation of colonial constitutional independence. The Australian governor-general informed Elgin of Seddon's intention, adding that he felt sure that the Commonwealth government would be in complete agreement. In the circumstances he suggested that undesirable discussion could be avoided by temporary or final withdrawal of the dispatch. The Colonial Office neglected to follow this sound advice. Consequently, in April 1906, Elgin received a typically aggressive memorandum from Deakin demanding the withdrawal of the offending circular.

The Australian prime minister considered the instruction a 'new departure of grave constitutional importance' implying 'a serious diminution of the Constitutional powers of all self-governing dependencies'. He devoted some effort to refuting the legality of the dispatch in connection with the Commonwealth's legislation: 'The Constitution ... sets out, *inter alia*, the powers and authority of the Governor-General, and it is submitted with all respect that its provisions in that regard may no more be overridden by instructions from one of His Majesty's Secretaries of State than may any other sections.' He claimed that, unlike the constitutions of Canada, the Australian States or New Zealand, the Commonwealth Constitution (Section 58) conferred 'absolute and unfettered' discretionary power on the governor-general to give the Royal Assent. Deakin submitted that the instruction in Lyttelton's dispatch was contrary to the Constitution in that it purported to control the discretion expressly and directly conferred by the Imperial parliament upon the governor-general. It was extremely undesirable to attempt to restrict, by confidential instructions, the discretion publicly reposed in an officer of the governor-general's high standing.

In asserting the discretionary power of the governor-general, Deakin was not setting him up as an irresponsible sovereign. As would be indicated in a subsequent dispute, the government still had the ultimate weapon of resignation to fall back upon. Nor was he denying the basic constitutional rule that a governor-general must find advisers to support whatever action he might take. Rather was he asserting the principle of dominion independence.

This ranging shot from the Commonwealth was followed shortly after by a broadside from the State premiers, assembled in conference at Sydney in April 1906. They resolved unanimously that 'any increase in the power of reservation at present held by the Governor-General of the Commonwealth or the State

Governors, would be viewed with disfavor'.

In the face of this opposition and New Zealand's earlier stand, Elgin was obliged to withdraw his predecessor's circular and cancel the instructions. It was no longer possible for the British government to coerce colonial governments into softening their restrictive legislation against Asians. It was also no longer possible for the Colonial Office to hold the threat of reservation over the heads of self-governing colonies. If changes were desired in colonial legislation, they would have to be accomplished by negotiation, as befitted sovereign states.

In his dispatch of May 1906 summarising the situation, Elgin salvaged what remnants of influence the Imperial government still retained, and its character was revealed to be essentially quasi-diplomatic. The crux of the problem was that, if assent were not reserved in the case of colonial bills affecting the relations of the Empire with foreign powers or other matters of Imperial interest, the British government had no opportunity of considering how their interests could be protected or of suggesting amendments which they thought desirable. It was true that the King could be advised to exercise his powers of disallowance, but Elgin considered, with justification, that these powers should be exercised as seldom as possible. Consequently the best solution to the difficulty lay in formalising the practice already operating informally in Australia. Colonial ministers in all self-govering colonies were asked to furnish the governor-general or governor with copies of any bill touching upon Imperial matters, for immediate transmission to the secretary of state. Though this arrangement did not meet the difficulty of bills which were passed rapidly through both Houses, or of amendments introduced during their passage, such problems could be overcome by the action of the governor-general or governor. These officers were instructed to keep the British government fully informed, by telegram if necessary, when any legislation touching upon Imperial matters was before parliament.

The British government's attempt to regain some of the initiative over colonial legislation imposing restrictions upon Asians had been short lived. Though the Indian government protested at amendments to Australia's Immigration Restriction Act in March 1906, and requested that the Royal Assent be withheld, it was persuaded by the secretary of state not to press its objection. The final resort in any matter of concern to the British government had to be the diplomatic role of the governor or governor-general as its representative in a sovereign state.

The Customs Tariff (British Preference) Bill introduced into the Australian parliament in September 1906 raised a similar, though less emotionally charged, problem. As first envisaged, the bill made British goods imported in foreign ships dutiable at a higher rate than the same goods imported in British vessels. This was Deakin's unilateral attempt to implement a policy of Imperial trade preference. But it was altered materially by the Labor Party, to provide that this preference would only operate if the British vessels were manned exclusively by white seamen. Though this was an unforeseen complication, it was not the major obstruction until, in October, the secretary of state pointed out to Northcote that, by imposing restrictions upon foreign shipping, the bill ran counter to certain treaty obligations of the Imperial government. Attempts to amend the bill and make it more acceptable to the British government were defeated by the Senate. Consequently the prime minister had little alternative but to advise Northcote to reserve assent. The attorney-general, Isaacs, tendered written advice to this effect, as did Deakin, and the bill was reserved on 17 October. When it reached Downing Street in November, consideration was deferred by the Colonial Office until after the colonial conference due to be held in April of the following year.

The 1907 Colonial Conference, like others of its type, was a disappointment to both colonial nationalists and closer unionists. Yet it was another shuffling step forward in the developing sovereign status of the self-governing colonies or, as they were thenceforward called, Dominions. The major item at this conference was the attempt by colonial ministers to convince Britain of the merits of Imperial preference. Deakin conducted a vigorous publicity campaign in its favour, but he was aware that he had little prospect of persuading Britain's Liberal government to alter its free trade policy. In the circumstances there was no point in pressing his Customs Preference Bill, particularly in view of the amendment forced upon him by the Labor Party. Accordingly he asked Elgin not to take any action with regard to the reserved bill which was allowed to lapse.

Deakin's conviction remained unchanged that it was generally undesirable for the governor-general to withhold Royal Assent to Australian legislation. This was revealed in a brief but decisive confrontation over Australia's Judiciary Bill, 1907. Once again in this dispute Northcote tended to support his Australian ministers rather than his British masters.

In October 1907 the attention of the Colonial Office had been drawn to a bill which was intended to make the High Court of Australia the final authority in all cases involving the division of power between Commonwealth and States. Its immediate objective was to resolve a deadlock resulting from the conflicting judgements of the Privy Council and the High Court on the question of State power to impose income tax on federal officers. The Colonial Office decided to seek the opinion of Loreburn, the lord chancellor, upon this legislation. Though he expressed himself to be in favour of the bill, Loreburn preferred to await the decision in a case pending before the Privy Council before offering his observations. Elgin thereupon telegraphed to Northcote: 'Perhaps you will consider whether Bill should not be reserved'. The colonial secretary's suggestion was interpreted by the governor-general as an instruction. He replied that he would reserve the bill.

When first informed of Northcote's intention to reserve the Royal Assent, Deakin appeared undisturbed by the implications. However, on second thoughts, he decided to take a firm stand and oppose any such action. He informed the governor-general that this change of attitude was the result of agitation by one of his parliamentary supporters, who asked him what had become of the Customs Tariff (British Preference) Bill 1906, and threatened to put a formal question on the subject to the government. As Northcote related the incident to the secretary of state: 'This caused the Prime Minister to reconsider his attitude on the Judiciary Bill; and he came to the conclusion that he could not defend either mine or his own position if he acquiesced in my reservation of a Bill, formally recommended to me by himself, without my assigning some specific reason for my action'. It is not exactly clear why Northcote refused to communicate his reasons to Deakin. His explanation to Elgin was that the telegraphed dispatch was marked 'secret'. But, whatever the motivation, the outcome of the dispute was another strongly worded memorandum from Deakin. The prime minister submitted that, while the governor-general's full power of reservation was not challenged, ministers could not retain office if His Excellency rejected their advice without assigning strong reasons for his actions. He warned that, if the cabinet resigned, Northcote 'could not hope for a Ministry that would take a different view of the Constitutional position of the Governor-General'. His fear was that the reservation of such a bill would be 'misunderstood and would lead to all sorts of wild rumours of sinister intentions of the Home Government towards the Commonwealth'.

Consequently Northcote dispatched a secret telegram on 10 October conveying Deakin's emphatic protest at the governor-general's proposed action against the advice of his responsible ministers. Fearing that the cabinet would resign if he ignored this warning, Northcote postponed his decision pending further instructions. His own opinion was that the secretary of state should give him leave to assent or permission to explain to ministers his reasons for reservation.

This dispatch caused a considerable flurry. Berriedale Keith, then a clerk at the Colonial Office, thought that Deakin had raised 'a very serious matter of principle' by attempting to limit a governor's discretion. He accused the Australian prime minister of seeking to set up a 'new and dangerous precedent'. The ministry's threat of resignation, in Keith's opinion, was 'hardly serious' since he considered that, having resigned, it would hardly get back into office. He suggested that the governor-general be instructed to reserve assent but to explain his reasons. Others at the Colonial Office agreed with this advice. But softer counsel prevailed. Northcote was warned that the question of reservation was entrusted to his personal discretion by the Constitution Act, and was advised to stall until the lord chancellor was consulted. On 11 October Northcote was informed by telegram that the lord chancellor had no desire that he should exercise his discretion in favour of reservation. Relieved, the governor-general immediately assented to the bill.

The exchange over Deakin's Judiciary Bill confirmed the lesson drawn from the earlier dispute over Lyttelton's withdrawn circular. The Australian government's indignant attitude towards British interference in Commonwealth legislation reminded the Colonial Office that the ultimate weapon available to a colonial cabinet was to resign and force His Excellency to seek alternative advisers. Downing Street was always reluctant to suggest such a confrontation, and Northcote was too sensible to blunder into such a position on his own accord. Consequently the governor-general's discretionary authority to reserve Royal Assent to Commonwealth legislation lapsed in practice, though not in theory. There were still a few subjects upon which the representative of the

Crown had no authority to grant the Royal Assent locally, but in such cases he would act upon the advice of his ministers.

Though, in retrospect, it is evident that the office of governor-general had been stripped of one of the last vestiges of its former power, the Colonial Office was reluctant to concede this in principle. In a long memorandum drawn up as a result of these disputes over reservation of the Royal Assent, Keith summarised the position as he interpreted it. He conceded that 'the Governor will never withhold assent except on the advice of Ministers'. But neither he nor the Colonial Office admitted Deakin's view that in any question of reservation the governor-general was bound to accept his ministers' advice or to satisfy them that his reasons for reserving a bill were adequate. It was clear, however, that if a similar case arose again Deakin and probably other Australian prime ministers would be ready to resign unless the governor-general could assign strong reasons for his action. Keith concluded by suggesting that when a governor-general considered it desirable to reserve a bill, he should communicate with the secretary of state to ensure that he did not place himself in conflict with his ministers unless the Imperial government desired reservation of the bill.

In February 1908 Deakin heard 'with alarm and regret' that the governor-general proposed to retire after the completion of four and a half years of his term of office. The prime minister's regret was genuine. He recognised that the Commonwealth was losing the services of an able official who had gathered valuable experience in the exercise of his role. It was a fundamental problem in the system. No matter how successful the governor-general was in exercising his role, he lacked that essential function, namely permanence, provided by a constitutional monarch. The nineteenth-century constitutional authority, Bagehot, had remarked on this as an advantage to the Imperial power. He considered that a governor who overstayed his normal time would identify with the colony too much and therefore lose some of his value as guardian of Imperial interests. Deakin, no doubt, would have regarded this tendency as desirable rather than not. He urged Northcote to stay on longer, but the governor-general felt unable to alter his plans. On 8 September 1908, after acting as host at ceremonies connected with the visit of the American Great White Fleet, he went home.

Northcote was the most successful governor-general to hold office in the first decade of the Commonwealth. His tour of duty had provided the stability and consolidation which had been generally hoped for upon his appointment, though there had been the predictable complaints from Sydney about the length of time each year during which its Government House was vacant. The general satisfaction with Australia's third governor-general enabled Deakin to settle, temporarily, some of the more troublesome problems raised by Northcote's predecessors. The Governor-General's Residences Act 1906 had at last established a workable and business-like agreement between the Commonwealth and the two senior colonies over the occupancy of Government Houses in Sydney and Melbourne. Though this was to prove only a temporary solution pending the building of a national capital, and the delay in achieving this ambition was to lead to further difficulties, there seemed no cause for concern in 1907. In addition an agreement had been reached whereby the Commonwealth repaid the

States for the governor-general's use of State railways.

In his assessment of the practical aspects of his post as head of state, Northcote had been cautious and realistic. He was not a rubber-stamp and held strong, sometimes stubborn views. But his strength of character was tempered by prudence. He had never had any serious disagreement or confrontation with his ministers. On the one occasion when his view of the role of governor-general had differed from that of his Australian advisers, in the matter of the Arbitration Bill, he had kept the affair secret and, in the end, given way. When the Colonial Office had come into conflict with the Australian government, he had usually supported the latter, though never provocatively. When supported by ministers he was prepared to assert the independent function of the representative of the Crown in the Commonwealth, as in the disputes over honours and the channel of communication with Britain. When called upon to exercise his emergency constitutional functions in the machinery of government he did so with good judgement and propriety. Though not a man of commanding personality he was widely liked and respected in Australia. His retirement to England encouraged hopes for further assistance to Australia in the future.

In a tribute to Northcote at a farewell banquet in Melbourne, the prime minister echoed the anticipation that the ex-governor-general would prove a valuable friend to Australia in Britain. Deakin's regret at His Excellency's departure was also a personal sadness. Northcote had been a welcome friend and ally for him during the political changes of the early years of the Commonwealth. Though his speech was appropriately light-hearted in tone, the compliments were sincere. The prime minister forecast that when the history of the previous four years of the Commonwealth was written, 'it would be found . . . how friction had been avoided; how popular feeling when it rose to too great a height had been calmed and how Australia had been guided with clear insight and cautious sagacity. In the darkest and most difficult hour they had always one man who never despaired of Australia — trusted its people and even its politicians'.

Illness prevented Northcote from taking an active part in British politics after his return, though he was a prominent 'diehard' in the controversy over reform of the House of Lords. He died on 29 September 1911. Historians have neglected to give him the credit which Deakin forecast. It was the touchstone of Northcote's success that he took decisions which might have been controversial but are now, as they were then, considered unexceptionable. That they were so is the best tribute to this unassuming Englishman who, with stolid, rather melancholy dignity, exercised the role of governor-general for five formative years of the Commonwealth.

Lady Northcote continued to take an interest in Australia, supporting, by gifts of money and music, the Lady Northcote Permanent Orchestra Trust Fund, which had been set up in Melbourne in 1908. At her death in June 1934, the *Argus* recalled her kindness to many Australian soldiers and travellers after she had returned to England.

The true foundations of the office of governor-general in Australia had been laid by Tennyson and Northcote, rather than by Hopetoun. During their terms the lasting bureaucratic machinery of the office was set up. Both unspectacular sons of eminent Victorians, they brought caution and frugality to their public duties. They showed that a governor-general might wield influence in the Australian political and administrative system, provided he was discreet about it.

3   The Edwardians

Though Queen Victoria had died three years before he took office, it was she rather than Edward VII, who provided the inspiration for Northcote's concept of the governor-general's role. Restraint and decorum were the hall-marks of his exercise of the duties of representative of the Crown in Australia. His natural reticence conformed with the general Australian desire, discovered painfully by Hopetoun, that the governor-general be unostentatious and inexpensive. In contrast, William Humble Ward, second Earl of Dudley, was a man in the mould of the former Prince of Wales; his ideas of monarchy had been shaped by the colourful and ceremonial court of Edward VII.

He was born on 25 May 1867 in London, son of William Ward, first earl, and his second wife Georgiana Elizabeth, née Moncreiffe. At the age of seventeen, while still a schoolboy at Eton, Dudley had inherited great wealth, landed estate and social position. His family owned 30 000 acres in Britain, including profitable iron-works, and also had estates in Jamaica. Relieved of the necessity to provide for himself, in 1885 he set out 'like the hero in a boy's novel' on an adventurous cruise around the world in his yacht 'Marchesa', during which he stayed for some months in the Australian colonies. Leaving large unpaid debts in Sydney, he returned to England in 1886 and became a prominent member of the wealthy nobility.

During the latter years of Victoria's reign, many British aristocrats displayed an ostentation and self-indulgence which scandalised the Queen. At the apex of this society, typifying its tastes and exemplifying its hedonistic values, was her son, the Prince of Wales. The future governor-general of Australia was closely associated with the patrician society which surrounded the heir to the throne. In 1891, in the presence of the Prince of Wales, Dudley's marriage to Miss Rachel Gurney, cousin and protégé of the Duchess of Bedford, was one of the great social events of the year. Subsequently, their splendid homes in Worcestershire and London joined the select circle of fashionable residences where long, weekend house parties helped to relieve the boredom engendered by great wealth and excessive leisure.

It was a society which prided itself, under royal patronage, on its handsome women. Dudley's mother, Georgiana, dowager countess, a prominent and successful hostess in this competitive social set, was reputed to be the most beautiful society woman of her generation. Her association with the Prince of Wales led to high-placed patronage for her eldest son. Compared to the homely Northcote, Dudley was a handsome man, tall and broadshouldered. Photographs show he had a condescending smile and a haughty posture. He was prevented by a slight lameness from excelling in cricket, rowing, or the other gentlemanly sports. Though at one time he had ambitions in the sphere of horse-racing, success on the turf eluded him and he sold his valuable stud. In spite of his physical disability, he achieved some reputation as a successful competitor in big yacht racing, a sport lifted to unprecedented prestige by the patronage of the Prince of Wales.

Like others of his class, Dudley believed that inherited ownership of land conferred upon the British nobleman a superior fitness for public office. For a time he toyed with politics, began to speak in the House of Lords and was rewarded with a post as parliamentary secretary to the Board of Trade in Lord Salisbury's government of 1895, the 'last government in the Western world to possess all the attributes of aristocracy in working condition'. But he lacked the fixity of purpose needed for a successful political career. The army offered an alternative. Responding impulsively to the mood of the time, in 1899 Dudley hastened to serve in the South African war. But he had not attended Sandhurst; his lack of professional training was a bar to any significant achievement in the military field and he returned to England in 1900. A vice-regal career seemed the best way to achieve the prominence he desired. It was possibly due to the support of his high-placed friends, including the King himself, that in 1902 he was appointed to the post of lord lieutenant of Ireland.

In Dublin Dudley distinguished himself by great extravagance and by an independence of spirit unusual in one of such a conservative background. His support of a policy of devolution for Ireland was much criticised by some British politicians. However, he was not regarded unfavourably by the Liberal government which took office shortly thereafter. Accordingly, when the King suggested Dudley as a possible replacement for Northcote in Australia, a position which was proving difficult to fill from Liberal ranks, Campbell-Bannerman acquiesced. Dudley accepted, with the firm intention of using Australia as a spring-board for the greater Imperial proconsular posts of Canada and India. Again, the Australian government played no part in the appointment, being merely notified of a selection already made and accepted.

Personal considerations influenced Dudley's decision to take up the governor-generalship of the Commonwealth. He hoped to save money in Australia, after his prodigality in Ireland. Also, by 1908 his marriage was unhappy. Ten years later, Lady Dudley stated that 'though a deeply injured wife' she had accompanied her husband to Australia 'hoping that matters would amend'. It was a mistaken anticipation for, while the mask of respectability may have been maintained in the bosom of Edwardian society, it was impossible to conceal impropriety in the exposed conditions of vice-regal life in Australia.

On 8 September 1908, having visited Canada *en route* to Australia, Dudley arrived in Sydney, where he briefly met his departing predecessor, Northcote. After an impressive swearing-in ceremony in the New South Wales capital, described by *Labor Call* as 'a gorgeous affair — gold braid galore', he proceeded to Melbourne to enter upon his duties with splendid pomp and ostentation. Bewigged postilions, outriders and footmen in livery escorted the fourth

Lord Dudley

governor-general as he drove ceremonially through Melbourne in a handsome four-horse carriage which, as the *Australasian* remarked, 'recalled the splendour of' Hopetoun's term of office.

The *Daily Telegraph* welcomed Dudley with the advice that 'the most successful Governor of an autonomous colony is the one under whom the wheels of Government run without creaking, and without calling any special attention to his presence'. The *Worker* was less restrained. In an article headed 'A Sham Australian Court of St. James' it rejected any suggestion that the flamboyant, regal ceremonial of Edward VII should be transplanted to Australia, and reminded its readers that 'The ideas of the courtier are not compatible with those of a vigorous and progressive democracy'.

The *Worker*'s outburst, reflecting radical antipathy towards those 'malign' European influences which 'tainted' Australia's egalitarian society, was echoed in parliament by the Labor Party. Northcote's judicious restraint had subdued but not eliminated the sort of criticism which had driven Linlithgow back to England. After 1908, parliamentary disapproval of increased vice-regal allowances again rose to a significant level, in response to Dudley's grandiose style and his misunderstanding of the function of his office.

In Britain, where its image had been refurbished by Edward VII, the Crown was an embodiment of the nation in a way which was never possible for the office of governor-general in the Commonwealth. The most important reason for this was that the monarch was as much a national symbol for Australians as he was for Britons elsewhere; the King was permanent, the King's man in Australia only a passing representative.

It was not wholly Dudley's fault that he failed to recognise the need for public restraint. In spite of Hopetoun's problems, Tennyson's strictures and Northcote's example, British politicians remained convinced that the Commonwealth required its chief executive officer to be enormously wealthy. Dudley had been chosen in the first place because Elgin had thought that there was not a sufficiently wealthy peer of the appropriate background in the ranks of the Liberal party. Moreover there was still a small but prominent group in Australia who aped the English aristocracy. Dudley's air of nobility was alluring to those Australians, who encouraged his ambitions for the social role of the representative of the Crown.

The new governor-general found an early opportunity to display these ideas in November, during the Melbourne Cup carnival, as close an equivalent to the 'London Season' as could be obtained in the antipodes. Balls, receptions, race meetings and banquets followed each other in swift succession and the Dudleys conscientiously displayed themselves to those who came to ogle. Government House in Melbourne, customarily the meeting-place for expatriate British officials during cup-time, was redolent with the atmosphere of an exclusive vice-regal club. If Dudley considered that he was required to cut a figure at the apex of this society, it is perhaps not to be wondered at, but his behaviour invited a confrontation with those Australians who objected to vice-regal extravagance.

Cup Week festivities at Government House were interrupted by affairs of state, when the Labor Party caucus decided to withdraw the parliamentary support it had given the Deakin administration since 1905. On 10 November 1908 the government was defeated on a procedural motion which it rightly interpreted as a question of confidence. The following day Deakin called at Government House to tender his resignation.

It was Dudley's clear constitutional duty to commission the leader of the Labor Party, Andrew Fisher, to form an administration and this he did. Fisher had become party leader upon the resignation of Watson in 1907 and since then had proved a cautious, constructive leader. He had moved the amendment which brought down the Deakin government. On 12 November, after caucus had elected the cabinet and Fisher had allocated portfolios, the second Commonwealth Labor government was sworn in.

Relations between the governor-general and Labor members during Fisher's first government were unremarkable. But there were signs of an opposition to Dudley's gubernatorial style that was to culminate in an open clash with members of the second Fisher administration during 1910.

Pursuing his broad concept of vice-regal duty, Dudley set out to change the residential pattern established by his predecessors. They had resided mainly in Melbourne and, less regularly, in Sydney, paying the other State capitals short visits during parliamentary recess. Dudley determined to reside in the State capitals for extended periods of time. To this purpose he decided to accept the South Australian government's invitation to visit Adelaide during January and February 1909, when the vice-regal country residence of Marble Hill was temporarily unoccupied.

Dudley admitted to the new secretary of state, Lord Crewe, that his scheme involved rather greater personal expenditure on the part of the governor-general than had hitherto been the case, but he thought that any such disadvantage was 'more than outweighted by the opportunities such a plan affords of meeting people who hardly, if ever, come to Melbourne or Sydney', and he thought it 'quite probable that in years to come, when the finances of the Commonwealth are in a more settled condition it may be possible to obtain for the Governor-General a somewhat larger salary than is now paid, in view of his obligations over the larger area'.

This analysis badly misread Australian opinion. Since parliament had in 1902 approved payment of an allowance of £5500 in addition to the £10 000 salary, expenditure had increased markedly, reaching £22 553 for the year 1908–09. This had not been without occasional protest, particularly from Labor members. Dudley's hopes for a 'somewhat larger salary' were unrealistic.

Expense was only one obstacle to Dudley's concept of the roving viceroy. Another was the determination, in most States, to retain State governors. Dudley's term of office coincided with a significant agitation for Australians to be appointed as State governors.

At federation it had been assumed by many that the establishment of the office of governor-general would render obsolete the office of State governor, and that considerable savings would be thus effected. By 1908 the salaries of governors in all the States except Western Australia had been lowered. The following table shows the salaries, in £s, of State governors in 1907, compared to those of colonial governors in 1893. Figures are from *Victorian* and *Commonwealth Year Books*:

	Vic.	NSW	S.Aust.	Qld	W.Aust.	Tas.
1893:	£10 000	£7000	£5000	£5000	£4000	£3500
1907:	5000	5000	4000	3000	4000	2750

But, insofar as State Government Houses continued to be occupied by British officials, it was evident that reduction of governors' salaries appeared to be the furthest that State parliaments were prepared to go towards change.

Nevertheless, there was a spasmodic but persistent movement during the first decade of federation aiming to abolish the office of State governor altogether, or to end the importation of British officials to fill these posts. These attempts became identified with the policy of the Labor Party. Though in the Commonwealth parliament Labor members generally limited their concern with these matters to occasionally tilting at vice-regal expenditure, a more radical spirit was evident in State Labor Parties: high on the party platform in every State were proposals for the abolition of the office of State governor. But, as this could not be achieved without drastically re-writing State constitutions Labor came to pursue a more attainable goal, namely the selection of Australian citizens as governors. In Victoria, both the *Age* and the Australian Natives' Association supported this contention. During the first decade of the century the question of appointing local governors was debated, usually briefly, in several State assemblies and at occasional conferences of State premiers.

The first real attempt to implement Labor policy in this respect was made in South Australia. At the 1907 Premiers Conference in Brisbane a motion declaring that 'the present is not an opportune time to alter the system of appointing State Governors' was opposed by the South Australian Labor premier, Thomas Price. Visiting London shortly afterwards, Price discussed with Elgin the possibility of appointing Australian lieutenant-governors instead of British governors. The consummation of these moves came in August 1908. In a carefully worded dispatch to the secretary of state the premier requested that the next South Australian governor be selected locally.

Price reasonably asserted that no position of honour in South Australia should be regarded as beyond the reach of its most distinguished citizens. Yet when the dispatch was tabled in the Adelaide Legislative Assembly there was an immediate outcry from conservatives in several States, foreshadowing the opposition raised by such proposals for the following 50 years. As late as 1947, R.G. Menzies considered the appointment of William McKell as governor-general of Australia to be 'shocking and humiliating'. In Adelaide in 1908 the Legislative Council declared that the method of appointing non-Australian governors was satisfactory and the representations in the premier's dispatch mistaken and unauthorised.

Press reaction was generally unfavourable, only the *Age* supporting Price's proposal. In South Australia neither of the two major newspapers approved of the dispatch. The *Argus* in Melbourne and the *Mercury* in Hobart vigorously denounced what they regarded as an attempt to sever Australia's Imperial ties, deprecating the 'tendency among Labor politicians' to 'let the Empire be whittled away'. The *Sydney Morning Herald* contented itself with a gentler editorial reproof, but it stressed the value as a link with the Empire which the system of appointing distinguished Britons to Australian State governorships provided. Most papers felt that the office would become a political party prize if local celebrities were appointed.

At the Colonial Office the dispatch was given short shrift. Crewe politely rejected Price's suggestion, requiring that any change in the system of appointing Australian governors could only be made at the unanimous insistence of all State governments. A suitable British replacement for the retiring governor in Adelaide was promptly suggested for the consideration of the South Australian cabinet. Leading a coalition ministry and lacking the support of any other State government, Price was unable to bring any effective pressure to bear upon the Colonial Office and he acquiesced in the selection of Sir Day Bosanquet, an affable, experienced naval officer who had served for some years with the British Navy in Australian waters.

The reaction to Price's attempt to implement Labor policy indicated that for most Australians national consciousness was still firmly within the Imperial mould. Those who urged that Australian citizens be selected to represent the Crown in the States, and who resented the implication that an Australian would lack the necessary impartiality of judgement, remained in the minority. Agitation for local appointments continued in the legislatures of Victoria, Western Australia and Queensland, but without effect. In February 1913 Sir John Forrest joined the ranks of those publicly advocating local State governors (Governor Sir Gerald Strickland believed that Forrest coveted the post for himself). Later that year the Western Australian Labor ministry of J. Scaddan forwarded a resolution petitioning for reconsideration of the question. But Harcourt, the secretary of state at the time, was unwilling to disturb the ruling made by Crewe and there the matter rested until the 1920s. Part of the reason for the failure of these attempts lay in a general reluctance in Australia to alter a system which seemed to be working well enough. State governments were also disinclined to reduce the prestige of their governors lest in doing so they surrendered more of their sovereignty to the federal government. In addition, the declared Labor policy of abolition tended to divide opinion along party lines. Such a polarisation allowed critics to claim that this item of Labor policy reflected the fundamentally disloyal attitude of the party towards the British Empire.

During the first decade of the Commonwealth the gathering strength of the Labor movement had provoked considerable alarm about its attitude towards the Imperial connection. The political and industrial developments of the late nineteenth century had produced a party whose aims were practical, social and industrial rather than theoretical or doctrinal. For this group local issues were of prime importance, the subtleties of the Imperial relationship less vital. While containing many who were staunchly loyal to Britain, in the absence of any other effective radical political party in Australia Labor had attracted to its banner a small band of independent-minded reformers and anti-Imperialists who helped to keep alight the radical conscience. As a result, the party's attitude towards the British Empire was a hybrid thing, neither rejection nor whole-hearted acceptance. Yet, more by accident than by design, and partly as a reaction to the extreme attitudes of Imperialists, a coherent policy of national self-sufficiency within the Empire did emerge. While the far-sighted among them might have foreseen that this policy would lead to complete independence in foreign affairs, Labor politicians usually disclaimed this goal. Defence policy and particularly naval defence policy became the cutting edge of this trend to independence.

To a certain extent the implementation by the Labor Party of its declared policy for an Australian navy was stimulated by an agitation generally known as 'the naval scare'. Revelations during a House of Commons debate on the naval estimates in March 1909 caused a wave of alarm to spread throughout the Empire — a fear that Germany had passed Britain in the naval race. Australia's isolation entailed a particular dependence upon the British Navy. Faced with the frightening possibility of Britain's loss of naval supremacy, the *Age* and soon most other Australian newspapers proposed that Australia assist Britain immediately by offering to the British government a battle cruiser of the 'Dreadnought' type. New Zealand, also affected by geographic isolation, did so immediately. A wave of Imperial patriotism, fanned by public meetings and excited speeches, engulfed Australia. The flavour of the public mood is captured by a description of one demonstration in Sydney which coincided with the festival Empire Day, on 24 May 1909. At a 'stupendous gathering on the great cricket ground at Moore Park ... ten thousand school children massed and drilled to form the giant letters of the words: One Flag One Fleet'. Even Deakin, previously a supporter of the concept of a local navy, hastily endorsed the proposal that Australia give a dreadnought to Britain.

To this public pressure on Fisher was added the private counsel of the governor-general. Though he quite properly refrained from open endorsement, Dudley suggested in private to the prime minister that 'the moral effect of presenting a Dreadnought might be very great, as illustrating the solidarity of the Empire'.

In the face of considerable public agitation, the Labor government remained calm and moderate. Fisher and his colleagues considered that available funds would be more usefully spent in creating a local flotilla. In February, one month earlier, the government had placed orders for three destroyers which were intended to form the first elements of an Australian naval force as advocated for several years by Labor and also by Deakin. For this purpose Fisher utilised a sum of £250 000 set aside by Deakin's government the previous year 'for such naval expenditure as Parliament may hereafter approve'. In a policy speech in late March 1909, goaded by the naval scare, Fisher announced Labor's ambitious plans for a fleet of coastal destroyers.

The proposal for a local navy was an important step towards international maturity. But the Labor government carefully endorsed Australia's continued attachment to the Empire. The prime minister reassured the governor-general that there need be no fear that Australia's loyalty to Britain was in any way diminished. Dudley elicited an assurance from Fisher that while the government's policy was 'to provide for its own defence, still, in the event of any emergency, the resources of the Commonwealth would be cheerfully placed at the disposal of the Mother Country'.

The governor-general's cautious advocacy of the dreadnought proposal was not authorised by any specific instruction from Britain. There was no indication in March 1909 that the British government welcomed the offer of a battle cruiser. Dudley can therefore be criticised not only for interfering in a matter of Australian concern, but also as exceeding his diplomatic instructions. But he had been prudent in not pressing his point of view in public and it was undoubtedly true that the offer of a dreadnought (later made by the Deakin government) emphasised the solidarity of the Empire.

At the 1907 Colonial Conference Deakin had been concerned to ensure that constitutional control over the local naval force should be vested securely in Australian hands. Yet it was clear that 'unity of control' was of great strategic importance in the disposition of fleet units. In April 1909 Fisher prepared a memorandum on the control of Australian war vessels in time of war or emergency. When shown a draft of this document, Dudley objected to a clause which provided that the consent of the Commonwealth should be obtained before any Australian vessel were placed under British command. Though again this was without specific authorisation from Britain, the governor-general's action was in accord with the 'watching brief' which it was his duty to hold over Imperial interests. On this occasion the cabinet bowed to the governor-general's wishes and the clause was re-drafted, largely by Dudley himself, to make the transfer automatic. Fisher declined to implement other changes to the draft suggested by Dudley.

In June 1909 Deakin replaced Fisher as prime minister. Again, the change of governments involved the governor-general's discretionary powers. For the third time in a decade, a ministry had advised a governor-general to dissolve parliament prematurely, and for the third time such advice was refused.

The seeds of Fisher's defeat and the formation of Deakin's third ministry had been sown six months earlier. In November 1908 the retirement of Reid from the leadership of the Free Trade Party in favour of the colourless but pragmatic Joseph Cook opened the way for discussions between Deakin's followers and the other elements opposing Fisher's ministry. These negotiations culminated in a joint meeting on 26 May 1909 which elected Deakin as leader of a united opposition. The following day saw the defeat of the seven-month-old Labor government — a defeat which Labor regarded, justifiably, as being ill-mannered in its haste and unnatural in its parentage. For two days tempers ran high and Australian parliamentary invective reached unprecedented heights, a fitting uproar for such a turning point in the evolution of the Australian party system.

Following its defeat the cabinet resolved to appeal for a dissolution from the governor-general. Over the last weekend in May William Morris Hughes, Fisher's attorney-general, worked on a memorandum which the prime minister presented to Dudley on Monday. Hughes argued that sound constitutional precedents existed for the grant of a dissolution and that the electors deserved an opportunity to test the new alignment of parties.

There was very little speculation in the press upon Dudley's likely response; it was almost a foregone conclusion that Deakin would be commissioned. Not even the radical press ventured to suggest that the governor-general ought to follow his government's advice, although a few, admittedly small, voices raised the possibility. The *Tamworth Observer* pointed out: 'Mr Fisher ... is His Excellency's responsible adviser. As such, it is quite conceivable that his advice may be taken'. And while the Hobart *Mercury* suggested without elaboration that there was a chance that the governor-general might grant an immediate dissolution, these were isolated opinions; the overwhelming expectation was that the request would be refused.

In retrospect there was considerable weight in the government's argument. Discussing the matter in his book *The royal power of dissolution* ... (1943) Eugene Forsey comments: 'If two opposition parties, both at issue on some great question of public policy, drop their opposition to each other and fuse, then it certainly seems reasonable for the minority Government to challenge the new, fused party in the country'. But there was also a strong opposing case. The coalition ranged against the Labor Party in the House of Representatives was numerically powerful and gave every indication of stability. There were approximately twelve months before parliament was bound to go to the electors again. Moreover, if an election for only the lower house were held, Senate elections would become out of step.

As a governor-general who was not only ignorant of Australian politics but lacked any experience of the operation of the House of Commons, Dudley faced a difficult task. It was not surprising that he should turn to Australia's most eminent constitutional authority, Sir Samuel Griffith. In a private memorandum the chief justice advised him to decline Fisher's request; Dudley immediately followed Griffith's advice. Reportedly, he later told Hughes he did not even read the government's memorandum! On 2 June 1909 Fisher resigned and Deakin formed his third and last ministry.

Subsequent judgements of Dudley's action have usually been neutral. Evatt commented that it was 'in accord with previous Australian practice'. But Keith thought it was '*prima facie* ... contrary to constitutional usage', and the proximity of the dreadnought controversy prompted him to suggest that the governor-general's action might have been influenced by 'the desire to see effective aid rendered to the Empire'. I have found insufficient evidence to determine whether or not Dudley was so influenced, but the inference was likely to arise in the future, as Australia grew in status.

An anonymous letter (signed 'Politician') in Melbourne's *Punch* suggested that 'the substitution of the Chief Justice of the High Court for the Governor-General would relieve the situation of all risk and all unfairness'. It was not difficult to imagine a situation in which it might be of the greatest political importance to the party in power in Great Britain that a certain statesman or a certain party should not obtain office in Australia. Can it be expected that the knowledge of this would fail to influence — even unconsciously — the judgment of a Governor-General whose very position was the reward for faithful service to the ruling party in Great Britain?

The proposal that the chief justice should exercise a discretionary role in the political affairs of the Commonwealth was impracticable and contrary to British parliamentary practice. But the contributor to *Punch* foreshadowed an inference which the still relatively immature Australian parliament was unwilling to draw. The governor-general was provided with constitutional advisers. It was time that his confidence in such advisers was extended to incorporate the dissolution of parliament. The situation was to rise again. Though at times some argued that the governor-general's discretionary power to refuse his ministers' advice remained, in practice the refusal of Fisher's request in June 1909 was the last such occasion in the Commonwealth.

In reporting the events to the secretary of state, Dudley paid credit to the attitude of Fisher and his colleagues. They had been 'most loyal and considerate . . . [and] carefully refrained from saying a word which might have the effect of exciting popular hostility against the decision which in the course of my constitutional duty I had been called upon to make'. Assuring Crewe that he himself held the Labor Party in high regard, he complimented Fisher's ministers as 'very earnest, painstaking and well meaning men'. Another contributor to *Punch*, however, suggested that the governor-general's refusal to dissolve parliament had 'convinced every labour man in the Commonwealth that the Earl of Dudley is the most uncompromising foe Labour ever had'. During his next experience of a Labor administration few of the signs of cordiality about which he had written to Crewe were to be evident.

Deakin's ministry lasted less than eleven months. It was an energetic government. Many measures of considerable importance to Australia's future were passed with the sure majority guaranteed to a ministry for the first time in the Commonwealth's history. But it was a relatively quiet time politically for the governor-general. In December 1909 he and his wife left Australia on a cruise to Colombo. During their vacation the Commonwealth was administered by the governor of New South Wales, Lord Chelmsford. Dudley returned to Australia on 27 January 1910; his wife, for both personal and public reasons, proceeded to England.

The wives of governors-general were prominent public figures. Lady Hopetoun had not been especially successful. She was shy in public and disliked the social activities which her position as leader of society obliged her to take while Hopetoun was governor of Victoria, and illness had curtailed her public duties during the eighteen months that she spent in Australia after federation. In contrast Lady Tennyson had relished the public duties of governor's wife in Adelaide and was only restrained from continuing to do so when Tennyson became governor-general by the conviction that, if she were too prominent, she might offend the wives of State governors. In a parting letter to Lady Northcote

Lady Dudley

Lord Dudley in Sydney
c.1909

she had explained the difficulties in advice which was still valid in 1909:

> Having been in both positions I must candidly own that I infinitely prefer
> being Governor's wife to Governor-General's, for in the one everything is
> open to you and you take part and interest in anything you like, — whereas as
> G.G.'s wife there is *very* little you can do without encroaching on the rights of
> the State Governor's wife, which even if she herself does not mind, the
> Governor minds for her ... Both Lady Clarke and Lady Rawson have been
> extremely nice and kind to me and we are all *great* friends but I have always
> *steadily* refused to do anything that they would consider State and therefore
> their work. You will find that people will be always asking you to open things,
> preside at meetings etc. etc. — my advice is if you want to keep peace, explain
> to them from the first that you would love to do it — and hate refusing but
> that they must remember you are Federal and not State and that you would
> not like to encroach on the rights of the Governor's wife.
>   It is a position, I can assure you, that requires an enormous amount of self
> denial and tact.

Lady Northcote seems to have taken her predecessor's advice to heart. Though
a quiet, friendly hostess at dinner parties, she said and did little in public,

Lady Dudley in Sydney c.1909 with her three youngest children: Roderick John (born 1902), Gladys Honor (born 1892) and Morvyth Lillian (born 1896). Her eldest son, William Humble Eric, Viscount Ednam (born 1894) remained at school in England.

seeming keener to devote her attention to the cultivation of the garden at Melbourne's Government House. However, she was a woman of independent wealth and opinion, and she did organize an exhibition of women's work in Melbourne in 1906.

Less conscious than Lady Tennyson or Lady Northcote of the need for public reticence, Lady Dudley determined to assert herself in the public forum. She was a strikingly beautiful woman of considerable intelligence and drive. A visitor to the Dudleys in Ireland later described Lady Dudley as 'the cleverer of the two' with 'great imagination'. But she was said to have a 'reserved, even absent manner'. Ada Holman, wife of the New South Wales Labor leader W.A. Holman, described Lady Dudley as: 'a marble statue, expressionless and almost dumb, keeping her long white gloves on throughout as was her wont even at dinner; toying with one salted almond and one cheese wafer at supper ... She was the goddess Artemis, a carved lily ...' Perhaps the Countess' manner on this occasion was exacerbated by her proximity to the effervescent Mrs Holman. A more sympathetic portrayal is given by 'Banjo' Paterson, who described Lady Dudley as 'cultivated and altogether feminine', and as 'a singularly beautiful woman, graceful and with a voice that had the range of an organ and had been carefully trained by professors of elocution'. But even he commented upon the 'steel in her composition'.

In May 1909 Her Excellency had accompanied her husband at the formal ceremony opening the Commonwealth parliament. The writer of *Punch*'s Ladies' Letter remarked on this with approval. 'In solemn truth', the correspondent continued, 'the Countess of Dudley is something of a politician. She is a talker herself — a conversationalist and a speech maker'. Certainly the governor-general's wife was interested in politics; in 1908 she had observed from the public gallery the Deakin government's defeat. She resolved to take an active role in Australia, in a sphere which was appropriate. The provision of health services outside city centres was, in those days before aviation, less than adequate. Speaking to a meeting of the Women's National Council in Brisbane on 21 August 1909, Lady Dudley urged the extension of the existing district nursing scheme so that patients in the outback could obtain the benefits of trained nursing care.

Having embarked upon the project, it was not in Lady Dudley's nature to leave the implementation to others. During the next two years she laboured to put her scheme into practice. In Melbourne she summoned a public meeting which called for expert opinion on the merits of a practical scheme. In early 1910, during a visit of several months to England, she set out to attract support from British Nursing Institutes and King Edward himself. On her return to Australia, and after the visit of two British advisers, a federal constitution was presented for public approval. This proposed to set up a federal council with the governor-general's wife as patroness, and six State councils each under the patronage of the wife of the State governor.

Lady Dudley's bush nursing scheme was an ambitious project commended by both Deakin and Fisher. But neither devoted any of the Commonwealth's public funds and the scheme failed to secure the public donations that it needed to become effective. A suggestion that it be set up as a memorial to the late King Edward VII was dropped when, as the *Argus* reported in July 1910, the public showed a preference to erect a statue. Finally opposition from the Australian medical profession meant the end of the proposal as it was originally conceived, though some State associations survived. By September 1910 Lady Dudley was forced to conclude that her bush nursing scheme was 'not wholly acceptable' to Australia. This was a matter of some disappointment for her.

Far more embarrassing was the disappointment of her hopes for an improvement in her marriage. Ada Holman wrote in 1947 that it was 'common knowledge' that Dudley and his wife were 'on very distant terms ... seen together only at strictly official functions'. In September 1910 John Norton published in *Truth* a scurrilous article charging the Earl of Dudley with 'concupiscent capers ... libidinous lecheries and lascivious lapses'. By October the relationship between the Dudleys had degenerated to the stage where 'terms of arrangement were embodied in a document'.

Other troubles multiplied. In September the Sydney *Sun* published a report headed: 'Lord Dudley — Trouble with the Ministry — Sharp Notes Sent to Government House'. It claimed that, for some time past, 'the happiest relations have not existed between the Governor-General and the Labor Ministry' which had secured office at the elections of April 1910. The *Sun* cited three reasons: the appointment of Reid as Australian high commissioner and the corresponding reduction in the importance of the governor-general as channel of communication; discontent at His Excellency's infrequent residence in Melbourne, which, the *Sun* asserted, had led to delay of assent to certain legislation which the government wished to hurry through; and the failure of Lady Dudley's bush nursing scheme.

In at least one respect this report had a kernel of truth. The governor-general had been disturbed about the effect upon his position of Reid's appointment as Australia's first high commissioner to London. In June he had written to Fisher expressing the hope that he would not be 'superseded as the recognised channel of communication between the Commonwealth Government and the Imperial authorities'. This was the first indication of what was to be an increasingly serious problem for his successors as representative of the Crown in the Commonwealth. But it had not reached the stage that could be described as 'strained' in 1910.

Though Fisher strongly denied any friction between his cabinet and the governor-general, there was no doubt that their relations were hardly as cordial as had been the case in Dudley's earlier experience of a Labor government. Perhaps, as *Punch* had hinted, some Labor parliamentarians were embittered by his refusal of a dissolution in 1909. If so, then the problem of paying for the vice-regal establishment provided an ideal opportunity for dissatisfaction to make itself felt. In November 1910 Higgs, the Labor back-bencher, made a vigorous attack upon the amount which the government proposed to expend upon the governor-general and on the two Government Houses. In a brief but lively debate many Labor parliamentarians expressed agreement with Higgs. J.H. Scullin was one who commented upon the 'growing scandal in the increasing expenditure upon Government Houses'. Eventually the acting prime minister intervened. Only after Hughes had promised to give every consideration to exercising 'proper economy . . . with a view to curtailing unnecessary expenditure' did Higgs withdraw his amendment.

Fisher had not needed this warning. A few months earlier he had rebuffed Dudley on an expenditure question. His Excellency had wanted to circumnavigate the continent by sea and had proposed that the Commonwealth government should charter a steam-yacht. He had urged that 'some expenditure is justifiable to enable the Governor-General to visit the more distant parts of the Commonwealth in a convenient and dignified manner'. At first Fisher was favourable, but when the costs were presented to him he decided against the proposal. *Punch* commented: 'even a Governor-General has his disappointments'.

In the face of the several public setbacks which Their Excellencies had received, not to mention their personal difficulties, it was clear by late 1910 that they could not remain much longer in Australia. On 7 October Dudley formally asked to be relieved of his post. In his explanatory letter to the secretary of state he cited his wife's ill health, the expense of the post and the scandalous gossip, for which, he assured Crewe there was '*not the smallest fraction of foundation*'.

After months of rumours about impending retirement, it was announced in March 1911 that, for personal reasons, Dudley was returning to England.

Relations between the governor-general and the Labor government continued to be strained in the late months of Dudley's term of office. In June 1911 Dudley was furious when none of his ministers attended a levee held to celebrate the coronation of George V. An account of his vexation is given by Deakin who attended the levee in his capacity as leader of the opposition and, upon walking accidentally into the governor-general's room, received 'an angry denunciation of Ministers for their absence which he took as a direct reflection upon him and an insult to the King ... He was openly fuming and pacing up and down his room, quite forgetting the exhibition of himself he was making'. Though on the following day Hughes apologised, claiming that the absence of ministerial representation had been an oversight, it was evident that between the government and the governor-general there was an unprecedented coolness.

Dudley relinquished office on 31 July 1911. His departure from Australia a few days later was 'unmarked by any official ceremony' and Hughes, the acting prime minister, was prevented at the last moment from carrying out his original intention of being present in the farewell party. Even after his return to England Dudley aroused controversy in Australia. In October 1911 a speech in which he condemned the system of payment for members of parliament in Australia was criticised by Labor ministers and provoked Higgs to renew his attack upon the unfortunate ex-governor-general for 'neglect of his duties' and other 'vagaries'.

The death of his Royal patron, the degeneration in his marriage and his unsatisfactory experience in Australia had brought Dudley's public career to a close. He never again held public office. A deed of separation drawn up in October 1912 marked the formal end of his marriage. During World War 1 he commanded a Yeomanry unit in Egypt and Gallipoli and Lady Dudley set up an Australian military hospital in France. She drowned on 26 June 1920 while sea-bathing in Ireland. Four years later Dudley married the former musical comedy actress, Gertie Millar (the original 'Our Miss Gibbs'). He died in London on 29 June 1932.

There was no doubt that Dudley's exercise of the office of governor-general in Australia had been unsuccessful. His concept of the role as primarily ceremonial and ostentatious was badly out of touch with Australian public opinion. Conflicts and scandal reduced any influence he might have had. Deakin summed up the failures of Australia's fourth governor-general:

> His ambition was high but his interests were short-lived and subordinate to those belonging to what may be termed his private life, though there was little privacy as to much of it ... He did nothing really important, nothing thoroughly, nothing consistently ... He should have been an 'impossible' Governor-General. He remained to the last a very ineffective and not very popular figurehead.

'It puts the clock back so', lamented Northcote, writing to Deakin. By 1911 it was clear that, far from being a sinecure, the post was beset with difficulties. 'Gov. Gen. of Australia is a thankless task', minuted one senior Colonial Office

man. Melbourne's *Punch* considered it 'not a pleasant position for any man ...
one is on a pedestal, not for aggrandisement, but as a fair mark for public
inspection, criticism and eventual judgment'. To a great extent the office had
become the focus of much discontent with federation. Rivalry between Sydney
and Melbourne; concern at the cost of central government; opposition by the
States to further Commonwealth incursion on their sovereign rights; and
difficulties over the changing relationship of the Dominion with Britain; all
complicated the problems of the representative of the Crown in the Commonwealth.

Only Northcote had negotiated the difficult path successfully, yet even he
proved unable to remain an effective 'ex-Australian' in London. Ill-health and
his early death in 1911 prevented the realisation of these anticipations.
Hopetoun had died in 1908, Tennyson lacked influence in British governing
circles and Dudley was disgraced and out of sympathy with Australian
aspirations. Evidently those constitution makers who had hoped that the
governor-generalship would be a 'great office' (Sir George Grey) and its
incumbent 'equal to the ... Governor-General of India ... capable of being a
cabinet minister in England' (James Munro) were astray in their anticipations.
Australians did not even seem to want him to be a 'ceremonial ... a glittering
and gaudy toy' (Deakin) if Commonwealth taxpayers were expected to pay for
the glitter. It was not surprising, therefore, that those leading British politicians
who were prepared to leave home to govern colonies preferred the less remote
and more satisfying posts in South Africa or Canada. Lord Gladstone, appointed
as first governor-general of South Africa in 1910, had been a cabinet minister. In
1912 a royal governor-general, the Duke of Connaught, took office in Canada.
In contrast Dudley's successor in Australia was a very minor political figure.

Thomas, third Baron Denman, was only 37 when appointed fifth governor-
general of Australia. He was born on 16 November 1874 in London, son of
Richard Denman, assistant clerk of assize, and his wife Helen Mary, née
McMicking. In 1894 he succeeded his great-uncle as baron, but he was so
penniless he could not afford his own horse, despite being a champion
steeplechase rider. Educated for a military career at Sandhurst, he had served
for a short time in a regiment of the Royal Scots before turning his attention to
politics in the House of Lords.

Like Dudley he remained interested in military affairs throughout his career
and saw action in a Yeomanry unit during the South African war, where he was
wounded in action and invalided home. He had obtained a minor court
appointment in Campbell-Bannerman's administration of 1905 and at the time
of his selection for Australia was acting as chief Liberal whip in the Lords —
Lord Ripon thought 'it might be a good thing to get him out of' that position.
Denman lacked political and administrative experience. Moreover his health
was poor and his personal qualities uninspiring. Dudley regarded him as
'pleasantly casual, narrow, ineffective & likely to have little influence on either
... politics or politicians', and Deakin agreed with this assessment. Northcote,
too, had little confidence in Denman's abilities: 'As regards the new G.G. I will
say nothing, as I hardly know him — except that the appt caused general

Lord Denman

surprise. The idea here is that large private means form an indispensible or "the" indispensible condition . . . Of course Lady Denman has all the money — he is a good rider; & keen about soldiering'. Youth and fondness for polo were advantageous for a vice-regal representative in Australia. In the previous century, young and wealthy governors such as Carrington, Hopetoun and Beauchamp had proved popular and, upon their return to London, had attained considerable influence in British affairs. But Denman lacked their personal vigour.

In 1903 he had married Gertrude, the only daughter of Sir Weetman Pearson (later Lord Cowdray). Denman's father-in-law was a wealthy Yorkshire contractor whose international business activities and generous donations to party funds had raised him to prominence in Liberal circles. Eventually he secured a viscountcy. Lady Pearson, an ambitious, single-minded woman, had successfully bridged the social gap between Bradford and London to become a leading hostess in late Victorian and Edwardian society. She, too, was an active worker in the Liberal cause and a generous benefactor to various humanitarian institutions. Her daughter inherited the considerable talents of both parents. Lady Denman was tall and slim, with an aquiline nose and red hair; in appearance the complete antithesis of the classically beautiful Rachel Dudley, though she lacked none of her predecessor's strength of character. Possessing

Lady Denman, about the
time of her marriage

far more drive and intelligence than her husband, and aged only 26, 'Trudie'
Denman was unlikely to take readily to the stuffy routine of vice-regal life in the
colonies, especially as their marriage was unhappy. Matters were not improved
by the Australian climate, which aggravated Denman's disposition to hay fever
and asthma.

The Denmans arrived in Australia on 31 July 1911 'keen to work hard'. They
found the Commonwealth 'lapped by a flood of prosperity'. The droughts which
earlier in the decade had held back pastoral industry had given way to seasons of
plenty. It was a period of steady growth. The population had grown from 3 773
801 in 1901 to 4 455 005 at the 1911 census. Politically the country was more
stable than at any other time since federation. A strong Labor government was
firmly in control of the Australian parliament and pursuing vigorous, progressive, national policies. The ministry was experienced and well-balanced.
Fisher's cautious leadership, and the administrative strength of G.F. Pearce as
defence minister, were supported by the more spectacular showmanship of the

attorney-general, Hughes, and the flamboyant unpredictability of the minister for home affairs, King O'Malley. Though the cabinet was weakened in October 1911 by the death of E.L. Batchelor, a wise and experienced minister for external affairs, its competence and confidence contrasted strongly with the ageing opposition front bench, which, as the visiting writer H. Rider Haggard observed, was 'singularly destitute of captains'.

Deakin, whose political skill and intellect had dominated the first decade of the Commonwealth, was only a shadow of his former self. Of his former Protectionist colleagues only Forrest and Littleton Groom remained to sit with him in the ranks of men who had for years been his political opponents. As leader of the erstwhile Free Trade group, Joseph Cook (later Sir Joseph) attempted without conviction to fill the breeches of the sadly missed Reid, assisted by William Hill Irvine (later Sir William), an aloof and narrow lawyer, and the diligent but ineffectual Senator Edward Davis Millen.

'The people I like best', wrote Lady Denman to her brother, 'are the Labour people. They are very simple and nice'. Lord and Lady Denman's relations with Fisher and his ministers were remarkably cordial throughout their whole period in Australia. Even after an election in 1913 returned Cook's Liberal Party with a narrow majority it was no secret that the governor-general remained in close contact with Labor leaders. Denman displayed no inclination to interfere in political affairs. Nor did he expect to be recompensed by the national parliament for his vice-regal entertainment. The Denmans' generosity was guaranteed by financial support of up to £50 000 from Lord Cowdray. 'We spend money like water', commented Lady Denman in a letter. The *Bulletin* remarked: 'the joyous Denmans hand out their money with both hands on the slightest provocation'.

Their Excellencies' popularity with Labor parliamentarians owed much to the way in which they struggled against the excessive formality of their official position. Younger and politically more progressive than their predecessors, they introduced a more relaxed atmosphere to vice-regal activities.

A writer for Melbourne's *Punch* complimented Lady Denman on refusing 'to adopt that pose of haughty disdain which has been so characteristic of some Vice-Regal ladies in the past'. In spite of constant poor health, Denman won Australians' praise for his enthusiasm for sport. His wife, too, was prominent in public. She followed her predecessor's support for the bush nursing project. Spurred on by a somewhat naive enthusiasm for the Australian bush, she zealously visited outback towns to install nurses in this scheme, which achieved some measure of operational success between 1911 and 1914 largely due to her efforts.

Both the governor-general and his lady were bravely prepared to travel extensively throughout the continent in what had become the obligatory gubernatorial fashion. Dudley had warned Denman that 'Travelling about visiting country towns and districts is one of the principal functions of the Gov. Gen'. The Denmans officiated at innumerable ceremonies in every State, opening anything from an agricultural show to the trans-continental railway. This activity had its repercussions. Denman found that relations with the

Reception line at levee for the naming of Canberra, March 1913. (Professor Hayden about to doff his mortar-board, Professor Hosking is shaking Lady Denman's hand.)

representatives of the Crown in the States were 'often difficult ... the Governors themselves are difficult to deal with'. In March 1913 Denman laid the foundation stone of the future national capital at a dusty but picturesque rural site which Lady Denman, with much ceremony, announced would be named Canberra.

Although it was to be many years before the national capital took shape, its founding was indicative of the growing self-assurance of the Australian government in both internal and external affairs. Though attempts to extend its powers under the Constitution were defeated in two separate referenda between 1911 and 1914, other measures such as the establishment of the Commonwealth Bank and the institution of maternity allowances were permanent and substantial legislative achievements. In 1911 the Australian government created a citizen military force for home defence under a system of universal compulsory training. A Navigation Act to provide additional protection for Australian shipping and Australian seamen was enacted despite opposition from British shipping interests. The Fisher government also brought to fruition plans to establish an Australian Navy.

The Imperial Conference of 1911, which coincided with the Denmans' arrival in Australia, provided evidence of further change in the relationship between the Dominions and Mother Country. This conference, the first attended by a representative of the newly established Union of South Africa, was chaired by the prime minister of the United Kingdom instead of by the secretary of state for the colonies as had been the case since 1887. Reluctantly, the British government recognised that the self-governing Dominions could no longer be completely excluded from the fields of Imperial defence and international affairs. Though Asquith was not prepared to concede to them any direct role in the conduct of policy, Dominion ministers were vouchsafed audience to an exposition of Imperial defence and foreign policy more comprehensive than had been revealed to the British cabinet. For the future they gained access to the Committee of Imperial Defence and a recognition that they would be consulted on matters affecting their external concerns and defence needs.

These changes in the status of Australia as a Dominion within the British Empire had a significant effect on the role of governor-general. The emergence of the Colonial and Imperial Conference as a central co-operative organ, albeit limited and discontinuous, left the governor-general and his superior, the secretary of state for the colonies, rather on the periphery. In little over a decade, Australian leaders had come into contact with British statesmen far more intimately and regularly than had been the case in the colonial period.

As British cabinet ministers lost some of their remoteness the governor-general inevitably lost prestige. His close association with the Colonial Office, which Australian leaders had long regarded as an unsatisfactory intermediary, also diminished his standing. It was becoming clear to colonial statesmen that the secretary of state for colonies was not as important a member of the British cabinet as had been the case during Chamberlain's tenure of office. At the 1907 conference Deakin had attempted to transfer Dominion affairs from the responsibility of the Colonial Office, which he regarded as inept and impenetrable, to a conference secretarist. But lack of support from the Canadian prime minister, Laurier, and skilful manoeuvring by the secretary of state, Lord Elgin, had defeated his proposal. A secretariat was set up, but it was securely under the control of the Colonial Office. Consequently the governor-general remained the principal channel of communication between Australia and the British government.

Despite their irregularity and the lack of a permanent independent secretariat, Imperial conferences enabled Dominion politicians to put their case personally to the British government. In addition, by 1911 the Dominions (Canada, New Zealand, Australia and South Africa) had stationed high commissioners in London charged with important quasi-diplomatic responsibilities. In 1910, after considerable delay, Australia had appointed former prime minister George Houston Reid as its first such official. Behind this appointment was the constantly expressed wish that Australian national interests be represented in Britain. The high commissioner was a potentially formidable agent of the Commonwealth in London, particularly one as enthusiastic and energetic as Reid. Conflicts soon arose between his office and the governor-general over their respective responsibilities.

The Colonial Office regarded with suspicion any evidence that Dominions were using the high commissioner as an alternative channel of communication. Early in 1911, after incidents involving New Zealand and South African representatives, Lewis Harcourt, who had succeeded Crewe as secretary of state in November 1910, reminded his cabinet colleagues that the sole intermediary between British and Dominion governments should be the Colonial Office. But the problem persisted, particularly with regard to defence matters. The most intransigent offender was the Admiralty in its negotiations with the Dominions over the establishment of Dominion navies. During 1911 a new naval agreement, conceding to the Dominions their right to flotillas of their own, took shape at meetings between Admiralty and Dominion representatives in London. Significantly, the Colonial Office was not represented at these negotiations and the bill to carry the agreement into effect was drafted without its concurrence. The agreement provided, amongst other things, that communications concerning technical matters such as equipment and armament should be channelled through Reid.

The Colonial Office was prepared to countenance such correspondence in routine matters. But in August 1912 Harcourt drew the attention of the first lord of the admiralty, Winston Churchill, to several instances of direct communication between the Admiralty and the Dominion governments, via the high. commissioners, which involved policy, not routine. Denman had complained that communications between his Australian ministers and the Admiralty had passed without his knowledge. Harcourt pointed out to Churchill that this practice placed the governor-general in an unfortunate position. Seeing nothing of the correspondence he would not be in a position to understand the nature of the Admiralty's policy. In the case of an emergency he would not be able to 'exercise the personal influence which he should have with his Government' in favour of those views.

Churchill agreed that in policy matters within the sphere of 'Colonial diplomacy', it was essential that the Colonial Office should be the Admiralty's ambassador. But he pointed out that 'a large and multiplying series of questions mostly of technical detail' were arising, many of which required to be dealt with by telegraph, while others had to be 'discussed verbally with the High Commissioner or with the naval representatives of the Dominions on the High Commissioners' Staffs'. Though he suggested an interdepartmental committee to consider the principles to be observed in dealing with the problem, it was becoming clear that the growing independence of the Dominions and their establishment of institutions such as local navies threatened to reduce the influence of the Colonial Office and the governor-general. In Australia, the official secretary, Steward, was also concerned at the 'direction in which things are drifting'. On 9 July 1912 he had forwarded to M.L. Shepherd, the prime minister's private secretary, a memorandum objecting to the tendency to 'transfer portion of the functions of the Governor-General to the High Commissioner's Office'. But, despite protests in London and in Melbourne, irregularities continued.

The development of alternative channels of communication between Britain and the Dominions led a contributor to *Round Table* in 1913 to suggest that the Colonial Office had become no more than a 'clearing house', while other departments, especially the Foreign Office and the Board of Trade, dealt with the more important aspects of Dominion affairs. While it was true that the appointment of a British trade commissioner to Australia in 1908, who reported direct to the Board of Trade, added yet another avenue of contact between the two countries, it was premature to suggest that the traditional channel of communication had been superseded.

The focal point of the Empire was still Downing Street and Whitehall. In the existing system of two-way dispatches there was a permanent, reasonably efficient instrument for the transmission of communications to that focal point. Without a foreign service, each Dominion and Dominion government still depended upon those dispatches, or upon press reports also emanating from London, for their information about foreign affairs. Except for the special occasions when Dominion ministers were attending conferences in London, the office of the governor-general remained the most convenient channel for any representation which the Commonwealth government wished to make to Britain or any other country. Moreover, Dominion cabinets were reluctant to grant their high commissioners any authority to bind the distant government. Canada's appointment in 1914 of Sir George Perley as cabinet minister in residence at London was the first attempt to give the high commissioner effective responsibility. But the outbreak of war quickly ended this experiment. In the case of Reid, whose term in London coincided mainly with a Labor administration in the Commonwealth, it would have been politically impossible for the government to allow him extra-territorial authority. Consequently the governor-general retained his function as principal link with and ambassadorial representative of the British government.

To the consternation of the Colonial Office Denman appeared not to recognise this aspect of his role. In particular his ready acceptance of Australian views on the establishment of a local flotilla led to disapproval in London. Perhaps unduly influenced by his friendship with Labor ministers in Australia, Denman made the Dominion navy the subject for enthusiastic public addresses. The permanent under secretary at the Colonial Office thought Denman should leave 'matters of policy alone, unless he has explicit instructions in regard to them'. Harcourt agreed. In March 1913 Denman welcomed the delivery of Australia's new cruiser, the 'Melbourne', by asserting that 'in view of Australia's sacrifices of men and money and her isolated position in the southern Pacific no-one could question her right to complete control of her own fleet unit'. But by 1913 the British government, particularly Churchill, was less satisfied with the proposition of Dominion navies than it had been only a few years earlier. In this situation Denman's March 1913 speech was considered at the Colonial Office to be 'most ill timed and injudicious'.

As this incident showed, Australia's emergence from colonial dependence upon Great Britain made it more difficult for the representative of the Crown to reconcile his function as agent of the British government with his role as Australian head of state. Australians wanted a constitutional monarch, sympathetic to Australian aspirations and able to make influential representations on their behalf in London. The British government saw him more in the role of diplomat and intelligence officer, exercising 'the personal influence which he should have with his Government' in favour of the British government's policy. On matters such as immigration and tariff policies, which had passed to local control before 1910, the governor-general was expected to act as guardian of Imperial interests. For example, Denman watched closely the passage of the Navigation Bill through the Commonwealth parliament, conveying representations on Britain's behalf.

For the governor-general to have such influence required considerable personal prestige and strength of character. Denman, though popular and conscientious, was ineffectual and inexperienced, unable to arrest the declining prestige of the position and, like his predecessor, unable to realise the potentialities of the role. In addition his term in Australia was overshadowed by a dispute which damaged the dignity of both the office of governor-general and its occupant.

The quarrel over occupancy of Sydney Government House which reached its climax during Denman's tenure of office had a long history. Prior to federation, the premier of New South Wales, Lyne, had undertaken to make ample provision for the governor-general's residence in Sydney. For this purpose he offered the existing Government House and arranged for the lease of 'Cranbrook', a smaller house at Bellevue Hill, as a residence for future State governors. The last colonial governor in New South Wales, Beauchamp, returned to England prematurely to enable Hopetoun to move into the premises in Sydney Domain. Reluctantly conceding that the governor-general must reside mainly in Melbourne during sessions of Commonwealth parliament,

Lyne had offered Sydney Government House to establish the principle that during parliamentary recess the representative of the Crown in the Commonwealth should live at Sydney.

The problem contributed to Hopetoun's early return to England. As sittings of the national parliament were more prolonged than had ever been anticipated, the representative of the Crown tended to spend more time in Melbourne than in Sydney. Most governors-general regretted this development. The picturesque Gothic building in Sydney Domain, with its magnificent setting and fine harbour views, was a far more comfortable residence than the large draughty mansion on the banks of the Yarra. Even when parliament was in recess, visits to other States cut into the time which could be devoted to Sydney.

As early as December 1902 Barton warned Tennyson of Sydney's sense of vice-regal neglect. Tennyson attempted to heed Barton's advice during the remainder of his term and advised his successor to follow suit and 'spend at least four and a half months in Sydney . . . if possible and four and a half months in Melbourne'. Northcote tried to continue this practice. But in July 1905 J.H. Carruthers, premier of New South Wales, reopened the issue. In a strongly worded letter to Deakin he expressed his State's dissatisfaction with the fact that 'the Vice-Regal residence has for all practical purposes been permanently fixed in Melbourne'. On his estimate the governor-general had spent on the average only 89 days yearly in Sydney since federation. For 'the greater portion of the year the . . . Government House . . . is empty and unused'. In providing other quarters for the State governor, great expense was incurred without adequate return. He asked the Commonwealth to 'hand back Government House, Sydney, to New South Wales, and accept other arrangements for the occasional residence of the Governor-General' in that State.

Carruthers' complaint was only one aspect of general discontent with the Commonwealth. Federation had proven costlier and more damaging to States' sovereignty than had been expected. Faced with the tendency of Commonwealth governments to increase their power still further, the States fought back with what methods they could. One way was to retain governors as channels of communication with Britain. Another was to insist that the Commonwealth make adequate recompense for property it had acquired from the colonies as a result of federation. The delay in establishing a federal capital made it inevitable that the question of vice-regal residences would cause difficulties. The tendency of most governors-general to identify themselves with the centralist impulses of the Commonwealth government also offended the State governments.

Replying to Carruthers in July 1905, Deakin had produced figures to prove that since Northcote's assumption of office the governor-general had spent no less time in Sydney than in Melbourne. He pointed out that absences from the capitals of the two most populous States were inevitable if other parts of the Commonwealth were to be visited. In these circumstances he hoped that Government House Sydney could be retained for the use of the representative of the Crown in the Commonwealth. After further correspondence with Deakin and Victoria's premier, Thomas Bent, a temporary solution was found. The earlier informal arrangement, whereby both premises were provided free of charge, was replaced by more business-like five-year leases. No rent was paid but the Commonwealth undertook to maintain the house and grounds of both properties.

Such an *ad hoc* arrangement postponed rather than solved the problem. As the federal capital was unlikely to be erected within five years the quarrel threatened to reappear when the time came to renegotiate the leases. This likelihood increased in early 1911 when a Labor government came to office in New South Wales. Though led by J.S. McGowen, its intellectual force resided in the energetic and resourceful attorney-general, W.A. Holman. While both McGowen and Fisher were absent in London in May 1911, Holman as acting premier informed the Commonwealth that he proposed to resume Government House for public purposes.

To some extent Holman's action reflected the general dissatisfaction in Australia with Lord Dudley's style of office. Though figures had been published to show that Melbourne was obtaining no more vice-regal patronage than Sydney it was undeniable that for over half the year both residences were unoccupied. Holman argued that the Sydney public should have more access to the magnificent site occupied by Government House. It was suggested that the grounds be added to the Domain as a park. The house itself could be used as a library, hospital, museum of arts or conservatorium. But in addition Holman stressed that the matter was simply a business proposition between the governments of New South Wales and of the Commonwealth. The Surplus Revenue Act of 1910 had effected the complete separation of Commonwealth and State finances. The governor-general was a federal rather than an Imperial officer. The time had gone when it was the duty of the State 'to find the appliances with which the Federal [Government was] to carry out its functions'.

Although the lease expired in August 1911, the New South Wales government agreed to enable the newly arrived Denman to occupy the old Government House until December. Subsequently, this period was again extended while negotiations between the two governments continued. In July 1912, McGowen offered to make available to the Commonwealth the house and all excluding about 25 acres of the grounds at an annual rental of 3.5 per cent of the capital value, on condition that the arrangement would terminate when Denman returned to England. But Fisher, aware of the Commonwealth parliament's persistent unwillingness to sanction expenditure on the governor-general's establishment, refused McGowen's offer. On 7 October 1912 Lord and Lady Denman left Sydney for Melbourne. An enormous crowd gathered at Central Railway Station to watch them depart.

The State government's action aroused a barrage of criticism in New South Wales. Both major Sydney newspapers were indignant at the treatment accorded to the representative of the Crown. The *Sydney Morning Herald* feared that, deprived of Government House, the governor-general might refrain from visiting Sydney altogether. The *Daily Telegraph* regarded 'the eviction' as 'boorish' and 'shabby'. Even the *Worker* criticised the treatment of the governor-general as 'inhospitable and un-Australian' and blamed the government's concern for 'States Spites' for its 'precipitate action'. At the ceremony on

THAT MATTER OF SYDNEY GOVERNMENT HOUSE
The second expulsion from Paradise. And there seems to be more fuss about this second
expulsion than there was about the first one. *Bulletin* cartoon by Lionel Lindsay,
18 January 1912. [Holman points the finger. McGowen looks on].

Central Station Sydney's mayor had castigated the Labor government for its
'wanton act of disloyalty . . . [and] personal insult to the highest representative
of the King in Australia'. A censure motion was initiated in the State Legislative
Assembly. Public protest meetings were held in Sydney and country centres.

One of these meetings set up a Citizens' Committee, with Sir William McMillan as its chairman, to consider the most effective form of opposition.

Though much of the motivation for what the *Bulletin* called 'an amazing Tory uproar' stemmed from narrow political motives, there was a real undercurrent of concern about the attitude of Labor towards the Empire. The Government House issue was revived at a time when Australia's place in the Empire was the subject of considerable scrutiny. The accession to power of Labor parties in Commonwealth and State parliaments and growing world tensions prompted careful attention to the details of Australia's links with Empire and Labor's attitude to those links.

Despite Australia's distance from London, the coronation of George V in 1911 was an opportunity for a renewal of spiritual fervour. Fisher's attendance at the Imperial Conference was watched very closely. Indignation swept Australia when the prime minister was alleged to have envisaged a time when Australia might be 'free to either take part in or to abstain from British wars as it thinks fit — and . . . to haul down the Union Jack, hoist our own flag, and start on our own'. Fisher immediately repudiated the report and the Australian press breathed its relief and approval. The incident revealed that Labor politicians needed to be constantly on the defensive regarding their attitude towards the Empire.

In 1911, no less than in 1901, the office of governor-general was the focus of Australian attachment to the Empire. Labor politicians tended to be pragmatic about such links. Whenever this pragmatism could be construed as threatening the Imperial attachment, 'loyalists' tended to assert the necessity of maintaining a spiritual bond. The *Sydney Morning Herald*, in July 1911, put the case for the loyalists accurately, if somewhat clumsily: 'There is a body of opinion — and one worth considering even by a Government situated as this is — which believes enthusiastically in sentiment as of the very fibre of the national as of the individual life'. It deprecated the action of McGowen's government which 'for the sake of a popular cry . . . would sacrifice an ideal'. The *Daily Telegraph* editorial on Denman's departure from Sydney seems alarmist and exaggerated today, but it expressed a widely held sentiment in 1912:

> At a time like the present when clouds gather quickly on the international horizon and when other parts of the Empire respond to the vague menaces that fill the air by approaching the British Government with new pledges of loyalty and spontaneous offers of assistance in the work of national defence, it ill becomes the parent State of the Commonwealth . . . to deprive the Governor-General of his official residence in Sydney.

The affair created little disturbance outside New South Wales. Most newspapers in other States either ignored the incident or referred slightingly to Sydney's 'petty and discreditable' attitude. The *Argus*, smugly self-righteous, congratulated Melbourne on its treatment of the governor-general. The *Age*, on the other hand, applauded McGowen's government for 'ending an untenable and utterly false position'. It considered that 'there never was any reason why the Governor-General should have had two vice-regal residences in Australia' and used the opportunity to press once again for ending the system whereby 'Downing Street officials' filled State vice-regal offices.

The overwhelmingly conservative nature of the Sydney press ensured that the public controversy should continue there throughout the latter part of 1912. Appropriately, the climax of the furore was reached in the grounds of Government House itself. On Saturday 14 December the gates were opened to allow the public to inspect the gardens and peer through the windows of the gubernatorial residence. Ministers had hoped for a demonstration of support and a crowd of two to three thousand gathered to witness what had all the signs of developing into an outright confrontation. Premier McGowen, obviously worried by the accusations of disloyalty being flung at him and his ministers, clutched a miniature Union Jack in his hand as he formally declared the grounds open for inspection. Holman spoke also, but when several speakers tried to put the opposing view, police removed the speakers' platform. As ministers hastily retreated, scuffles broke out in the crowd and the proceedings ended in uproarious scenes and near riot.

Though he had stubbornly clung to the State's demand that the Commonwealth either pay for the residence of its chief executive officer or relinquish its occupation of Government House, Holman was forced to retreat from his original proposal that the house be made available to the public. The old stables were transformed into a conservatorium of music, but Government House remained empty and unused while a lengthy court action, initiated by McMillan's Citizens' Committee, proceeded in State, Commonwealth and eventually Imperial courts, to determine whether the New South Wales government's action was constitutional. It was not until 1915 that the Privy Council verdict upheld the State government's right to put the house and grounds to any use it saw fit. By then doubts about Holman's loyalty to the Empire had been dispelled by his whole hearted support for the war. In October 1915, to the disgust of the *Bulletin* and the satisfaction of the remainder of the New South Wales press, the State governor, Sir Gerald Strickland, moved back into the house vacated by his counterpart, Beauchamp, fifteen years earlier. 'Cranbrook' was sold in 1918 and became a private school. By then Denman's successor as governor-general had secured possession of Admiralty House, in Kirribilli, for his use when in Sydney. Although this beautiful house, which faced the rival vice-regal residence across Sydney Harbour, was too small to hold large entertainments, it was rent free, and provided a useful *pied-à-terre* for the governor-general on his visits to the New South Wales capital.

The controversy over Sydney Government House, as Denman himself remarked, had 'tended seriously to impair the prestige and position of the Governor-General'. It was undignified for the governor-general, when he was obliged to visit Sydney, to have to remain in his railway carriage or make do as a guest of the admiral. Unfortunately Denman himself had exacerbated the regrettable situation. Instead of remaining discreetly aloof from the debate he had publicly associated himself with McMillan's Citizens' Committee. He even prepared a memo setting out his views of the necessity of retaining Government House for the governor-general, which prompted one Colonial Office functionary to minute: 'he should not have meddled'. Denman's tactless memorandum earned him a warning from the secretary of state not to give any encouragement to the Citizens' Committee. Lady Denman, too, was guilty of an indiscretion: after the State government had resumed the premises she asked for certain furniture from the drawing room of the old building. This only occasioned further humiliation, as the premier declined her request.

The eviction of Denman from Government House in Sydney marked the lowest point reached by the governor-general since Hopetoun had been forced to return to England, mortified, ten years earlier. Though the reasons behind Holman's action were complex, involving dissatisfaction with the Commonwealth rather than with the representative of the Crown, the effect was to reduce the influence which the governor-general might be expected to bring to bear upon Australian ministers. Moreover, Denman's relations with the government of Joseph Cook, which came into office in 1913, never reached the cordiality that had existed while Fisher had been prime minister. Denman found himself involved in a dispute with the Liberal minister for defence, Millen, over his exercise of the role of commander-in-chief. The details of this minor dispute have not been fully preserved, but it seems to have centred upon Denman's inclination to become too closely involved with senior Australian military staff, perhaps understandable considering his Sandhurst education and interest in military affairs. In April 1912 he had sent to the secretary of state a private report on the military forces of the Commonwealth, critical of the standard of Australian officers.

At the Colonial Office the 'extraordinary deterioration in the position of the Governor-General' under Dudley and Denman caused some concern. Another problem was the position of Steward, the governor-general's official secretary. Ten years in the post, Steward had come to exercise a strong influence upon successive representatives of the Crown. In matters concerning Australian political affairs his experience was invaluable to a new governor-general. But it was his possible influence upon the latter's role as representative of the British government that disturbed the Colonial Office. By May 1911 it was felt in London that 'far too much rests with the Official Secretary'. Twelve months later Berriedale Keith composed a long memorandum in which he noted the tendency for the governor-general to become 'a somewhat expensive and useless figurehead'. This deterioration he dated to the administration of Dudley, who, he claimed, had 'completely neglected' the official side of the governor-general's work, on occasions signing documents in blank and leaving them to be completed by the official secretary. Nor did Keith believe matters had improved noticeably under Denman. He concluded that the situation whereby 'Major Steward continued to enjoy the unofficial position of Governor-General' was 'profoundly unsatisfactory'.

Keith's memorandum on the position raised the whole question of the dual role of the governor-general. The 'official' work to which he was referring was the representation of the interests of the British government. The Colonial Office had always been concerned with this aspect of the governor-general's role. By February 1914 Keith considered that experience was tending 'more and more to show that Governors-General are not of much assistance in dealing with difficult questions'. Steward's influence upon Dudley and Denman, and his access to confidential instructions from Downing Street, were seen as a restriction upon the usefulness of the representative of the Crown as diplomatic agent of the British government. These were the first signs of doubt about the governor-general's ability to exercise such a role effectively. With regard to the position of the official secretary, the Colonial Office felt that little could be achieved while Denman remained in office. Careful instructions were given to his successor in an attempt to retrieve the position.

In mid-1913 Lady Denman had returned alone to London for a short visit. There, at a meeting with the colonial secretary, she had hinted that her husband was determined to resign. Though Harcourt urged the governor-general to remain for his full term, Denman replied in November 1913 that, for private reasons, he must ask Harcourt to accept his resignation. He had been constantly ill with colds, asthma and hay fever — Australia's national flower, the wattle, had caused him considerable discomfort. Lady Denman's biographer relates that Denman was 'moody and difficult' and his marriage unhappy; matters were made more difficult by the presence of one of Denman's staff (later to die on Gallipoli) 'who shared all Trudie's tastes ... admired her and was interested in her as a person'. In January 1914 Denman announced at the annual luncheon of the Australian Natives' Association that he intended to return to England.

In his cabled resignation of 11 November Denman had asked that he be allowed to stay until July 1914. This was to enable him to complete three years service and handle the threatening constitutional crisis. But Harcourt insisted that he leave in May, to suit the wishes of his successor. Denman left Australia on 18 May 1914. Though his marriage survived, it was for 'outward appearances' only. His later career was unexceptional, tied as it was to the Asquith Liberals. Lady Denman, on the other hand, had a long, distinguished public career as chairman of the Women's Institutes and the Family Planning Association and, during World War II, director of the Women's Land Army. She died on 2 June 1954. Three weeks later, on 24 June, Lord Denman died.

In the sense that Australians judged the role of governor-general, Denman had been a partial success. He had erred in opposing too openly, and without his federal ministers' support, the New South Wales government's resumption of Sydney Government House. But the *Sydney Morning Herald* considered that he had 'justified his selection to a degree which those who appointed him are probably not fully aware'. It complimented him for 'seeing eye to eye with Australians in their national policy of defence' and for winning 'the confidence of the Ministry which he found in office on his arrival'. Other Australian newspapers echoed these comments. The *Advertiser* felt that regret should be tempered with 'satisfaction at the thought that we shall have hereafter at the seat of the Empire a man ready to show interest in and sympathy for the Commonwealth when its affairs are discussed by the outside world'.

A more surprising source of approbation was the *Bulletin*, in which one contributor pronounced His Excellency 'the most successful Governor-General since Lord Tennyson's day', justifying this with a string of negative achievements which were a fair indication of the difficulties faced by representatives of the Crown in Australia:

> Denman has neither irritated nor scandalised any one section of society . . . his private life has been . . . flagrantly blameless . . . He has not exasperated either political party . . . His sporting tastes have not been sufficiently marked to depress Wowserdom. No one knows for certain if his sympathies lie in the direction of Orangism or Hibernianism . . . Add to these things the fact that he has travelled and speechified conscientiously, despite . . . rotten health and you get a very admirable record.

Even the labor newspapers, such as the *Westralian Worker*, though its tone was hardly effusive, felt that Denman had carried out his duties adequately.

Denman had proved to be the type of governor-general most Australians wanted — an unostentatious but visible link with the British Empire. But he had failed to provide the representation which Britain still felt it should have in the Commonwealth. The Colonial Office considered that, in addition to their monarchical functions, the Kings' men should safeguard Imperial interests by an active influence upon Australian ministers. Both Dudley and Denman seemed less successful in this aspect of their role than had Northcote — Dudley because he lacked influence, Denman because he identified too closely with Australian national aspirations. In 1874 the then governor-general of Canada, Lord Dufferin, had expressed succinctly the dilemma of his office. 'A Colonial Governor', he wrote, 'is like a man riding two horses in a circus'. A man needed to be exceptionally resourceful, politically experienced and diplomatic to hold together the diverging roles of the governor-general's office in Australia by 1914.

4   Imperial proconsul

By 1914 the office of governor-general of Australian had diminished in prestige. The hopes of those who considered that the post would be one of prestige and importance both within Australia and in the Empire as a whole had been constantly set back. None of the five occupants who had held office since federation had served a full term. Even the loyalist *Argus* conceded that 'five years in so remote a country as Australia may to many men of position seem an unduly long period of exile from the scene of their permanent interests and ambitions'.

From the beginning of the federation movement in Australia it had been hoped that experienced statesmen would be sent out from Britain as governors-general — in 1900 Lyne's reaction to Hopetoun's appointment had been regret that a 'statesman of cabinet rank' had not been selected! This reflected Australia's desire for maximum symbolic reassurance. But in addition it arose from the belief among conservatives that the more prestigious a statesman appointed governor-general, the more likelihood that he could exert an influence sympathetic to Australia in Imperial councils. By 1914, however, as the *Argus* had recognized, Australia's distance from Britain had to some extent defeated these anticipations.

More radical elements in the Australian community had no hesitation in asserting by 1914 that governors and governors-general appointed from Britain were no longer necessary. Echoing the arguments of their predecessors in the nineteenth century, they persisted in regarding the office as simply a constitutional figurehead, a point of view which allowed little scope for the personal qualities of the occupants. The *Westralian Worker* asserted, for example, that 'one rubber stamp is very much like another'. A related attitude was that the functions still retained by the representatives of the Crown in the Commonwealth should be exercised by Australian democrats rather than by British aristocrats.

But this was the view of a minority. For the majority, the very remoteness of Australia, which made distinguished British statesmen reluctant to venture so far from home, was the most pressing argument for retaining the office. As an early 1914 editorial in the *Sydney Morning Herald* put the point: 'although the wide ocean may sunder us physically, we are members of the same great family of nations ... The representative of the King typifies the bonds which unite us in these distant seas to both mother country, upon whose power we still depend in a large measure for our liberties and peaceful development, and to the sister dominions...' This was the prevailing Australian conviction. The governor-general was both the symbol of Imperial security and the guarantee of racial unity.

In July 1914 a writer for Melbourne *Punch* reflected on the qualities necessary for the governor-general. Although he was the representative of the King he was a paid servant of the Commonwealth. A monarch had personal, charismatic advantages which a governor-general lacked. In general, a King's appointment was for life whereas a governor-general's tenure of office was usually brief, and in the early years of federation had been extremely brief. With these disadvantages and other drawbacks a governor-general needed to be a 'model of tact and urbanity, with a figure sufficiently commanding to inspire respect and maintain the dignity of the high office'. *Punch*'s judgement of previous occupants was that though some had been singularly successful, others had been 'mere colourless personages' and still others 'arrant failures'. A governor-general needed to be well versed in politics so that he could avoid being used as a party tool in local political disputes. He required special qualities of judgement of men and affairs to enable him to deal not only with politicians, but with every other kind of person. He must have the knowledge and experience necessary to handle them all, to manage them all, and yet keep himself apart, so that he avoided identification with any one class or section. Though these were rare gifts, *Punch* considered that they were possessed by the man selected to succeed Denman as governor-general.

Ronald Crawford Munro Ferguson was born on 6 March 1860, eldest son of Colonel Robert Munro Ferguson, member of parliament for Kirkcaldy, and his wife Emma, née Mandeville. His family was aristocratic, Scottish and wealthy, with a strong military and political tradition and large landholdings, including coal mines. His home, Raith, standing in its park overlooking Kirkcaldy, north of the Firth of Forth, is not a palace in the scale of Hopetoun House, but it is an elegant and beautiful mansion. From his Munro ancestors he had inherited the Novar estates on Cromarty Firth in Ross-shire. He was educated privately, mostly at home, and then went to Sandhurst. From 1879 to 1884 he served in the Grenadier Guards.

Unlike Hopetoun, Dudley and Denman, Munro Ferguson had neither knowledge of nor interest in sports and games. Apart from managing his estates, politics had been his life-time preoccupation. In 1884 he had entered the House of Commons as a Liberal sitting for Ross and Cromarty, but was defeated in November 1885. He won Keith Burghs in August 1886, and became private secretary to Lord Rosebery. From very early in his political career Munro Ferguson had, like Rosebery, identified himself with the Liberal Imperialists. He became a council member of the Imperial Federation League in 1888. In 1886 he had visited India, where he had met his future wife, Lady Helen Hermione Blackwood, daughter of the viceroy, Lord Dufferin. They were married in 1889.

His close political and personal connection with Rosebery both shaped and stunted Munro Ferguson's public career. In 1892 he again became his mentor's private secretary and two years later was appointed lord of the treasury in the

Sir Ronald Munro
Ferguson in the
grounds of
Government House,
Melbourne

Liberal government which took office upon Gladstone's final resignation. In 1895 he declined the governorship of South Australia. During the Boer War he was a prominent Liberal supporter of the Unionist government's war policy.

Munro Ferguson's 'Lib-Imp' attitudes and an identification with Rosebery made him less than satisfactory to the radical Campbell-Bannerman government of 1905. Nor was his relationship with Asquith, Campbell-Bannerman's successor as prime minister, particularly close. His chances of preferment to a cabinet post were defeated less by lack of ability than by a personal reluctance to adhere to strict party discipline. After some years of being more of an independent than a Liberal, in June 1913 he voted against the Asquith government in the Commons over ministers' share transactions in the Marconi contract. In February 1914, after the Australian Government had been informed of the selection, it was announced that Munro Ferguson would succeed Denman.

To some in Australia there was a distasteful air of political manoeuvring in the new appointment. A few days prior to the announcement, the *Argus* commented on the impression created that 'the office is being hawked about and that no one who would be considered as at all eligible is particularly anxious to take it'. In fact this was less true of this appointment than of any since Hopetoun. Anxious to help Munro Ferguson find a billet, Harcourt had offered him the governor-

Lady Helen Munro
Ferguson

ship of Victoria, which he had declined. Once it had become clear that Denman was resolved to go, Harcourt had moved quickly to obtain Munro Ferguson for the higher post.

To the Brisbane *Worker* the new appointee was 'a rabid politician', 'cantankerous' and 'of a retrogressive type', sent to Australia, the 'happy hunting ground of the party dumpings of Britain', to avoid his proving embarrassing to Asquith in the next election campaign. Even the more circumspect *Brisbane Courier* was uneasy about this possibility, assuring its readers, more in hope rather than in confidence, that 'the days have passed when [British] Governments sent either difficult colleagues or impecunious friends to govern in the overseas dominions'. But there was more truth in these hints than in the *Argus'* fears about 'hawking about'. Disillusioned with political life, having earlier fallen out even with Rosebery, Munro Ferguson had become a difficult colleague for his Liberal friends. Moreover, he had quixotically assumed the debts of his wife's family and optimistically saw Australia as an opportunity to economise. He was knighted after his selection for Australia, but declined the offer of a peerage.

Grey-haired, tall, with a strong physique and an upright, military bearing, Sir Ronald had a 'splendid presence'. He was a successful, practical forester and would chop down a tree for exercise. Keenly interested in literature and art, he had a fine collection of paintings, some of which he took to decorate the walls of Government House, Melbourne. Bede Clifford (later Sir Bede), his private secretary from 1919 to 1920, described him as 'essentially kind' but 'choleric' and 'subject to outbursts of temper ... often followed by quite touching displays of remorse'.

The political situation facing Munro Ferguson upon his arrival in Australia in May 1914 again raised constitutional perplexities. Elections the previous year had returned Cook's Liberal Party with a majority of one in the House of Representatives but hopelessly outnumbered in the Senate. Consequently, government legislation faced the constant threat of amendment or delay at the hands of the Labor majority in the upper house. It was widely anticipated that Cook would attempt to end this situation by seeking an early dissolution of both houses of parliament. Two bills were drafted which were calculated to create a confrontation between the House of Representatives and the Senate.

The question of the governor-general's power to grant or refuse a prime minister's request for a dissolution had never been far from the surface during the first decade of federation. In three political crises the advice of ministers to dissolve parliament had been refused. George Reid noted that the practice in the Dominions differed from that in Great Britain, where His Majesty's ministers 'have their own way in such matters'. This discretionary power of the governor-general was one of the last vestiges of earlier gubernatorial authority. It reflected the pre-federation feeling that some constitutional guardian was needed to curb the possibly irresponsible action of colonial politicians.

The pertinent question in 1914 was, had the Commonwealth gained sufficient maturity and political stability to dispense with such a protector? It was ironic that in the ensuing controversy radicals claimed for the governor-general an independence which belied their view of him as 'rubber stamp', while those who claimed that the governor-general should act solely upon the advice of his cabinet were the conservatives.

Section 57 of the Commonwealth Constitution was devised to solve a deadlock between the House of Representatives and the Senate. It states that a bill passed by the House of Representatives but not agreed to by the Senate, can be presented again after an interval of three months. If the measure is again rejected, the governor-general is empowered to dissolve both houses simultaneously. The makers of the Constitution had envisaged that the electorate would be able to express an opinion upon the specific piece of legislation which was at issue. If an election failed to resolve the deadlock, further action was stipulated to lead to that end.

In 1914 it was clear, however, that the section could be utilised for a quite different purpose, namely, to resolve a discrepancy between party forces in the Senate and the House of Representatives. Most of the founding fathers had failed to anticipate that party groupings rather than provincial loyalties would determine voting patterns in the Commonwealth parliament. Consequently they made no provision for the situation which arose in 1914. The two brief bills which were introduced and forced through the House of Representatives on the Speaker's casting vote were not vital issues of public policy but merely convenient measures to establish the formal conditions required by Section 57 before a double dissolution could be granted. On 2 June 1914 the prime minister called upon the governor-general and asked that as a result of the action of the Senate, both houses of the Commonwealth parliament be dissolved simultaneously.

Though he had been in the country only three weeks, the new governor-general was well prepared for the decision which was now his to make. The very wording of Section 57 meant that for at least three months the likelihood of such a request had existed, and the Australian press had regularly canvassed the position. On several occasions Denman had warned the British government of the approaching crisis, thus enabling Munro Ferguson to seek advice before he left England.

There was some press speculation that the governor-general had been given special instructions by the Colonial Office regarding the expected request for a double dissolution. This was not so. It was true that he had asked for such instructions but the permanent under secretary had specifically declined to advise him. The prevailing Colonial Office opinion, at least as conveyed in a memorandum by Keith, was that the governor-general should exercise his own discretion based on his opinion of the political situation.

But there was one man in England whose knowledge of the Australian Constitution, and in particular its practical political application, was unique: George Reid, the Australian high commissioner in London. Munro Ferguson did not hesitate to ask for Reid's advice, and the old campaigner was, characteristically, happy to respond. At their interview in April 1914 Reid confirmed Denman's forecast that Cook would undoubtedly demand a double dissolution. He warned that whatever decision the governor-general made would attract keen criticism.

Munro Ferguson's political career had equipped him to deal with criticism. But it had also endowed him with a respect for the British system of responsible or parliamentary government. He asked Reid several questions on the practice in Australia. Could he see the leader of the opposition without the consent of the prime minister? Reid agreed that it would be necessary to see Fisher but he did not anticipate any objection from Cook. In 1905 when Reid himself had requested a dissolution, the governor-general had not considered it necessary to obtain the prime minister's consent before consulting Deakin, then leader of the opposition. Reid felt that Cook could not be refused a double dissolution if a single dissolution were later to be granted to Fisher. This would be to give one side what the other had been denied. The high commissioner's advice supported Munro Ferguson's natural respect for parliamentary government grounded in 30 years experience of the House of Commons.

A long letter from Denman awaited the new governor-general on his arrival in Melbourne on 18 May. This letter revealed rather less concern for the conventions of responsible government than for the necessity to maintain the position of the governor-general. Denman did 'not presume to advise' his successor, but he felt constrained to submit certain considerations evolving from his three years experience, such as a warning that the Australian press was overwhelmingly pro-Liberal while the Labor Party had 'practically no press behind them, so cannot so well voice their opinion'. Shrewdly, he doubted whether Liberals stood to gain very much by a double dissolution. He expediently suggested that it might be more advantageous for the governor-general to avoid offending the Labor Party, 'undoubtedly the most powerful political organisation in Australia'. Suggesting that his successor seek advice from the High Court judges, he recommended Barton in particular.

Denman's advice accorded the governor-general more responsibility than had Reid, and revealed his sympathy with the Labor Party. It is idle to speculate what course he would have taken had be remained to deal with Cook's request. To a certain extent, however, Denman's advice, if Munro Ferguson accorded it any weight, counter-balanced Reid's in so far as it considered the Labor point of view and regarded the governor-general's role as less restricted by constitutional custom.

Munro Ferguson's first intimation of the proximity of the approaching crisis came on 29 May when, during a ministerial dinner, the prime minister expressed a wish to see the governor-general in a day or two. On 2 June Cook arrived for an Executive Council meeting with W.H. Irvine, the attorney-general, and two other ministers, remaining after they withdrew to make the long-awaited request. Cook gave his reasons for a double dissolution and presented three memoranda which were 'put aside to be read later'. The governor-general then put certain questions to the prime minister. Cook stated that his government would resign if their request were refused and that 'there was not the slightest chance' of Fisher being able to form a government out of the current parliamentary situation. Like Reid, the prime minister stressed that if Fisher were later granted a dissolution of the House of Representatives, the governor-general would be giving to the opposition that which the government had been refused.

Strictly speaking, this advice was not accurate. Cook was not requesting a single dissolution because that would not solve his party's problem of a hostile majority in the Senate. It could be charged that Cook's difficulty arose from his determination to use Section 57 of the Constitution for a purpose other than that intended by its drafters. On such a view, the governor-general, as constitutional guardian, might have refused the prime minister's request to dissolve a parliament which still had two years to run. At least there seemed a case for obtaining the opposition's interpretation of the situation, if the governor-general were to be allowed to make an independent judgement. But when, towards the close of the interview, Munro Ferguson expressed a wish to see Fisher, the prime minister indicated that he opposed such a course. This was clearly contrary to established procedure and indicated that Cook was either unaware of the precedents or unsure of the weight of his arguments in favour of a double dissolution.

When Munro Ferguson came to read the documents presented by the prime minister in support of his request, he found that one memorandum, apparently drafted by Irvine, argued strongly that the governor-general was constitutionally bound to follow his prime minister's advice. Relying heavily on Keith's

Responsible government in the Dominions (second edition, 1912), the attorney-general claimed that the representative of the Crown in Australia, like the King in Britain, could act only on the advice of his cabinet except when the ministry was defeated in the lower house. If such a view of the role of a constitutional monarch sounded strange from the pen of a conservative such as Irvine, it was no less than had been claimed by Australian radicals since the late nineteenth century.

Munro Ferguson was reluctant to accept Irvine's interpretation. There was no unanimity among constitutional authorities in 1914 that the action of the British King was as restricted as both Keith and Irvine assumed. But quite apart from that, the governor-general in Australia, particularly in respect of dissolution of parliament, had previously refused the advice of ministers. Munro Ferguson's instincts were against the surrender of such a position, and he soon found one eminent authority who disagreed with the attorney-general's proposition.

Though Cook had opposed Munro Ferguson's intention of seeing Fisher, he had not been averse to a consultation with the chief justice. Sir Samuel Griffith came to lunch at Government House the next day. He impressed the governor-general, who later described him as standing 'head and shoulders above all Australians in knowledge, decision, and quickness of vision'. While the chief justice believed that the governor-general was 'in the position of an independent arbiter', in the immediate case at issue he considered that Cook was entitled to a dissolution. Somewhat illogically, Griffith concurred with the prime minister's advice against seeking the opinion of the leader of the opposition.

The influences upon Munro Ferguson were thus Reid, Cook and Griffith. He seems to have given scant attention to Denman's advice and, in view of what both Cook and Griffith advised, he decided against speaking to Fisher. As a Liberal, and fresh from the constitutional battle with the Lords, his own sympathies lay with Cook's Australian Liberal Party, faced with a hostile majority in an upper house. He seems not to have taken into consideration the Constitution-makers' view of the Senate as a States' house. In the event, although he declined to accept the government's interpretation of the Constitution, he accepted Cook's view of the political situation and decided that the only solution to the deadlock lay in a double dissolution.

For his interview with Cook on 4 June, Munro Ferguson armed himself with a brief pencilled memo concealed in his desk diary. Taking pains to retain for the governor-general a discretionary role, he specifically denied the proposition put forward by Irvine that he was bound to act according to his ministers' advice. His determination not to be a cypher is evident from his unwillingness to grant Cook a promise of a double dissolution in two or three months time, and his requirement that Cook obtain supply before proroguing parliament. But the essential substance of his decision was that, as the parliament was unworkable, if Cook wished an immediate double dissolution, it would be granted. Cook assured him that the government intended to dissolve parliament immediately after the necessary formalities, including parliamentary approval of supply, had been completed, though it appears that his action in advising a double dissolution at that time had not been authorised by the Liberal Party caucus.

Nevertheless an exchange of formal communications confirmed these arrangements, and on the following morning the decision was conveyed to both the
House of Representatives and the Senate.

Munro Ferguson was prepared for 'some ebullitions of wrath from the
Opposition'. One of the strongest came from the pen of W.M. Hughes, attorney-
general in the previous Fisher administration, who called the decision 'constitutional butchery'. But the *Daily Telegraph* considered that Hughes' memorandum
displayed 'the peevishness characteristic of Labor when denied its own political
way', lacking its author's customary plausibility.

In the Senate supply was granted though the governor-general's action was
vigorously criticised and an attempt was made to obtain publication of the
correspondence leading to the decision. His Excellency, acting on cabinet's
advice, declined to do so. The Senate also petitioned the governor-general to
authorise a referendum to be held simultaneously with the election. Again
acting upon the cabinet's advice, Munro Ferguson refused the request. There
was little justification for the strictures of the opposition. The most that Fisher
could have demanded was the right to personally put the opposition's point of
view to the governor-general, a right later supported by the secretary of state.
But some of the arguments for the governor-general's independence of action
were expressions more of pique than of principle.

Forgetting earlier allegations that the representative of the Crown was a
'constitutional dummy', the radical press in Australia launched quickly into an
attack upon the decision of this 'rubber stamp' to follow the advice of his
ministers. To the *Bulletin* the governor-general was 'technically, if for no other
reason ... utterly wrong' in granting the double dissolution. The *Westralian
Worker* discerned a more sinister fact. Noting that the governor-general dined
with the president and members of the Melbourne Club on the evening of 7
June, it concluded that 'the imported viceroy has proved loyal to the interests of
his class'. The *Australian Worker* criticised the decision as 'ludicrous'. *Labor
Call* accused His Excellency of 'partisanship' and 'unfairness', while the Brisbane *Worker* considered that 'lack of knowledge' had led to Munro Ferguson
being 'misled by his constitutional advisers'. But these were the opinions of a
minority only. With the notable exception of the *Age* and Melbourne's *Punch*
which favoured a dissolution of the House of Representatives only, Australian
newspapers supported the governor-general's decision.

Some commentators after 1914 claimed that Munro Ferguson's action
pointed to an acceptance of the doctrine that the governor-general must act
upon the advice of his ministers. The chief exponent of this point of view was
A.B. Keith. In his *Imperial unity and the Dominions* (1916) he hailed Munro
Ferguson's action as a 'landmark in the history of responsible Government in
the Commonwealth', indicating that Australia had finally become a constitutional monarchy on the British pattern and sloughed off the remaining vestiges of
colonial status. Though this point of view was challenged both at the time and
later, it had considerable force. Prior to 1914, Australian ministries had not
possessed the right to dissolve parliament at will. Keith's earlier book,
Responsible government in the Dominions, published in 1912, had emphasised the

'serious responsibility devolving upon a Governor by discretion in matters of dissolution'. Four years later Keith considered that this no longer held true, and that in acting upon the advice of the Cook government Munro Ferguson had established a significant precedent.

Keith's opinion echoed the arguments of Irvine in his memorandum of 2 June, and supported the comment in the authoritative *Annotated Constitution of the Australian Commonwealth* (1901) by (Sir) John Quick and (Sir) Robert Garran that the power of simultaneous dissolution would be exercised according to the advice of ministers. In his later work, *Legislative powers of the Commonwealth and States of Australia* (1919), Quick developed this line, arguing that the governor-general had 'little if any discretion left in such a great crisis'. Like other powers and prerogatives of the Crown (he later wrote privately to Munro Ferguson) the power of dissolution is exercised according to the advice of responsible ministers. Munro Ferguson struggled manfully to correct what he considered to be a misinterpretation of his action. He gathered opinions from distinguished legal authorities such as Griffith and the professor of law at Melbourne University, William Harrison Moore, which challenged Keith's assertions. Sir Ronald continued to emphasise that he had granted Cook's request on his own discretion in view of his own interpretation of the parliamentary situation. His reliance on the extra-parliamentary advice of Reid and Griffith, unknown at the time, supports this view.

In later decades Munro Ferguson's view of his action found weighty champions, notably H.V. Evatt and E.A. Forsey. Evatt denies Keith's conclusions and asserts that in coming to a decision based on the 'parliamentary situation' Munro Ferguson was exercising the customary discretionary role of the governor-general. This argument would be stronger had the opinion of the opposition leader been obtained. By failing to see Fisher the governor-general had, to a certain extent, compromised his independence of action.

It was undoubtedly true that in strict legal terms His Excellency's power of discretionary action, in the matter of dissolution of parliament, remained intact. But the significant fact is that no governor-general has since refused a prime minister's request for either a single or double dissolution. If the trend of British monarchical government be relevant in Australia, Munro Ferguson's action was a step in the direction of ministerial responsibility. In this scenario any subsequent governor-general would be unlikely to have sufficient confidence in his discretionary power to put it to the test by refusing his ministers' advice; that is, the longer power remained unused the rustier it became. In practical terms Keith's 1916 judgement seems correct. But the Australian Constitution, since it is a written document, differs significantly from its unwritten British model, in which the Crown has fought essentially a rearguard action as it retreated from its prerogatives, concerned chiefly with the need to preserve the dynasty. Munro Ferguson's action in granting Cook a double dissolution certainly reflected both the political stability of the Commonwealth parliament and the growing status of Australia. But because his powers were specified in the Constitution and his office lacked any dynastic nature, there seems no way his successors could be bound by this precedent.

The argument about the effect of Munro Ferguson's action may remain unresolved, but there seems little doubt that his decision was, in Professor Geoffrey Sawer's words, 'constitutionally correct and politically wise'. In the event, to the surprise of many, the double dissolution sought by the government, opposed by the opposition and granted by the governor-general, resulted in a return to power of Fisher's Labor Party. By the time the election had led to this result, however, Australian attention was absorbed by external rather than internal conflicts.

The Australian government was slow to deliberate upon the shattering events in Europe. In part this reluctance reflected unwillingness to interfere in Britain's conduct of foreign policy. But also pertinent was the peculiarly inconvenient time. The Commonwealth parliament had been formally dissolved on 30 July and campaigning for the election was in full swing. Government ministers and opposition leaders were spread widely throughout the continent. For a few crucial days Australian affairs were conducted not in the seat of government, Melbourne, but in Sydney, and not by the cabinet, but by the minister for defence, acting in consultation with the governor-general and defence advisers.

Munro Ferguson had arrived for a routine visit to Sydney on 10 July, determined to re-establish good feelings with the State which had declined to provide the governor-general with a permanent residence. After appropriate welcoming ceremonies and with a regretful glance at the still unoccupied home of his precedecessors in the Domain, he proceeded to 'Yaralla'. This was a palatial but remote property on the Parramatta River, near Concord (now a hospital), owned by Miss (later Dame) Eadith Walker, a supporter of the Liberal Party and a prominent Sydney philanthropist who, at Cook's urging, had vacated her home for the governor-general. Temporary offices were established at 'Craignish' (now demolished) in Macquarie Street, where callers could enter their names in the visitors' book and where Steward, the official secretary, carried on the administrative work of the governor-general's office. Immediately after his arrival Munro Ferguson commenced a vigorous round of social activities: presenting prizes at a polo carnival, attending banquets and holding a levee. The programme was scheduled to continue for approximately one month, after which His Excellency intended to visit Brisbane, but these plans were to be halted by the outbreak of war.

Australia's first steps towards war were confused, almost comic, reflecting its relative immaturity in international affairs. The first official warning from the British government that war was likely was a cable which reached Steward at 'Craignish' at 3 p.m. on 30 July. The telegram should have read, 'See preface defence scheme adopt precautionary stage . . .', a pre-arranged message which meant that preliminary steps laid down in 1907 by the Committee of Imperial Defence were to be effected immediately. But an error in deciphering the cable delayed Australia's implementation of the instruction, and Cook's absence led to further difficulties.

Normally such a telegram would be deciphered and a copy sent to the prime minister and governor-general. In this case, the prime minister being inaccessible, a copy was handed to the minister for defence. Millen's unpreparedness (he had to cable to Melbourne to have both the naval war orders and the defence scheme brought to Sydney), and his understandable unwillingness to take important decisions in the absence of the prime minister, led to further delay. Pressed by the British commander of the Australian squadron, rear-admiral Sir George Patey (who had already received his orders from the Navy), and by the Naval Board, Millen agreed to effect the necessary naval measures. They were in full train by 10.30 p.m. on 30 July 1914. But he was reluctant to put in train the appropriate military arrangements without Cook's authority. It was not until the attorney-general, Irvine, arrived in Sydney that Millen could be persuaded. Eventually, on 2 August, at a conference between Millen, Irvine and Munro Ferguson it was decided that orders should be issued to commence the first stages of mobilisation.

In these difficult circumstances the governor-general's role was far more than a watching brief. For the harassed minister for defence he was a welcome counsellor whose advice carried considerable weight. Writing to Harcourt on 2 August 1914 His Excellency described Millen as 'extremely business-like and helpful in these anxious days, when in the absence of the prime minister a good deal of responsibility rested upon us two'. Nor did his influence cease when Irvine joined them in Sydney on the Saturday. He later informed Harcourt, in words which indicated how deeply he was involved in these deliberations: 'we had rather a delicate matter to deal with, namely whether we should hold up for the day a cypher presumably from the German Government to a small German ship ... We decided to do so'. Earlier, he had taken the unusual step of suggesting to the prime minister, by both letter and telegram, that a cabinet meeting should be summoned 'in order that Imperial Government may know what support to expect from Australia'.

Even in 1914 it was no part of the function of the representative of the Crown in the Commonwealth to take part in policy discussions. Nor was it strictly proper for Munro Ferguson to advise his prime minister to call a cabinet meeting. But in the unusual circumstances of those confusing days prior to the declaration of war the energetic and dedicated governor-general interpreted his role far more actively than under more normal conditions. As representative of the British government and in the absence of Cook, he had taken action to assist in Australia's prompt commitment to the European war.

There was no doubt of the Commonwealth's support for the Empire in Britain's hostilities. The distant Dominion's attitude towards the Empire was instinctive tribal solidarity. The office of governor-general was itself an embodiment of this sentiment. On 11 July 1914, commenting on Munro Ferguson's visit to Sydney, the *Sydney Morning Herald* had described him as the representative 'of the King and of the race'. When 'real trouble threatens', it continued, 'trouble from outside — why then, for better or for worse, in victory or in disaster, whether it means eventual success or absolute irremediable ruin, through cloud or sunshine, or rain, or snow, or whatever the future holds, until that trouble is through, we are in it with the rest of our race'.

Within one month the time had come for such pledges to be redeemed. On the night of 31 July 1914 both Millen in Sydney and Fisher at Colac, where he happened to be campaigning, reaffirmed Australia's support for Britain. Millen's assurance that 'Australia is no fair weather partner' received wide publicity in Australia and was greeted with enthusiasm in London. In contrast Fisher's subsequently famous pledge to help and defend the mother country 'to our last man and our last shilling' received relatively little notice in Australia, only the *Argus* reporting it.

Cook scheduled the cabinet meeting suggested by the governor-general for Monday 3 August at 3 p.m. That day Munro Ferguson returned to Melbourne in the company of the two ministers with whom he had been acting during the previous few days. Also on the train were the chief Australian naval and military advisers, Admiral Creswell and General White. Grim-faced, they were met at the platform by the prime minister. After a few words the governor-general drove off to Government House while ministers proceeded to hold the long-delayed cabinet meeting to discuss the war.

In one respect this cabinet meeting was a formality. The precautionary steps committing Australian naval and military forces had already been taken by Millen in Sydney, acting in consultation with the attorney-general and the governor-general. Cabinet needed only to give retrospective approval of actions already taken. The real purpose for the gathering of ministers, as the governor-general had prompted, was to decide merely the extent of the support. On 3 August Munro Ferguson presided at an extended session of the Federal Executive Council at which the decisions of the earlier cabinet meeting were given executive authority. After this meeting the prime minister announced that the Australian Navy would be placed under the orders of the British Admiralty and that the Commonwealth offered an expeditionary force of 20 000 men to be placed at the complete disposal of the British government. Thus was born the Australian Imperial Force (AIF). The governor-general described the general mood which surrounded its formation as one of 'indescribable enthusiasm and entire unanimity', and observed that '20 000 men represent but a fraction of what the Commonwealth could contribute to the Imperial Forces'.

At noon on Wednesday 5 August 1914 the cable announcing that war had broken out with Germany arrived in Melbourne. Munro Ferguson could feel satisfied with his role during the preceding week. He had been in constant consultation with Australian ministers and military advisers, partaking at crucial moments in their decisions. Australia's solidarity with the Empire, of which the office of governor-general was both symbol and guarantee, had been pledged as promptly as circumstances had allowed. In the crisis the governor-general's function as channel of communication between the British and Australian governments had safeguarded his role as ambassador with special access to the Commonwealth executive.

Munro Ferguson realised that the outbreak of war would significantly change his activities. Writing to Harcourt in August 1914, he anticipated that as commander-in-chief of Australian defence forces nearly all his work would be with soldiers and sailors. He saw it as particularly advantageous 'for the G.G. to have either naval or military experience, for Ministers are usually strange to both services, and a G.G. who is regarded as a brother officer, will always find a useful sphere of influence'. Despite the self-congratulatory tone of these remarks, they were essentially accurate. As a Sandhurst graduate and former Guards officer, Munro Ferguson was regarded with esteem by Australian army and naval staff. One Australian officer later described how his 'influence and example were greatly felt and appreciated in the military training establishments in Australia during the war'.

Munro Ferguson took very seriously his titular position as head of the fighting services. To some extent his involvement was ceremonial. He had a soldier's respect for military demonstrations. During his visits to all States he constantly made himself available for presentations of colours or medals, or for parades at which he would take the salute, resplendent in plumes and official uniform. But he liked to mingle with the Australian officers and men more informally. Early in the war he took upon himself the task of inspecting military camps. On these tours of inspection he was sympathetic to the needs of the soldiers and interested in standards of health and training, conveying complaints direct to Pearce, the minister for defence. In November 1915 he even visited 'the venereal camp'. On these visits he came to know the officers and, less often, the men of Australia's fighting services, and in this way was able to feel himself to be more involved in the practical affairs of the war than his otherwise formal position would have allowed.

Letters to Pearce reporting shortages of blankets or inadequate drying facilities indicated Munro Ferguson's dedication to what was really a subordinate military task. On a higher level he took a close interest in the senior Australian Staff appointments, an interest encouraged by his personal friendship with the senior British commanders in the Mediterranean, Sir John Maxwell and Sir Ian Hamilton.

Prior to federation the *Bulletin* and others had warned that a British official in the position of governor-general might exercise his influence against the best interests of Australia in the event of a conflict between those and British interests. Defenders of the office of governor-general had dismissed such objections, emphasising instead the argument that such an official would be specially well-placed to understand the Australian point of view and represent that attitude to the British government. It was later claimed by Berriedale Keith that a governor-general 'felt it to be at least as important a part of his duties to impress Dominion views on British Ministers as British views on Dominion Ministers'. Early in the war there occurred one occasion where this was the case. The incident concerned the protection of naval convoys in the Pacific.

Munro Ferguson had from the first shown a close interest in the fledgling Australian fleet. Despite British disapproval, he quickly appreciated that 'nothing could be more disturbing in naval circles in the Pacific than to cast doubt on the value of separate Fleet Units. Australia could not now conceive any alternative'. The approach of war found him even more attentive to the matter. On Sunday 2 August, he made an informal visit to Garden Island Naval Depot, arriving at an early hour and remaining all morning to observe the great activity there as preparations were made for the fleet to sail. Later in the day he had an interview with Admiral Patey when the latter arrived in Sydney. But despite this interest, Munro Ferguson's knowledge of naval affairs was limited and his awareness of the strategic situation in the Pacific was superficial.

One month after the outbreak of war New Zealand's Expeditionary Force was ready to be transported across the Tasman Sea. On 14 September reported sightings of two big German cruisers near Samoa, and news of the exploits of the 'Emden' in the Bay of Bengal, led to apprehension in Australia and New Zealand about the security of troop convoys. But, since Patey and the Admiralty discounted such fears, the New Zealand government decided to transport its troops across the Tasman Sea with virtually no protection. Several of the vessels had already sailed when a telegram was received in New Zealand from Munro Ferguson conveying his private opinion that the transports ran a grave risk and should not sail until the Admiralty had been further consulted. The convoy was recalled immediately.

Although the British government later approved the Australian governor-general's action his concern was unfounded. The assessments of Patey and the Admiralty of the unlikelihood of a raid by the German warships proved accurate. But Munro Ferguson's direct interference had caused the delay of both New Zealand and Australian Expeditionary Forces. In the opinion of official war historian A.W. Jose:

> Sir Ronald had in this matter acted not as Governor-General advised by his Ministers, but as an influential citizen of the Empire, informing its officials in England and New Zealand of his personal view . . . In this crisis he acted on his own responsibility; and, though the event proved his action needless, it would not therefore be safe to contend that its motive was unsound.

Jose's assessment needs reconsideration in a study of the role of governor-general.

Though Munro Ferguson sent the cable on his personal responsibility, his action had stemmed from the attitude of Fisher. The Australian government, only a few weeks in office, was concerned almost to the point of obsession by the possibility that troops might be lost in a naval attack so close to Australian shores. In response to this anxiety, which he personally shared, the governor-general was prepared to support his ministers. He later expressed Australia's resentment at 'the assumption made by the Admiralty that we "funked" the embarkation of Troops'. In his secret report of the incident to the secretary of state, Munro Ferguson also justified his action on the grounds that loss of the unescorted transports would have entailed 'a loss of confidence in the Admiralty which would raise the question of the advisability of handing over the Australian Fleet to Admiralty control'. The intervention can therefore be seen as ambassadorial rather than personal, revealing sensitivity to opinion in Australia and preparedness to support his Australian ministers when by so doing he was promoting Imperial unity.

If the cable to New Zealand showed Munro Ferguson's willingness to intervene in support of his cabinet, there were occasions when he was equally as firm in asserting a point of view contrary to ministerial advice. In August 1914 the treasurer, Forrest, had attempted to have the governor-general sign an authority for the expenditure of £500 000 upon war preparations. As this had not been considered by parliament, Munro Ferguson questioned the lack of authority, asking whether it would not be wise to consult the leader of the opposition in the circumstances. Forrest had to leave without the signed authority. The strength of such interventions lay in Munro Ferguson's grasp of parliamentary procedures and his confident assertion of the monarch's active role in the executive and administrative areas of government.

Nor did the accession to power of the Labor government deter him from asserting his supervisory role in Australian affairs. In early 1915 he detected signs that the new ministry, 'with the exception of Mr Fisher himself who is always most punctilious, is inclined to treat H.M.'s representative somewhat cavalierly'. The occasion for this comment was an announcement by Hughes, acting as prime minister during Fisher's visit to New Zealand, that he intended to administer the government from Sydney rather than Melbourne, without consulting the governor-general or giving him the reasons for the move. Munro Ferguson protested to both Fisher and Harcourt about the matter and Hughes apologised, but the problem of lack of consultation was to recur.

In March 1915, a document setting up a royal commission on the New Hebrides, Norfolk Island and Lord Howe Island was brought before a meeting of the Executive Council. After the meeting Munro Ferguson warned Hughes, still acting prime minister, that such an investigation infringed upon the jurisdiction of the British Foreign Office and that France was likely to misconstrue an Australian investigation in a colony jointly administered by her. Having raised these considerations, he indicated that he was willing to sign the commission if Hughes advised him to do so. Having no knowledge of the matter himself, Hughes undertook to contact his colleagues. He thereupon cabled Fisher his opinion that the proposed commission 'might easily do much harm', and suggested that the Foreign Office be notified and its approval obtained before the commission acted.

Though he did not consider the proposition to be a 'dangerous innovation', Fisher agreed that the 'Home Govt should be fully advised of its friendly peaceful character' and invited to assist in making its mission successful. The government's policy on all war matters, the prime minister explained, was to 'avoid conflict with H.M. Govt when it decides there is danger [of] foreign complications'. In view of Munro Ferguson's concern at the possible French reaction, Fisher replied that the commission should be delayed and 'certainly should not go to the New Hebrides until it was assured of a friendly reception'. Though the commission in itself was not really significant and its secret report (recommending annexation) was never published, Munro Ferguson had guarded against clumsy and unauthorised Australian action in an area which was potentially controversial between Great Britain and France. Fisher wrote to the minister of external affairs on 16 September 1915, requestion that correct channels be followed in future.

By firm but tactful intervention in Australian political affairs Munro Ferguson was exercising the special advantages of the governor-general's position in a way not evidenced since Northcote's term. In diplomatic, military, naval and even domestic affairs Sir Ronald conveyed his own opinion and that of the British government to the Australian ministry. His tact and commonsense prevented him from insisting upon his own view when to do so would simply be counter-productive. In this delicate relationship between governor-general and cabinet, mutual respect between the prime minister and the representative of the Crown was of vital importance.

There was no doubt that Munro Ferguson regarded highly the government he found in office when he arrived in Australia. He later wrote: 'Sir Joseph Cook ... was my first Prime Minister and, from a Governor-General's point of view, quite the best, for he was always anxious to be thoroughly constitutional in his relations with the Kings representative and took pains to be "correct" in every particular.' In September 1914 he related to Harcourt how he had 'an almost touching exchange of adieux with the late Administration ... when it assembled in force to say goodbye. We had come to be very good friends', he wrote, 'and it was certainly a Government of high ability and Executive capacity'.

He considered Cook's successor, Fisher, to be 'a man of admirable character, of sound if restricted views ... [who] has exercised good influence upon his Party'. At first the new prime minister had 'laid stress on the expediency of all communications between the Governor-General and his Government passing through the Prime Minister'. However he soon relaxed this ruling and Munro Ferguson was 'quickly in the close relations with the Minister for Defence' to which he was accustomed. Fisher also suggested that it was not the practice to discuss business at meetings of the Executive Council. Munro Ferguson agreed, but he insisted on receiving the minutes of Executive Councils in sufficient time to give them due consideration. It was clear that he was determined to exercise conscientiously the role of constitutional monarch in Australia and to insist on his right to be consulted, to warn and to encourage. In August 1915 he complained that ministers were failing to observe the governor-general's rights. The prime minister apologised and instructed cabinet members to observe the correct forms of procedure in future.

In January 1915 Munro Ferguson was asked by Harcourt to use his influence upon Australian politicians. Five months earlier Japan had entered the war in support of Britain and her allies. At first, Britain had hoped that Japan's war effort would be restricted to China and the China Sea. But by October further assistance was required. The Japanese occupied German colonies in the Pacific, including Yap, an island north of the Equator which had been administered from Rabaul and on which wireless stations had already been destroyed by Australian and British ships. It was at first assumed that Japan would hand Yap and other islands north of the Equator over to an Australian occupation force. In late November, however, as such an expedition was preparing to depart from Australia a Colonial Office cable directed that the occupation be abandoned. Riots had broken out in Japan at the proposition that she should relinquish prizes won from Germany in the Pacific.

These events in late 1914 prompted a secret letter from Harcourt to Munro Ferguson, 'for your eye only, and under no circumstances ... to be seen by anyone else'. The governor-general was informed there was 'little doubt that it is the intention of the Japanese at the end of the war to claim for themselves all the German Islands North of the Equator'. The secretary of state continued: 'You ought in the most gradual & diplomatic way to begin to prepare the mind of your Ministers for the possibility that at the end of the war Japan may be left in possession of the Northern Islands and we with everything south of the Equator.' Knowing that the Australians would find this fact disturbing, Harcourt argued that the object of most importance was to obtain 'those territories most contiguous to Australia', to add German New Guinea to Papua and to bring the whole of the Solomon Island group under the British flag. He concluded: 'I fear I have set you a hard task but I am sure you will execute it with your usual skill and discretion'.

The governor-general scarcely needed a second invitation to enter the field of international diplomacy. He had already begun to take soundings in Australia on the future of the former German colonies in the Pacific. He replied that there would be little opposition to Japan keeping the Marianne and Caroline groups, but the Marshalls might cause more difficulty because of Australian trading interests there. He undertook, however, to consult Fisher and other leading Australians on the question. In these discussions Sir Ronald was clearly acting as ambassadorial representative of the British government. Moreover, he was not exactly sympathetic to the Australians' terror of the 'Yellow Peril'. In April 1915 he wrote: 'This fool's paradise needs a rude awakening, and if a Japanese naval base near the Line should act as a solvent then it would be a blessing in disguise'.

In the following months Munro Ferguson attempted to comply with Harcourt's instruction, seeing numerous politicians, and even Sir James Burns of Burns Philp and Co., whose company had extensive trading interests in the Pacific. The chief of general staff, Legge, was also consulted. His opinion that, from a military point of view, Australia should stay south of the Equator was seized upon by the governor-general to support his diplomatic initiatives. When in May 1915 Fisher seemed to be wavering from a previously expressed view that Australia would have her hands full in the south Pacific, Munro Ferguson referred him to Legge who had lately repeated his disbelief in the military value of the northern islands. Despite all the governor-general's efforts, Australians remained opposed to Japanese occupation of islands in the Pacific which might constitute a future threat to Australia. Later the question passed from the sphere of the governor-general's personal diplomacy to the sphere of direct diplomacy between Australia and Britain, after Hughes became prime minister.

For the rest of his term of office Munro Ferguson retained a close interest in the Pacific area and particularly the British island territories. For a time he employed as his private secretary E.C. Eliot, an official of the West Pacific High Commission. On several occasions Munro Ferguson urged the secretary of state to draw together all the Pacific colonies under one administrative authority and he suggested that this task might be entrusted to the governor-general of Australia. British power in the area could thereby be consolidated, its commercial interests protected and the welfare of the local inhabitants secured. This scheme was never regarded favourably in London, however, and would have

Sir Ronald Munro Ferguson
opening Tasmanian
hydro-electric scheme, May
1915. When he turned the
handle the assembled guests
were sprayed with water.

encountered opposition from New Zealand, where Australian influence in the
islands was regarded suspiciously.

The death of General Bridges at Gallipoli in late May 1915 was the occasion of
an unfortunate though unpublicised rift within the Imperial forces, in which
Munro Ferguson's role was more than just that of an observer. On 20 May a
cable nominating Colonel Legge as successor to Bridges was submitted for the
governor-general's signature. Seizing upon the opportunity to emphasise that he
did not regard such action as a formality, he enquired whether the appointment
had been fully considered by the government. Fisher replied that the matter had
been discussed at a cabinet meeting and the appointment agreed to. Munro
Ferguson signed the cable but was unwilling to let the matter rest there. He
subsequently saw the minister for defence and obtained an assurance that a copy
of the cable had gone to Hamilton. Pearce assured him also that Legge 'was the
only Australian officer capable of succeeding General Bridges but that there was
no desire to dictate to or to embarrass, the War Office or the G.O.C.' Munro

Ferguson was aware that, though a 'competent and experienced officer', Legge was unpopular, and he therefore took it upon himself to inform the secretary of state of this fact by personal and secret cable on 21 May.

The Army Council replied to the Commonwealth government's cable by confirming the appointment and Legge was promoted to brigadier general. But on 22 May Munro Ferguson received an intimation that Hamilton, who had not been consulted concerning the appointment, objected to the Australian government selecting his divisional commander. Legge was the senior permanent officer in the Australian defence forces. But two brigade commanders, Monash and McCay, citizen soldiers not regulars, were so upset by Legge's appointment over their heads as to talk of resignation. They preferred to serve under the British officer, General Walker, who had temporarily assumed command of the First Australian Division. The prospect of dissension among his Australian staff had prompted Hamilton to ask the Australian government to reconsider the appointment.

It was an embarrassing situation, made more so by the fact that Legge had already sailed for Gallipoli, and by the highly emotional atmosphere in Australia where the news of the Anzac landing had just been received. The cable from Hamilton raised the whole question of command of Australian troops in action, which had earlier been avoided only by Bridges' unchallengeable position as creator of the AIF. The problem was to be a continual source of irritation. Australian politicians were inexperienced as war leaders and far from the fields of battle. As members of a Labor government, ministers needed to heed nationalist pressures that Australian soldiers be commanded by Australian officers. In announcing Legge's appointment Pearce had said: 'we shall have the satisfaction of knowing that the Division is still in the command of an Australian officer'. But Australian army staff officers lacked experience and seniority. There was also an element of snobbery about the British commanders' lack of confidence in Dominion staff officers. Hamilton thought that even Bridges, 'fine character, brave soldier as he was, yet would not have been big enough to command a Corps', believing that a commander of men was 'not created so much by education as by birth . . . it takes a long time to manufacture a true military character and frame of mind'.

Fisher's immediate reaction to Hamilton's cable was a refusal to revoke an appointment which had already been made and announced. But he agreed that Pearce should also be consulted on the matter and later both ministers came to see the governor-general. His Excellency then pointed out to them the serious nature of a decision which forced a divisional commander upon a GOC against his wishes. Despite the governor-general's anxiety about the possible ill effects of the appointment, the two ministers refused to reverse the decision, arguing that it had been open to the Army Council to raise objections had it wished. They felt that to recall Legge after gazettal of his appointment could only lead to his resignation. Both Pearce and Fisher considered him a 'perfectly competent officer, the best in the Australian service, and accounted for some of his unpopularity by the fact that he had, through ability, passed over the heads of other Officers'. They were strongly of the opinion 'that it was expedient that an

Australian Officer should command the First Australian Division'. Munro Ferguson remarked that 'inured to Trade Unions and the Political Caucus, [Ministers] do not seem to appreciate generally the value of *bon cameraderie* in the Field'. Fisher, particularly, had been 'disposed to make light of "popularity" as a wholly superfluous quality'.

In the face of the Australian government's determination, there was little else for Munro Ferguson to do but to recommend that the appointment be accepted. Legge reached Gallipoli in June and took over from Walker for a few months, but later he was transferred to the command of the Second Australian Division. It was at this stage that command of the whole Australian Imperial Force was assumed by General W.R. Birdwood.

The Legge incident revealed that Munro Ferguson was by no means a cypher in the role of commander-in-chief. Though his interventions had been discreet, he had required his Australian ministers to justify their actions and decisions to him. Although he had not insisted upon his own opinion, he had impressed it upon the prime minister and the minister for defence who were, apparently, the only ministers who knew of Hamilton's cable. It was to be characteristic of Munro Ferguson's exercise of his role as governor-general that he asserted both his own point of view and his responsibility as representative of the British government as vigorously as discretion allowed. He continued to make it clear to the Australian parliamentary leaders that he was in close contact with the senior British officers in the Mediterranean. Birdwood wrote regularly to him from the front and selected passages from these letters were forwarded to Pearce, Fisher and later Hughes.

Even during wartime the constant problem of strained relations between governor-general and the State governors persisted. Although Sir Ronald was generally on good terms with the Victorian governor, Sir Arthur Stanley, differences between them arose over the perennial channel of communication issue. Later Munro Ferguson engaged in argument with the New South Wales and Western Australian governors Sir Walter Davidson and Sir Francis Newdegate. But the most prolonged and sharpest difference of opinion involved Davidson's predecessor in Sydney, Sir Gerald Strickland.

Prior to his appointment to New South Wales in March 1913, Strickland had held a series of governorships, first in the Leeward Islands, then in Tasmania and Western Australia. His gubernatorial experience, legal training and pugnacious personality led to conflicts with both Northcote and Dudley, who expressed annoyance at Strickland's zealous support of States' rights. By seniority, Strickland held the Dormant Commission to administer the Commonwealth, but neither the Colonial Office nor the Australian government wanted to see him exercise this authority. Munro Ferguson and Strickland quickly came to dislike each other and there was a series of petty incidents. In July 1914 Strickland complained to London that he had not been invited to the governor-general's levee. Sir Ronald even expressed doubts to the secretary of state about Sir Gerald's sanity. The situation was not eased when, in October 1915, Strickland triumphantly entered into occupation of what had formerly been the governor-general's Sydney residence. By 1916 the governor-general refused to conduct official business with the New South Wales governor except in writing. Their extended dispute only ended when Strickland was recalled to Britain in May 1917, having attempted the previous November to dismiss his premier, Holman.

The governor-general even encountered difficulties with the governor of New South Wales over so harmless a subject as afforestation. Munro Ferguson frequently urged Australia to better conserve and administer its timber resources. In May 1916 he chaired a conference on the subject in Adelaide, whereupon a dispatch to the secretary of state from Strickland accused him of taking an 'active part in matters of administration'. But the governor was the only one to object to this activity. Upon Sir Ronald's departure the *Australian Forestry Journal* expressed its appreciation of the value of His Excellency's contribution to forestry management.

Not only Sir Ronald, but also Lady Helen caused dissatisfaction in the States about the exercise of vice-regal authority in the Commonwealth. In March 1916 Governor Stanley reported to the Colonial Office a dispute that had arisen between her and Lady Madden, the wife of the lieutenant governor of Victoria. Lady Helen, as befitted the daughter of Dufferin, was possessed of an imperious disposition. Tall and 'of distinguished carriage and appearance', she had 'an iron constitution and inexhaustible energy. Her sight was weak but she seemed to be free from all other infirmities, as she never even caught a cold'. Early in August 1914, Lady Helen undertook the active organisation of the Australian Red Cross and remained its president throughout the war. Government House Melbourne became the headquarters for the Australian network and the ballroom was converted to a storage centre for Red Cross parcels. Lady Madden criticized Lady Helen for assuming 'functions that should properly belong to representatives of the States'. Stanley reported that Lady Madden was 'violently hostile to Lady Helen' and resented 'the autocratic management of the Red Cross'. Despite the State jealousies aroused by Her Excellency's methods, her work was a useful and practical contribution to both Australia and the Empire, for which she earned the appointment of Dame Grand Cross of the British Empire in 1918.

One earlier source of friction between the governor-general and State governors was absent in the early years of Munro Ferguson's term. Fisher was resolutely opposed to awarding honours and declined to submit any recommendations. In May 1914 Denman had informed his successor, 'I had to make recommendations off my own bat', Munro Ferguson believed that, when wisely distributed, honours were 'a source of local and imperial public advantage', but his attempts to persuade the prime minister of this were fruitless. Faced with this opposition Sir Ronald attempted to submit names upon his own initiative. But his recommendation of the former minister for defence, Millen, for a knighthood was strongly opposed by Fisher, and the secretary of state declined to submit the nomination to the King. While Fisher remained prime minister only the State governments and State governors could distribute such patronage.

As the war reached and passed its first anniversary, however, the pressures upon Fisher proved too much for him. On 29 October 1915 he resigned as prime minister, then proceeded to London in place of Reid as high commissioner. The political leadership of his party and the Commonwealth passed to William Morris Hughes. In the following dramatic but divisive years Munro Ferguson, though at the centre of events and an intimate confidante of Hughes, lost some of the ground he had succeeded in re-establishing for the office of governor-general. Moreover, in May 1915 his friend, Harcourt, had been replaced at the Colonial Office by the Conservative leader, Bonar Law. His Excellency's correspondence with the secretary of state never regained its former intimacy.

The departure of Fisher for England in late 1915 can be seen to mark the conclusion of Munro Ferguson's rehabilitation of the office. He had been remarkably successful. In barely eighteen months, working amicably with three prime ministers, he had revived the influence of the governor-general, which had declined under his two predecessors, and established himself as a man of significance not only in Imperial concerns but also in Australian domestic affairs. The British government recognised him to be an able and zealous diplomatic representative. Australian ministers accepted his active interpretation of the functions of local constitutional monarch without significant demur. The outbreak of the war had further strengthened his dual role for, as channel of communication between the Commonwealth and the British government, he was privy to all official correspondence. By the end of 1915 Munro Ferguson had already shown himself to be the most successful and active governor-general since federation.

The elevation of Hughes in late 1915 ushered in a new period of vigorous Australian nationalism. The next few years witnessed important changes in Australia's relationship with the mother country with consequent effect upon the role of the governor-general. With the other Dominions, Australia sought an improvement in status corresponding to the sacrifice involved in participation in the war. The war and its aftermath changed the Dominions' standing within the British Empire and their international identity as well. Consequently, the role of governor-general declined during the remainder of Munro Ferguson's term of office. Underlying these adjustments, as Australia moved towards maturity, was the force of Dominion nationalism. But personal factors, too, were involved, especially the character of the new prime minister.

In many ways the Welshman's quicksilver personality was in marked contrast to that of the Scottish laird who represented the Crown. Whereas Hughes was politically adroit, erratic and impulsive, the governor-general was inflexible, systematic and cautious. Yet Munro Ferguson quickly established a close personal relationship with his newly appointed chief minister, an association which later broadened into an intimacy which the more guarded Fisher had never countenanced.

Munro Ferguson was not uncritical of the sometimes unpredictable ways of the prime minister, and he soon realised that it was more necessary to be on his guard with him than with Fisher. Nevertheless he acknowledged that Hughes stood out 'above his whole party in intellect, courage and skill' and considered it in the interests of both Australia and the Empire that at the head of the government was a man who inspired 'his colleagues with some of his own go and grit'. In 1915 he conveyed his high opinion to the British prime minister, Asquith: 'Though stone deaf he is a remarkable personality. He has had greater educational advantages than most of his colleagues; is a natural leader of men; a delightful companion; bold in adversity; clear in his views; . . . sound on the question of economy; also he has elasticity of mind and the faculty for grappling with difficulties.' More importantly, Hughes was 'a most sincere Imperialist'.

No sooner was Hughes in office than he resolved to travel to the United Kingdom, accepting an invitation extended by the British government to all Dominion prime ministers. From January to July 1916 he was absent from Australia. The proposed conference did not eventuate, as the other colonial leaders had been unable to leave their own territories at that time. In their absence Hughes was lionised in London, feted by the British press and flatteringly accepted into the councils of the Empire. He attended meetings of the Imperial war cabinet, an unprecedented honour for a Dominion leader, and the Paris Economic Conference. He also visited Australian troops in the trenches and met Birdwood and the Australian commanders in the field. It was a formative period in Hughes' development, encouraging his ambitions for both his own and Australia's advancement within the Empire.

During Hughes' absence Munro Ferguson again found it necessary to correct the tendency of Labor leaders to disregard the role of the governor-general in the constitutional process. In March he protested at the failure of cabinet to inform him of its decision to fix the price of flour and bread, a far-reaching assumption of central power by the Commonwealth which the governor-general had first discovered not from his ministers but from the press. Though Pearce, the acting prime minister, apologised for the oversight, Munro Ferguson decided to use the occasion to re-establish his position. He asked that while he was resident in Sydney periodic letters should keep him posted on current affairs. Heads of state, he asserted, whether under a monarchical or republican constitution, ought to be 'informed of Public Policy in time to consider it before that Policy is announced'.

Pearce's non-committal reply — he would do his best to give effect to Munro Ferguson's wishes — goaded the governor-general to retort that the matter was not one of personal whim but of respect for the forms of the Constitution. He denied that these were 'merely empty survivals', claiming that 'the underlying meaning of the obligation to consult the Crown before giving effect to any Policy is that by so doing that Policy becomes a national instead of a Sectional Policy'. This correspondence resulted in a personal meeting at which the two men had what Munro Ferguson described as a 'frank exchange on Constitutional practice'. Faced with Pearce's evident reluctance to concede to the governor-general an active supervisory role in Australian public affairs, he determined to raise the question again when Hughes returned.

Munro Ferguson's concept of the monarchical aspects of his office was somewhat old fashioned; as the proper model for the relationship between monarch and cabinet he instanced Gladstone's treatment of Queen Victoria. But his interpretation of the role of governor-general as constitutional watch-dog in the Australian system of responsible government was, in theory, accurate enough at the time. It was also true that in the United Kingdom the monarch was still kept closely informed of cabinet's policy. Throughout his whole term of office Sir Ronald insisted that his position be accorded as much weight as was the King's. He demanded the right to advise, encourage or warn his ministers on policy matters, even when such matters were but tenuously linked to the category of 'Imperial interests'. It was a role which no governor-general since Northcote had attempted to assert and few of his successors imitated. It was also an interpretation which independent-minded democrats in the Labor movement were unlikely to accept, particularly when the office was filled by Britons appointed by the King on the recommendation of the British government. Munro Ferguson increasingly found his views challenged during the following years; Hughes' return presaged the eventual frustration of his persistent attempts to influence policy on an official level. However, such a comparatively minor matter of constitutional nicety was necessarily thrust aside by the far more important political controversy over conscription.

Munro Ferguson observed in August 1914 that the initial contingent of 20 000 men represented 'but a fraction of what the Commonwealth could contribute to the Imperial Forces'. Later he tried to ensure that Australia increased its commitment. From the first days of the war, watching his country struggling in the most destructive conflict in history, Munro Ferguson was understandably anxious to be of positive service to Britain. In December 1914 he informed Harcourt that the question of how to get more men to the front was under discussion and 'might easily lead to a party squabble, in which case my influence may be of use'. In October 1915, he suggested to Fisher that federal MPs might play a more active role in State government recruiting drives.

The governor-general and the State governors were prominent in efforts to induce young men to enlist voluntarily. Munro Ferguson officiated at parades, marches and military demonstrations in every State. He was not an impressive orator; but he spoke vigorously at call-up rallies and on other public occasions of the need to fight for the Empire. Public speeches were now much less dangerous occasions for governors. Patriotic exhortations and sabre rattling replaced the uncontroversial and usually dull dubjects of pre-1914 vice-regal orations. No doubt it was because he was so wholeheartedly involved in the recruiting campaigns himself that Munro Ferguson expressed his disappointment at the lack of enthusiasm evidenced by some Commonwealth ministers. But, in a typically cautious reply to His Excellency's gentle reproof, Fisher contended that too much could be made of ministers as recruiting agents. Munro Ferguson was forced to let the matter rest for the time being.

During 1915 the Commonwealth government came under increasing pressure to stiffen Australian military involvement by compulsory enlistment, particularly after Gallipoli had brought home the war's grim reality. The Universal Service League, a powerful pressure group cutting across traditional party lines, was prominent in New South Wales, largely due to the influence of the premier, Holman. Another influential group which took up the cause was the Australian Natives' Association, whose chief strength came from Victoria. The governor-general sympathised with these moves to strengthen Australia's war effort. He cautiously raised the subject with Hughes in November 1915, but the new prime minister replied that conscription was not a practicable proposal in Australia unless or until it were adopted in England. In December, reporting to the secretary of state that recruiting was 'not going as well as it might do', Munro Ferguson stated his belief that 'compulsion ... may be regarded as inevitable if voluntary enlistment fails'. A few months later, although he defended his government's reluctance to introduce conscription, he had decided that voluntarism had indeed failed. Writing to the leader of the opposition, Cook, he expressed the view that while the obstacles to compulsion were very real, they were less than they had been and would continue to diminish. He considered that 'in a war like this the doctrine of "equality of sacrifice" is ... bound, sooner or later, to prevail'.

Conscription was introduced into Britain, after considerable agitation, in early 1916. This increased pressure for similar legislation in Australia, but the prime minister's absence delayed resolution of the matter. The Australian press, almost universally in support of obligatory overseas service, widely speculated on Hughes' probable course of action. Simultaneously, forces opposed to the concept began to organise in preparation for the coming battle. Hughes returned in late July and a month of manoeuvring began.

The governor-general was more than merely a disinterested spectator during these crucial weeks. Shortly before Hughes' return he had written to Birdwood: 'We would certainly raise another quarter of a million men at a pinch & I am personally now in favour of conscription'. His letters to Hughes in England had conveyed increasing anxiety about the shortage of recruits and expressed the belief that some form of compulsion appeared to be necessary. Hughes' return enabled Munro Ferguson to plead the case for compulsion in person.

By late August Hughes had finally reached a decision. His problem was how to deal with doctrinal opposition to conscription within his own party. On 22 August both he and Munro Ferguson were in Sydney, at the opening of new head offices for the Commonwealth Bank. After the ceremonies Hughes asked if he would be allowed a dissolution on the question of compulsory service. He intended to use this promise, if the governor-general concurred, as a weapon in the caucus room, anticipating that his opponents would give way rather than risk a general election on the issue. Sir Ronald agreed to the request, saying that he 'saw no difficulty as to granting a Dissolution'. This was an important indication of His Excellency's commitment to Hughes and conscription. There were good reasons why a two-year-old parliament should not be dissolved in war time, especially over such a divisive issue, yet the governor-general was willing to hand Hughes this important political weapon.

In the event, though Hughes appears to have indicated to his colleagues that he had been fore-armed with such a promise, he decided to leave 'the sword in the scabbard' and caucus narrowly approved a compromise, whereby a plebiscite would be held on the question. The governor-general's promise of a dissolution was, therefore, not redeemed, but it had been a valuable indication for Hughes of the sympathy and support he had from the representative of the

Crown. Cabinet resolved that the question of conscription should be put to the people. On 30 August, in Munro Ferguson's words 'a memorable day in Australia's political history', the prime minister announced in parliament his party's decision on a question which 'easily transcends any matter which has been dealt with by the Government since the inception of Federation'.

Hughes' conviction that compulsion was necessary was chiefly the result of the increasingly sombre news he was receiving concerning the progress of the war in Europe. Convinced that Germany's defeat needed extraordinary measures of sacrifice he undertook to provide the men which Australian commanders in the field, and the War Council, estimated to be necessary. The responsibility for this decision must be sheeted home to the prime minister himself. But the governor-general's discreet, persistent advocacy of compulsion had reinforced Hughes' natural tendencies. Their similar Imperial patriotism made them natural allies. Consequently, just as a word of caution might have deflected Hughes from his course, Munro Ferguson's support must not be ignored as a factor in persuading Hughes to press ahead.

The nature of their relationship at this time is revealed in a notable incident towards the end of what had become a bitter plebiscite campaign. Hughes attempted to introduce a provision whereby men eligible for service within Australia could be questioned by returning officers at the polling booths. But the proposed regulation was rejected at a meeting of the Federal Executive Council in Melbourne on 25 October, at which the vice-president, Senator Albert Gardiner, presided. Two days later, without indication of the earlier rejection, the same regulation was presented to a different meeting, held in Sydney and chaired by the governor-general. On this occasion, because of the absence of the three who had opposed the measure in Melbourne, the regulation was passed. When the absent ministers (Gardiner, Senator Edward Russell and William Higgs) discovered what had been done they promptly resigned.

At about midnight on the evening before the poll the prime minister telephoned the governor-general (rousing him from his bed in Admiralty House) and asked if he could see him. Munro Ferguson crossed the harbour to find Hughes waiting for him in a taxi on the Quay. After informing him of the latest cabinet defections, 'The poor little man asked for advice and sympathy saying he "had not a brain wave left"'. But Hughes did not reveal that the offending regulation had been rejected by the earlier Executive Council. Touched by this appeal from the dejected prime minister, the governor-general suggested that the announcement of the resignations be censored until after the vote. Hughes hurried off to put this advice into effect, only to find that the three ministers had already communicated their decisions to the press.

The melodramatic meeting at midnight was more than a plea for sympathy. It can also be seen as a shrewd attempt to learn the governor-general's attitude and enlist his co-operation in what promised to be critical weeks. Hughes knew that the episode of the regulation and the ministers' resignations were fatal blows to his control of the Labor Party. His was a theatrical personality and no doubt the emotional depression and appeal for help were genuine enough. But he was always a master of persuasion and if his real intent had been to ensure the support of the constitutional head of state before he engaged in the in-fighting and political intrigue which loomed ahead, he succeeded completely. The governor-general could thenceforth be trusted almost as a fellow conspirator, though a little aggrieved that even while apparently pouring out his soul Hughes had not placed the full facts before him.

The 1916 conscription plebiscite led to important changes both in the governor-general's attitude towards Australia and the Labor Party's attitude towards him. Previously Munro Ferguson had regarded as 'almost unique in its touching simplicity' Australia's loyalty to the Crown. With many others he believed that there would be 'general acquiescence in universal service'. The narrow but undeniable victory for the 'Noes', therefore, was a 'most serious blow' to his 'confidence in the future of this country'. 'For the moment the anarchist and most ignorant section of society has shown itself more powerful than all the rest, & that in a community which is in the main the most irresponsible, self confident & inexperienced in the Empire, or even perhaps outside of it', he wrote to Bonar Law.

With his Whiggish background it was not surprising that he criticised the selfish class motives of Hughes' opponents and regarded the successful campaign as 'somewhat discreditable . . . to the Labour organization'. Moreover, as a Liberal Imperialist he was shocked by the anti-British outbursts of Archbishop Mannix throughout the struggle. The result was that he allowed these considerations to affect his previously balanced judgement. Writing on Christmas eve 1916 to the new secretary of state, Walter Long, with whom he corresponded more frankly than with Bonar Law, Sir Ronald criticised Australia's contribution to the war as 'much below' its fair proportion, an unjust remark, considering Australia's distance from fields of battle and meagre population. His Excellency also commented on the fact that Australian troops did not go into battle until April 1915, an implication of tardiness which ignores the fact that the AIF, recruited largely from civilians and with much further to go, was in action in Gallipoli before Kitchener's new armies took the field. Such judgements were not merely the reaction of a jingoistic British aristocrat. Many Australians felt likewise. For example Cook thought the result 'disgraceful . . . a disaster for Australia . . . a betrayal of national honour'.

In one camp were those who regarded themselves as loyal to the British Empire, with whose instincts the governor-general naturally sympathised. Elements of this group had always distrusted the attitude of the Labor Party towards the British connection, and they now considered their worst fears realised. The support which Labor branches and anti-conscriptionist party members gave to the 'No' campaign led many to the conclusion that the party was controlled by disloyal elements. This distrust was exacerbated by the loss in one stroke of all the Labor Party's leading figures. Control of the movement was left to unfamiliar men, vulnerable to the accusations of an Imperialist publication such as *All for Australia* that they were pawns in the hands of outside bodies which were 'luke-warm to the War, indifferent to the Empire, or strongly opposed to it'.

Munro Ferguson, previously seen as impartial as any of his predecessors, found himself irretrievably identified with one party, the 'Win the War' or 'Empire' party. He considered Hughes' defiance of caucus as a victory for responsible government and a defeat for the 'secret Trade Union Junta'. After the conscription plebiscite he regarded Labor as revolutionary and dangerous. This distrust was mutual. Despite occasional doubts about his impartiality, Labor leaders had previously been willing to give the governor-general the benefit of those doubts. They soon came to believe, with some justification, that the chief executive officer was firmly ensconced in the ranks of the pro-conscriptionists. Before the war there had been consistent Labor agitation for the abolition of imported State governors. To this was now added the demand that governors-general should also be chosen from the ranks of Australian citizens. There was to be little in the subsequent actions of Munro Ferguson to soften the impression gained by some Labor members that he was as partisan as their political opponents.

In his report of the result of the plebiscite, Munro Ferguson forecast a reconstruction of the government, followed by a general election. Though this eventually proved to be the case, several confusing months intervened. On 4 November Hughes again asked Munro Ferguson to promise a dissolution. Assuring the governor-general that he had no intention of using the promise, he explained that he needed a weapon in the forthcoming negotiations. Munro Ferguson replied by expressing his 'deep sense of confidence in Mr Hughes as P.M.; his conviction that this confidence was accorded to Mr Hughes by the people of the Commonwealth as a whole; and his determination to afford the P.M. the utmost support compatible with the limits of his action prescribed by the custom of the Constitution'. But he refused to commit himself in advance, reserving judgement until Hughes had allocated vacant portfolios and until he himself was convinced that the existing parliament could not provide a government to carry on for the remainder of its term. It was clear from this exchange that though Hughes could count on the governor-general's active sympathy, Munro Ferguson would not lightly relinquish his independence of action in advance.

By 14 November 1916 two more of Hughes' colleagues had resigned (Hugh Mahon and King O'Malley); only four out of a cabinet of ten remained with him. Finding himself opposed by a hostile caucus majority and preferring to take the initiative himself rather than be deposed, Hughes withdrew from the meeting, followed by 23 of his followers. He was left with only thirteen direct supporters out of the 75 members of the House of Representatives, and eleven out of 36 in the Senate. Yet, when later on the same day Hughes submitted his resignation and asked to be recommissioned, his request was granted.

Again Hughes appears to have been less than straightforward with the governor-general. After asking and receiving a new commission the prime minister revealed that the new ministers were already assembled at Government House, bibles at the ready, waiting to be sworn in. Though His Excellency required that Hughes give a written assurance that the Liberal Party would co-operate, this was a token exercise of his discretion. Munro Ferguson was, by this time, committed to Hughes as an individual. He informed the secretary of state that the former Labor leader was 'the one man who can fill the role of Prime Minister' but that it was not apparent at that 'stage from whence his Government is to come'.

Hughes' caretaker ministry, supported in parliament by the Liberals, retained office until February. During this period the prime minister once more attempted to obtain the active assistance of the governor-general in his cabinet-making. In early January he discussed the question of an early dissolution with Munro Ferguson who, while not specifically committing himself in advance, was obviously willing to consider the suggestion favourably. Eventually such a course was unnecessary as Hughes and Cook reached agreement and a Nationalist ministry was sworn in by the governor-general on 17 February 1917.

But the political turmoil continued. Hughes was reluctant to risk an election so soon after the plebiscite. He therefore introduced a resolution to procure an Imperial Act extending the life of parliament for the duration of the war. Unfortunately for Hughes' plan the Labor Party still controlled the Senate and were understandably hostile to such a proposal. In an atmosphere of suspicion and confusion considerable pressure was brought to bear upon waverers. Two Tasmanian Labor senators (J.J. Long and J. Guy) absented themselves from parliament and another, R.K. Ready, resigned suddenly in March on the plea of ill health. This enabled a hastily summoned meeting of the Tasmanian Executive Council to nominate as Ready's replacement a former Labor premier but pro-conscriptionist, John Earle, who was visiting Melbourne at that time. A series of cables passed between Melbourne and Hobart which resulted in Earle taking his seat in the Senate less than 24 hours after his predecessor had resigned. Despite his uneasiness that the business savoured too much of a trick, Munro Ferguson was involved in this discreditable episode not only as the channel of communication between the Commonwealth and Tasmanian governments but also as a witness to Earle's written resignation from the Tasmanian House of Assembly, a necessary pre-condition for membership of the Senate. However, these manoeuvres were rendered ineffective by the refusal of two other Tasmanian senators to support the obviously tarnished proposal to extend parliament's term, and Hughes was compelled to advise dissolution in May and seek re-election.

Though the 'Win-the-War' party triumphed in the Commonwealth elections and was supreme in all States except Queensland, eligible young men seemed to lack their political leaders' enthusiasm for the fighting. Enlistments in the Australian Imperial Force continued to decline. Notwithstanding the result of the earlier plebiscite the governor-general continued to regard compulsion as the only way to secure the necessary recruits. Others, such as the influential back-bencher Sir William Irvine and the former Liberals in the Nationalist coalition, were of the same opinion, and as the war news worsened, notably when Russia pulled out, the government came under pressure to do something about the problem. At first Hughes considered conscription to be impracticable but the grim news of Passchendaele persuaded him to make a further appeal to the electorate. Munro Ferguson agreed that compulsory service was the only solution, but attempted to dissuade cabinet from embarking upon a plebiscite. He suggested instead that a bill be brought into parliament, followed by a dissolution. Disregarding this proposal and Irvine's advocacy of conscription by executive action, Hughes decided on another referendum.

The second conscription plebiscite was more violent and bitter than the first, with the Catholic archbishop of Melbourne, Daniel Mannix, again vigorously leading the 'No' campaign. Hughes threw himself into the fight with energy and dedication but his vilification of the opponents of compulsory service inflamed feelings and proved in the end counter-productive. On occasions more than words were flung about. The governor-general reported that 'in one Queensland constituency a catapult was set up — the range having been carefully ascertained previous to the meeting — eggs and road metal were hurled with remarkable accuracy at the Honourable James Page'. At Warwick, also in Queensland, the prime minister himself was the target for an egg 'of indubitable antiquity'. It was an ill-omened and divisive campaign. Several times Hughes asserted that his ministry needed an affirmative vote in the plebiscite and would not attempt to carry on without it. Yet despite this threat, and a vigorous campaign by the government elected only six months previously, the Australian electorate again rejected the proposal to introduce conscription.

Jubilant anti-conscriptionists called upon the cabinet to honour its pledge to resign. Once again Hughes relied upon his close association with Munro Ferguson to assist him out of his difficulty. The governor-general was in residence at Admiralty House, Sydney, for Christmas 1917 but his official secretary had remained in Melbourne. On Boxing Day Steward was summoned to the prime minister's presence. Obviously agitated, and explaining that he dared not absent himself from the delicate cabinet negotiations then taking place, Hughes asked that Sir Ronald make a secret, unscheduled visit to Melbourne. Munro Ferguson cabled his willingness to travel south but rejected the undignified suggestion that he drive from the railway station to government house secretly and circuitously in an unmarked car.

Though aware of the general dilemma which faced the government, Munro Ferguson was not sure of the precise purpose of the proposed interview. He therefore sent Steward to enquire. But Hughes refused to be specific, merely subjecting the official secretary to a half-supplicatory, half-bellicose harangue, in which he warned that a government led by Labor leader Frank Tudor might take Australia out of the war altogether. It was clear to Steward that the government was looking to the governor-general 'either for such advice as will help them out of their difficulty, or for such assistance as will achieve the same end'.

Munro Ferguson and Hughes met for about two hours in Government House, Melbourne, on 29 December 1917. With characteristic assiduity the governor-general arrived well prepared. His written 'aide memoire' reveals his conviction that the best course was for Hughes to resign and recommend that another leading member of the Nationalist Party be sent for. Such a course of action would fulfil pledges made during the campaign and yet not risk the accession to power of the Labor Party. Probably Hughes repeated to Munro Ferguson the doubts he had expressed to Steward about Labor's loyalty to the Empire and commitment to the war. The interview concluded without any definite result and His Excellency returned to Sydney.

On the surface Munro Ferguson's solution to the government's moral and practical impasse was a feasible proposition. But, as Sir Ronald had earlier remarked (in December 1916): 'It is doing Mr Hughes no injustice to suggest that he was averse to the relinquishment of power'. Possibly Hughes believed his own forecasts of the dire consequences if Tudor came to power. It may also have been true that another Nationalist leader would have been unable to hold the coalition together, though if Hughes really had the interests of the nation and the Empire at heart he could surely have prevailed upon his followers. But, whatever his reasons, having with considerable effort obtained the governor-general's advice, Hughes failed to follow it.

Cancelling a scheduled visit to Bathurst, Munro Ferguson returned openly to Melbourne on 3 January. By this time there was no disguising the government crisis. Hughes fought resourcefully for his political life. A meeting of the National Party on 3 January overwhelmingly endorsed him as its leader and the following day resolved to oppose any course of action which would 'hand the government of the Commonwealth over to the Official Labour Party'. Finally on 8 January Hughes called again at Government House and resigned, stating that 'the resignation was unconditional and that he had no advice to offer'. The governor-general was left with the constitutional responsibility of finding a ministry capable of carrying on the government.

Though in theory Sir Ronald's discretion was absolute, in reality his choices were limited. His guiding principle was that another political battle should be avoided and that an election would further inflame already embittered feelings. The actions of the National Party in the first days of January had closed the avenue that he had thought to take. Hughes had not asked to be recommissioned but there was practically no other alternative available short of entrusting the government to the Labor Party. Quite apart from any personal bias His Excellency might have felt against the Labor Party, there were good reasons why Tudor should not be commissioned: supply had to be voted by Friday 11 January; therefore parliament could not be dissolved without re-assembling and a minority Labor government faced the prospect of being unable to control the business of the house.

Munro Ferguson went to elaborate lengths in appearing to exercise his responsibility impartially. He ostentatiously summoned to Government House no less than seven Commonwealth parliamentarians: F.G. Tudor (ALP), W.G. Higgs (ALP), J. Cook (Nationalist, former Liberal), W.A. Watt (Nationalist, former Liberal), Sir J. Forrest (Nationalist, former Liberal), A. Poynton (Nationalist, former ALP) and G.H. Wise (Nationalist, former Liberal). These interviews were not to offer any of them a commission, but simply to enlist their views. He even considered entrusting the government to the aged but still ambitious Forrest, but after discovering that Nationalist ministers refused to serve under the old man, he discarded that possibility. All other Nationalists consulted agreed that the only man who could keep the two elements of the party together was Hughes.

During his interview with Tudor, Munro Ferguson had 'enquired as to his ability to form an Administration'. The Labor leader had replied that his party was in an undoubted minority but that he had at least as good a chance of forming a government as had Hughes in November 1916. As the governor-general remarked, this claim was 'more ingenious than relevant'. It was obvious that if Tudor secured office he would need to dissolve parliament almost immediately. But the problem of passing a Supply Bill would still remain. In this situation the course which promised to involve the least disruption was to re-commission Hughes, as His Excellency was quick to perceive. After dinner he sent for Hughes. At this interview he stated that though previously he had believed that the prime minister's 'temporary withdrawal from office would enhance his credit in the country and satisfy public opinion', he had found it necessary to ask Hughes again to form an administration. In doing so he 'earnestly recommended that three places in the Government be offered to the Labour Party'.

Early the next morning Munro Ferguson attempted to inform Tudor and the press of his decision to recommission Hughes. But the official secretary, Steward, advised the governor-general that it was the invariable procedure in the Commonwealth for such announcements to be made by the prime minister. Steward was aware that an announcement made before Hughes had completed the formation of his cabinet, and while parliament was still in session, might embarrass the prime minister. It later appeared that Hughes' control of the National Party was not so secure as he would have liked. A 'plot' involving Irvine and a back-bencher, Austin Chapman, did emerge a few days later. But by then Hughes had been recommissioned. Reluctantly, after correspondence with Hughes, Munro Ferguson withdrew both messages. He considered that to allow the houses to meet and then adjourn without informing them that the dye had already been cast would be to reduce the prestige of parliament, which it had been his ambition to restore. Though he urged Hughes to make known the situation in the house, the prime minister was insistent that he be allowed to decide himself when and where he did so. The governor-general was forced to give way. Hughes did not announce that he had been recommissioned by the King's representative until after parliament had adjourned for the day, and he did so in the party caucus room.

At his interview with Munro Ferguson on 8 January the prime minister had pleaded that he had 'a very difficult row to hoe' and asked if the governor-general would provide an explanatory memorandum for presentation to parliament. Munro Ferguson agreed and, after unofficially consulting Professor Harrison Moore, prepared a memorandum which was tabled in both houses on 10 January. In his document Munro Ferguson stressed that he had been guided by a determination not to put the country to the expense of an election so soon after the previous one, nor to risk reviving controversy after two bitter plebiscites. His decision had been limited, therefore, by the parliamentary situation as it then existed and he had found that Hughes was the only man who could command a majority. His public emphasis upon the supremacy of parliament hinted at his private distrust of non-parliamentary organisations such as party caucuses.

Munro Ferguson's actions during 1917 and early 1918 led to some predictable hostility towards him in Labor circles. In September 1917 the Toorak branch of the party naively wrote to the 'Secretary, Labor Party, House of Commons, London' urging the recall of the governor-general 'on the grounds of his partiality and interference in party politics to the prejudice of the Labour Party'. The recommissioning of Hughes led to criticism in parliament of the King's representative. In the Senate, one Labor Party member protested vigorously against the partisanship which he alleged the governor-general had shown in the domestic affairs of the federal parliament. The Victorian weekly, *Labor Call*, labelled the affair 'a farce' and 'a bit of comic opera', exclaiming: 'How these imported titled gentry do hate labor'. The recommissioning of Hughes strengthened the already distinguishable demand in Labor circles for a change in the system of appointing governors-general. On 23 January the Victorian parliamentarian Frank Anstey addressed a mass meeting which demanded both a dissolution and the recall of the governor-general. A few months later Dr W. Maloney placed on record in the Commonwealth parliament resolutions of various meetings urging that Munro Ferguson be recalled. At a Labor Party conference in Sydney during 1919, a motion was carried calling for the governor-general to be Australian-born.

Maloney's comment — that the prime minister could do with the governor-general whatever he wished — was not entirely accurate. Munro Ferguson had favoured the more honest course of a genuine resignation by Hughes' ministry followed by a reconstructed, though still Nationalist, government. This solution proved impossible because of the prime minister's tenacity and his virtual indispensability to the coalition. Had Hughes tendered his resignation on 29 December the governor-general might have had real freedom of action. But by not resigning until 8 January, after he had demonstrated his strength as leader of the party, he rendered useless the apparent discretion of the governor-general, despite his ostentatious refusal to offer any specific advice.

In the passion of their opposition to the renegade Hughes, Labor Party members exaggerated the partisanship of the governor-general; but their point was none the less worth making. It can certainly be argued that over an extended period the governor-general had been a useful bolster for the Nationalist coalition. Hughes acknowledged his debt in a letter written shortly before he departed again for England. He wrote: 'You have been in many a serious & trying crisis a great help to me. Many times I should have thrown up the sponge but for your advice, your sympathy & the feeling that you believed in me.' The governor-general replied that it had occasionally been a solace, when so far removed from the scene of the war, 'to find it possible to help make smooth the path of the Government Car'.

The support which Munro Ferguson invariably gave non-Labor governments should be seen in the light of the governor-general's concept of his duty to the

Empire. There is no doubt that he regarded it as part of his contribution to the war effort to encourage the dispatch of as many Australian soldiers to the European war as could be spared. Moreover, from at least the formation of Hughes' minority government in November 1916 — an event which the Colonial Office recognised as being 'of great advantage of the Empire' — he had been sympathetic to the party which was committed to wholehearted support for Britain in the war. A contemporary piece of doggerel recognised this:

> True to trust that you held sacred,
> 'We must win the war', you said,
> And when party leaders failed you,
> You discarded them, and led!
>
> . . .
>
> Mouthing Billie served your purpose,
> And wisely you commissioned him
> To select, by your direction,
> A Government the war to win.

It is significant that the characteristic which Munro Ferguson most frequently praised in Hughes was his Imperial patriotism. A letter written to Long after the second conscription plebiscite reveals Munro Ferguson's overriding allegiance to Britain. He observed that:

> The better kind of people are very disappointed at the result of the Poll and suffer from a sense of humiliation and a feeling of hopelessness with regard to the future of Australia. It is difficult not to share these feelings and at such moments the desire to be at Home and share in the great war effort of Britain is strong. However there may be something done in spurring them on to build ships and to increase production.

Munro Ferguson's last attempt to stimulate enlistment was a 'governor-general's recruiting conference' of 1918. Suggested to him by a New South Wales Labor parliamentarian, Captain A.C. Carmichael, and supported by Hughes, this was a gathering of representatives of Australian employers and employees with parliamentary representatives from all States to discuss ways of resolving, by voluntary means, the recruiting problem. Not only was the initiative for the meeting taken by His Excellency but he organised it and it was held at Government House in Melbourne. Steward acted as secretary for the occasion. Talks lasted for seven days, from 12 to 19 April 1918, but the results were disappointing. Recruiting figures for the month of May did show an increase but thereafter they remained low. Though internal dissension prevented the conference from any substantial achievement, the fact that it was called and that bitter opponents were prepared to meet and discuss the problem of recruiting signified a much needed relaxation in tension and suspicion.

Steward's prominence behind the scenes during the government crisis following Hughes' resignation and his usefulness for such functions as the recruiting conference indicated how indispensable he had become to Munro Ferguson. During Dudley's and Denman's terms there had been uneasiness in

London about Steward's influence, and, apprised of these fears, Munro Ferguson arrived in Australia determined to reduce Steward's authority. In August 1914 he was still of the opinion that under normal conditions it would be best if 'the sums paid for maintenance of an Official Sec^y & his staff & of the official part of Gov^t Ho' be handed over to the governor-general. This reflected his ignorance of the Australian parliament's determination that the official business involved in the representation of the Crown in Australia should be transacted by an officer responsible to the Commonwealth parliament. Twelve months later he admitted that his earlier proposal had been impracticable. Steward continued to exercise the functions he had inherited from Wallington in 1902.

The official secretary's experience was a positive assistance to all governors-general. His zealous control of the expenditure of the establishment had helped to lessen criticism of extravagance. He had also been a consistent defender of the governor-general's role as sole channel of communication with the British government. His official duties included the encoding and decoding of confidential correspondence between Great Britain and Australia on both routine and secret subjects. In August 1915 the secretary of state dispatched a secret memorandum concerning counter-espionage to the Commonwealth government, requesting that its proposal be implemented in Australia. It was characteristic of Australian security arrangements at the time that this circular was lost. Steward's prior experience in the Australian Intelligence Corps and his access to classified correspondence between Britain and Australia made him the obvious choice to head the local branch.

In early 1916 the 'Commonwealth Counter Espionage Bureau' was set up with the governor-general's official secretary as officer-in-charge. Its function was 'to undertake the widest possible interchange with the British Government of confidential intelligence bearing especially upon the activities of hostile secret service agents throughout the Empire, both in time of peace and in war'. Munro Ferguson reported in April 1917 that Steward had been 'specially engaged in unravelling the schemes of the I.W.W. and following the doings of various malefactors of this type & of aliens', in which operations he appeared to have remarkable gifts.

Though pleased at access afforded by this arrangement to the 'subsoil activities' of Australia, His Excellency was also a little anxious about it. Quite apart from his pardonable concern at the occasional unsavoury character who called at the back door of Government House, there was the problem that the duties of official secretary suffered while Steward busied himself with his duties as chief spy. But the situation was never resolved to the governor-general's satisfaction. Indeed it worsened, for in June 1917 Munro Ferguson complained to the prime minister about other 'usages' to which his official secretary had been put. He informed Long that Hughes did not trust the secretary of the Prime Minister's Department and used Steward for confidential business of his own. In March 1919 Steward resigned to take up the post of commissioner of police for Victoria, in which capacity he was acting when he died in May 1920.

Steward's long career as official secretary to five governors-general and one acting governor-general had been beneficial both to the occupants of the office and to the Commonwealth. Though he was sometimes difficult and pompous he established amicable working arrangements with most of his superiors. Shortly after arriving in Australia, Munro Ferguson commented that Steward was 'a strange mortal . . . He says "No" to everything . . . I am sure he means well and does his best. He amuses me and I get along quite well with him'. His efficient exercise of the dual roles of secretary to both the governor-general and the Executive Council had assisted the representative of the Crown to retain access to Commonwealth affairs. As Munro Ferguson recognised, 'liaison officer between the Governor-General and his Advisers . . . was a delicate position demanding the exercise of considerable tact and judgment'. Steward's familiarity with the workings of Australia's governmental machinery was unexcelled. He was rewarded for his services with a KBE in 1918. Though less gifted than his contemporaries, Atlee Hunt and R.R. Garran, his name should be included among the leading pioneer Commonwealth civil servants.

Steward's activities in the counter-espionage field had led him to advocate in January 1917 the establishment of a 'small Federal Police Force'. Munro Ferguson supported this, but without success until the closing stages of the second conscription plebiscite. After the egg incident at Warwick, Hughes resolved to create such a force. As his chief purpose was to deal with the difficulties into which he had got in Queensland, he proposed to establish the Commonwealth police in that State, with headquarters at Brisbane. The governor-general immediately wrote to Hughes urging that the sphere of the federal police should not be entirely confined to one State since such a force was needed in other States to protect ships, guard Commonwealth property and 'support the Secret Service'. It was a sensible suggestion which Hughes accepted.

Another attempt by Munro Ferguson to exercise a more than nominal role in Executive Council meetings was less defensible. From 1903 to 1914 it had become common practice to delegate to the vice-president — a politician — authority to deal with business of a routine character during His Excellency's absence from Melbourne. But from the beginning of his term of office, Munro Ferguson was determined to actively exercise his functions as chairman of the Executive Council. In November 1916 he informed the prime minister that he proposed to revert to the practice of holding Executive Council meetings in the federal Government House, instead of in the cabinet room of the Commonwealth Offices. Hughes admitted that 'a certain looseness had crept in' and agreed to make whatever arrangements the governor-general thought proper. But His Excellency continued to express dissatisfaction at irregularities and objected to the prime minister's tendency to rush the formalities through without respect for the governor-general's right to consider policy matters before affixing his signature. He particularly deprecated the practice of dealing with important matters in his absence at councils chaired by the vice-president.

The culmination of these representations was a memorandum dated 22 January 1918 in which the governor-general attempted to use the temporary strength with which the recent political crisis had endowed him, and reform the procedure at Executive Council meetings. He recited past irregularities and suggested that no Executive Council should be held elsewhere than in the council chamber of Government House, save with the express consent of the governor-general, and that all minutes be delivered to the secretary to the council 24 hours before the meeting. In addition he suggested that the delegation of powers to the vice-president in the absence of the governor-general should be amended to preclude the discussion of anything other than business of a routine or formal character unless the governor-general had 'adequate time either to attend the meeting, should he consider it advisable to be present, or to give a considered opinion by telegraph or otherwise'.

Munro Ferguson was a vigorous, intelligent man who chafed at the enforced political inactivity of his position. In particular he resented the continued tendency of Australian cabinets to ignore the governor-general. His earlier remonstrances with Fisher and Pearce about such discourtesy were echoed in frequent, sometimes strongly worded, complaints to Hughes. Eventually, after Hughes had received what he described as 'a hell of a talking to from the G.G.', he agreed to see the governor-general once a week to discuss government business. But he was opposed to the governor-general's inclination to assert a supervisory role in any formal way through the Executive Council. He replied politely but firmly to Sir Ronald's memorandum of 22 January, reminding His Excellency, as Barton had reminded Tennyson, of the supremacy of the elected representatives of the people over the nominated representatives of the Crown. Admitting that it was desirable for proper procedures to be observed, Hughes was adamant, nevertheless, that the government had the right to submit matters to the Executive Council whenever it saw fit. He considered that 'to admit the right of the Governor-General to delay assenting to matters submitted to him personally at Executive would be to admit his right of review or even rejection of such matters: — but this would make the Gov-General the de facto Government of the Commonwealth which under our Constitution & that of Britain he is not'.

Despite this timely reminder that he must not push his role as constitutional watch-dog too far, Munro Ferguson was reluctant to concede defeat. Subsequent delegations of authority to the vice-president of the Executive Council were accompanied by a memorandum embodying his recommendations concerning procedure. Moreover, he continued to assert his executive independence. In May 1919, when presented with a form of credentials establishing Australian representation in the United States of America, he 'altered its terms so as to restrict his sphere to that of trade commissioner'. Six months later he declined to sign a proclamation submitted to him by the minister for customs until Hughes pressed him to do so.

These interventions were evidence of Munro Ferguson's concept of the monarch's active supervisory role in Australian affairs. He unquestionably retained an active influence over one sphere of policy, namely the conferral of honours. In January 1916 he had reported to the secretary of state that Hughes, unlike Fisher, had an open mind on this subject. But the Labor cabinet continued to oppose such recommendations and it was not until Hughes had formed his Nationalist ministry that the governor-general found a government which was prepared to sanction the award of titles and other distinctions.

Predictably, problems involving the channel of communication immediately arose. In February 1917 two State governors protested against the governor-general's action in announcing honours recommended by State governments. In this instance the secretary of state supported the objections and instructed Munro Ferguson that in future he should 'enable State governors to publish their own honours'. An exception to this general rule was the newly instituted British Empire Order. Both the governor-general and the Australian prime minister insisted that these distinctions, since awarded for war services, should be a Commonwealth responsibility. Despite pressure from State governments, the Colonial Office supported the proposition that the governor-general, advised by the Commonwealth government, should act as co-ordinating authority in respect of recommendations for the British Empire Order.

Munro Ferguson's exercise of office illustrated the opportunities available in war-time to a strong-minded governor-general to exercise an active rather than a passive role in the inner machinery of the Commonwealth government. But such opportunities were soon to be seriously undermined. Though he was as quick as his predecessors to protest at any tendency to by-pass his office, the occasions on which he was overlooked increased. These reached a peak in mid-1917 particularly in the case of correspondence between the Australian Naval Board and the Admiralty. Strongly worded complaints were sent to Hughes, Pearce and Cook but the problem remained unsolved.

It was not only in this sphere that the governor-general's role as channel of communication was being disregarded. Early in 1917 both Long and Munro Ferguson objected to Hughes' new tendency to cable direct to the British prime minister, Lloyd George. During the Australian leader's visit to London he had enjoyed unique access to British policy-making and to war reports. Upon his return to Australia he chafed at the lack of detailed information available to him and at the delay which occurred when he was forced to communicate via the governor-general and the Colonial Office. On occasion he by-passed the official channel to correspond directly with the British prime minister, often using Keith Murdoch (later Sir Keith), an ambitious Australian journalist then working in London, as intermediary.

In early 1918 the British government had invited Dominion ministers to London for an Imperial War Conference. Hughes had been unable to attend the Imperial War Conference of 1917 which had been an important turning point in the evolution of the Dominions as sovereign states. A resolution of this 1917 conference had recommended that a special conference be called after the war to consider the readjustment of constitutional relations, and it was resolved that 'any such readjustment, while thoroughly preserving all existing powers of self-government and complete control of domestic affairs, should be based upon a full recognition of the Dominions as autonomous nations of an Imperial Commonwealth, ... [with] an adequate voice in foreign policy ... and should provide effective arrangements for continuous consultation in all important matters of common Imperial concern ...' Twelve months later Hughes' local political position was secure enough for him to attend the next conference. En route to London he cabled a request (through the governor of Fiji) to add to the agenda for the approaching conference an additional subject, namely 'channels of communication between Britain and the self governing Dominions'.

The secretary of state was puzzled at this message and asked for further details. But the governor-general was no better informed. Hughes had not mentioned any such desire before his departure. Nor did he subsequently explain what he proposed, despite further cables from Munro Ferguson to Hughes in Honolulu and Vancouver. Not until the Imperial Conference itself did the governor-general discover Hughes' intention: to press strongly that Dominion prime ministers should be able to communicate directly with the prime minister of Great Britain.

The governor-general was dismayed at the prospect of losing access to important correspondence, recognising this proposal as a serious attack on the position of the King's representative as quasi-diplomatic agent of the British government. Without knowledge of such communications he would be unable to pass on his own comments and recommendations to the secretary of state, and his privileged influence on Australian politicians would decline. He conveyed these fears to the equally apprehensive secretary of state and at the same time lobbied governors-general in all the other Dominions in an effort to defeat or modify Hughes' proposals.

Though his fears were to prove justified, both his and Long's efforts were without effect. Faced with Hughes' conviction that Australia and the other Dominions had passed the stage when the Colonial Office and the governor-general should act as delaying buffers between them and the British government, the secretary of state had to give way. Hughes' tactics — securing in advance the concurrence of Canada's prime minister, R.L. Borden, and failing to give the Colonial Office time to organise opposition — were successful. The Imperial Conference resolved that 'the development which has taken place in the relations between the United Kingdom and the Dominions necessitates such a change in administrative arrangements and in the Channels of Communication between their Governments as will bring them more directly in touch with each other'.

This mildly worded resolution heralded a new period in the relationship between Australia and Great Britain, a period in which the Commonwealth and the other Dominions sought to exercise an influence upon British policy through consultation — and a period in which the term 'British Commonwealth' gradually replaced 'Empire'. In the new organisation the governor-general's role as intermediary was no longer relevant. The conference resolution was quickly given teeth by the Imperial war cabinet. Lloyd George proposed, at a meeting of the latter body, that prime ministers of the Dominions should communicate directly on cabinet business with the United Kingdom prime minister and vice versa, each being the judge of what was of sufficient importance to warrant such action. He also suggested that for the duration of the war each Dominion should keep a resident minister in Britain to attend meetings of the war cabinet.

Though the Colonial Office disclaimed the imputation that the new arrangements reflected dissatisfaction with its functioning, Hughes was voicing a consistent Australian point of view, dating back to Deakin. 'The present method of administration through the Colonial Office ... has ... become an anachronism', he said. He later referred to it as a 'tortuous channel'. In the Melbourne *Herald* Keith Murdoch asserted that the motive behind the changes was discontent with the 'crusted, procrastinating, bureaucratic inefficiency and ineptitude of the Colonial Office'. Munro Ferguson quickly found that 'the opinion that the Colonial Office had entirely ceased to be connected with Australian affairs' was rapidly gaining ground. There was a widespread feeling that the Dominions were being 'swept into the circle of world politics'; they had 'arrived at a stage at which they can no longer be considered merely as colonies'.

The governor-general was naturally disillusioned. Earlier in the war he had hoped that Australia's growing maturity would mean that his functions would become increasingly more important. In particular he had hoped and constantly urged that the additional role of high commissioner for the Pacific would be added to his duties. In a dispatch of October 1918 Munro Ferguson outlined his concept of the office and discussed the effect of the new developments under three headings, Imperial affairs, federal affairs and Commonwealth government administration.

There was some truth in Sir Ronald's assertion that the governor-general had 'federal' significance. His office was a reminder to the public of the unity of Australia, encouraging a wider patriotism than purely State loyalty. In 1918 his claim that it was 'important to strengthen the position of the one factor, viz., the Crown, which can enforce to a certain extent the observance of constitutional forms and provide a check on irregular or hasty action' was less persuasive. But the actions of Sir Philip Game, governor of New South Wales, in 1931 and Sir John Kerr in 1975 later revealed that Munro Ferguson's view of the role of a monarch in a democratic system of government was not dying as quickly as it seemed.

Concerning the governor-general's role as guardian of British interests, His Excellency stressed that he was the only independent source from which the British government received unbiased reports of Commonwealth policies and attitudes. The suggestion that his role ought to be limited to representing the King and not the British government he countered by pointing out that the latter would then be 'totally unrepresented in Australia' while a Commonwealth minister and high commissioner would resemble 'representatives accredited to Downing Street'. He was convinced of the need for Britain to watch closely Australian affairs, listing five occasions when he had intervened on behalf of the United Kingdom government 'to secure the observance of regular procedure in the conduct of international and inter-Imperial affairs': the commission to the New Hebrides; the channel of communications between the Commonwealth and the commissioner for the Solomon Islands; the exclusion of Maltese immigrants; enforcement of finger-print process on Japanese entering Australia; and the channel of communications between the minister of external affairs and the governor of Ceylon. He could also have mentioned the important conversations he had with Australian leaders concerning Japanese occupation of Pacific islands north of the Equator.

Munro Ferguson's assessment of the governor-general's Imperial role, though slightly exaggerated, was a reasonable summary of the situation as it had existed since federation. It was natural that he should deprecate a change which threatened that role. He failed to recognise that the diminished importance of the governor-general was a reflection of the significant alterations of Imperial structure effected during and by the war. But he was correct in concluding that 'a change which transforms the Representative of the Crown into a social figurehead, having less than ambassadorial responsibility, is one which must necessarily diminish his power of usefulness, both as the official head of the Government in Australia and as a factor in maintaining the unity of the Empire'. His successors were to find their ambassadorial responsibility reduced and then eliminated while the Empire lost the unity which had been maintained prior to the Great War.

For some time Munro Ferguson had shown anxiety at the Commonwealth's increasing drift away from the formerly intimate Imperial ties. This was especially true in the sphere of commerce. He viewed with distrust the Commonwealth's developing trade with Japan. But what caused him most alarm was Australia's relationship with the United States. As early as June 1916 he expressed concern that zeal for Australia's safety might induce Hughes to turn towards America. Indeed, the governor-general anticipated a 'growing orientation of this country towards the U.S. which may in time have a determining effect on Australia's future'. He had no doubt that this would be a retrograde step 'involving weakening of the sense of dependence on the Mother Country and a fostering of Republican sentiment'. This fear increased as the years 1917 and 1918 saw a steady growth of financial and commercial ties between Australia and the USA.

By far the most important evidence of Australia's suddenly enhanced international status was, as Munro Ferguson recognised, her involvement in the negotiations which followed the war. In March 1920, writing to Lord Milner who in 1919 had replaced Long as secretary of state, Sir Ronald commented: 'The formation of the League of Nations has put new aspirations into the heads of the Dominion Ministers, they see themselves transformed into world powers'. Hughes was still in Europe when peace came, having remained after the 1918 Imperial War Conference had adjourned. At the Peace Conference in Paris he was vigorous in defence of what he conceived to be Australia's national interests. This performance, in retrospect, may be seen as uncouth and short-sighted, but it was an impressive debut in world affairs. Australia's international status was later confirmed when, as an independent signatory to the Treaty of Versailles, it became an original member of the League of Nations.

Realising that further loosening of Imperial ties was inescapable, Munro Ferguson pressed for increased British representation in Australia. He pointed to the activity of commercial agents from America and suggested that Britain ought to follow suit. The retirement of Steward in 1919 prompted the suggestion that the moment had come for 'the Home Gov^t to have agents of the quasi Dip^{ic} or Secret Service type' in Australia. Since the Dominions had achieved a position of comparative independence, it was desirable that the British government should have as much information about their 'external condition and colonial activities as it possesses as to those of F[oreign] countries'. These recommendations reflected a recognition of the narrowing role of governor-general and an appreciation of the need for the structure of the Empire to be reshaped to meet the changing situation. It was to be another six years before the changes in the status of the governor-general were given formal recognition.

In the meantime the institution of the new channel of communication made it increasingly difficult for the governor-general to keep in touch with important developments in foreign policy, such as Australia's claim to mandates and her policy towards the League of Nations. The secretary of state expressed regret and forwarded certain relevant telegrams for the governor-general's files, but the likelihood was that the representative of the Crown would be overlooked more frequently in the future.

It was perhaps natural, given Munro Ferguson's background of Imperial federationism, that he viewed the drift of the Dominions away from the mother country with alarm. The announcement in July 1919 that an American fleet planned to visit Australia provoked him to protest against such a visit and suggest that a squadron of the British Navy would be preferable. While this specific suggestion was not followed, the post-war years saw a significant revival in the propaganda of Empire. Munro Ferguson commented approvingly upon the visits to Australia, first of Admiral Jellicoe and later of General Birdwood — 'shrewd emissaries of Imperial Federation' according to the *Australian Worker*. But these tours were far eclipsed in mid-1920 by the triumphal progress of Edward, Prince of Wales — a visit which the British government was anxious to make 'an Imperial event of wide significance'.

Australia's reception of 'The Prince of all the Britains' was wildly enthusiastic. From May to August thousands massed to witness the royal progress, which provided an opportunity for the people to participate in a ceremonial re-dedication to the British connection. Though mainly concentrated around various State Government Houses, the Prince's itinerary also included lengthy excursions into the back-blocks. At the end the unfortunate youth emerged battered and exhausted but with his popularity and the prestige of the Crown enormously enhanced. His tour stimulated Australian loyalty to the Crown and pride in British citizenship.

There were, of course, protesting voices. The Trades Hall Council in Sydney resolved to boycott functions connected with the visit. A few radical newspapers poured scorn on the 'nauseating drivel' and 'sordid extravagance'. But these were isolated criticisms, only serving to illustrate the gulf between radical opinion and the great majority. Australians may have rejected conscription but the majority had retained their fervour for monarchy and their pride in the British Empire. The Prince of Wales personified both. He left Australia in August 1920, followed, in October, by the governor-general.

Two years earlier, in August 1918, Munro Ferguson had been so depressed by his 'elimination as a constitutional factor' that he had been glad his five-year term of office was nearly over. His expressed intention to return to England in May 1919 aroused some consternation in Britain. It was clear that he would be hard to replace. Long reported that Hughes, too, was anxious that His Excellency should stay on. An attempt was made to obtain Admiral (later Earl) Jellicoe, but he preferred to wait until New Zealand became vacant. Eventually Munro Ferguson was persuaded to withdraw his tentative resignation and remain for an additional year. Subsequently this was twice extended, first to enable him to plan and supervise the tour of the Prince of Wales, and later to avoid an interregnum between the end of his tour of duty and the beginning of his successor's. He finally relinquished office on 6 October 1920, nearly six and a half years after he had arrived in Australia.

Munro Ferguson returned to Britain amid general acclamation. 'Oriel', the regular versifier for the *Argus*, lauded his achievements:

> You came among us for the years
>   When war hung heavy in our sky,
> Our hopes together with our fears
>   You shared in ready sympathy.
> No idle sham or vain display
>   Proclaimed a wish for fete or fuss —
> You did your job. And so to-day
>   We're proud to think you One of Us.

Most newspapers in all States lavished fulsome praise on Sir Ronald's exercise of office.

In the radical press His Excellency received a less complimentary farewell. The most embittered outburst was in *Labor Call* which exclaimed: 'Good riddance to bad rubbish ... Ferguson was never of the people, with the people or for the people'. His popularity was credited to 'smug vulgar society cliques ... lickspittles ... profiteers [and] ... perjured politicians'. The harshness of such comment reflected attitudes to the part he had played in the political crisis over conscription.

On returning to Britain Munro Ferguson was raised to the peerage as Viscount Novar of Raith on 6 December 1920. In October 1922, to general surprise in political circles, he was chosen by Bonar Law, after several others had declined, to be secretary for Scotland, thus finally completing his swing from Liberal to Conservative. He retained the post in Baldwin's first administration, to January 1924, but his independence again interfered with his political relationships (he opposed protection and the decision to dissolve parliament) and he was consequently not included in Baldwin's second ministry in November. Next year he became chairman of the committee reviewing political honours, and in 1926 he was appointed Knight of the Thistle. He died at his home, Raith, on 30 March 1934. Lady Helen died on 9 April 1941.

Munro Ferguson had presided at a time of hardship and sacrifice engendered by the war. The special opportunities which this provided he had seized with enthusiasm. As a result the King's representative had reached the apex of his influence as envisaged by Australia's founding fathers, exercising a central though subtle role in the machinery of government. In his close and cordial relationship with successive prime ministers, particularly Hughes, he provided a model of the way the personal influence of an Imperial proconsul should operate.

Nevertheless, the latter part of Sir Ronald's term had also witnessed a reduction in the role of King's representative in the internal affairs of the Commonwealth. To some extent he had over-extended his influence upon the formal organ of the Executive Council. In his concern to retain the governor-general's status it is possible that he had unwittingly contributed to a reduction in what had been one of the most important prerogatives remaining to him prior to his appointment, namely the discretion to refuse his minister's advice to dissolve parliament. He had refused, more than once, to give a promise of a future dissolution, but when his ministers had presented him with advice to dissolve parliament immediately, he had complied. Although he had insisted that in so doing he had been acting as an independent arbiter, the practical effect of his actions was to give weight to the argument that in cases of dissolution (as in the case of other prerogative powers of the Crown) the governor-general should act upon the advice of his ministers. After his retirement, with Australian leaders assuming a greater role in international and Imperial councils it was unlikely that the precedent which Munro Ferguson had set would be disregarded.

But developments in Australia's status had effected a more significant change in the function of the governor-general. Hughes' successful efforts to obtain the right of direct communication with the British prime minister had begun a process which, within a decade, was to see the elimination of the governor-general as representative of the British government. Although he was to retain the function of constitutional monarch, the quasi-ambassadorial duties he had undertaken on behalf of the Colonial Office were to be shorn from him. The result was a lowering in the status of governors-general and a change in the manner of their appointment, developments which were foreshadowed during Munro Ferguson's term of office.

Though Munro Ferguson himself did not clearly perceive the direction in which developments in the office of governor-general were moving, his dispatches and suggestions during the latter years of office pointed to separate representation for the British government in Australia. One man who did recognise the implications of evolving Dominion independence was L.S. Amery, who acted as secretary of state for six months during 1920. In an excellent appraisal of the situation which he conveyed to Munro Ferguson in May of that year, he pointed out that the dual function of governor-general was a 'survival of the process by which Dominion Self-Government gradually became established'. The principle of equality of status would lead inevitably to a point where the function of agent and mouthpiece for the British government would cease and the governor-general would be left in exactly the same position as the King, 'entitled to be consulted in every subject of importance, and to see copies of every important paper going in and out, but no longer himself an official channel of communication'.

5 'Pretending to be the King'

Munro Ferguson's successful exercise of office showed that unostentatious former members of parliament provided the qualities which Australians expected their governors-general to possess. 'Untried juvenile noblemen' like Hopetoun and Dudley had proven markedly less successful than mature, experienced politicians such as Northcote or Munro Ferguson.

The appointment of a successor to the latter was the occasion for a change in the method of selection. In 1902 Barton had suggested that several names should be supplied, from which the Australian cabinet could choose the most suitable, but the suggestion was ignored. A clerk at the Colonial Office minuted: 'there is no ground . . . for going further than the usual practice of first selecting someone and then asking the C'wealth Gov't whether he will be acceptable'. It was not until after World War I that the increased status of the Dominions within the Empire led to a departure from this procedure.

Shortly before returning to Australia in 1919 Hughes composed a memorandum concerning the appointment of governors-general. Asserting that the time had passed when the Commonwealth would be satisfied with a mere notification of an appointment which had already been made, he claimed the right, not only to be consulted, 'but to have a real and effective voice in the selection of the King's representative'. To this extent Hughes was echoing Barton's request nearly twenty years earlier, and following a suggestion cabled by acting prime minister William Watt earlier in 1919. But he went on to suggest that Dominion governments should be able to submit their own nominations and that 'the field of selection should not exclude citizens of the Dominion itself'.

This proposal caused consternation at the Colonial Office. Officials there realised that the governor-general's diplomatic role had justified the retention by the central authority of the right of selection. A senior official, Sir H.C. Lambert, argued that in so far as the governor-general was an agent of the British government, it would be absurd for the Australian ministry to have a greater, or even any, claim to nominate. He predicted that if the office were filled by a local, His Majesty's government would be forced to choose an alternative channel of communication, such as a high commissioner, for diplomatic representations between Britain and Australia. While he reminded Milner that 'an able and conciliatory Governor-General in constant personal touch with Ministers had often had a very real influence', he pointed out that a weak man in that position 'rapidly degenerates into a figurehead and once the influence is lost it is difficult to regain'. In Lambert's opinion the newly instituted channel of communication between prime ministers had greatly weakened the governor-general's position.

This minute was an indication of the Colonial Office's attitude to the changing structure of the Empire and of its recognition of the need for flexibility in the face of post-war demands. Hughes' attitude was supported by the South African prime minister, J.C. Smuts. While prepared to concede change if pressed, the British government was always inclined to wait until that pressure became explicit. Consequently, Hughes' memorandum was left unanswered. The secretary of state thought that the Australian leader was merely 'blowing off steam'.

Twelve months later Hughes proved that he had been in earnest. After reading a Melbourne *Herald* report in May 1920 that a successor to Munro Ferguson was about to be named he dispatched a peremptory telegram urging that the selection be in accordance with his earlier memorandum. The secretary of state was quick to deny any intention of making an appointment without first communicating with the Commonwealth government. He enquired whether Hughes had any name to suggest. If not, Milner was prepared to nominate a man who 'would fill the position admirably'. In any case he undertook not to submit any name for His Majesty's approval until they were in agreement about the choice. Mollified by this assurance, but still reserving the right to submit a name himself, Hughes asked Milner whom he had in mind, adding that any appointment should be for two years only, to allow the next Imperial Conference 'to make such readjustments of Imperial relations as war and other circumstances have made necessary'.

It appears that the man being considered as a suitable replacement for Munro Ferguson was Stanley Baldwin, then a member of the British coalition government with long parliamentary experience, mostly on the back-benches, and later to become British prime minister. Though it is interesting to speculate on the possible course of British history if Baldwin had accepted, the suggested appointment was not entirely appropriate. Hughes was unlikely to have welcomed such a man as representative of the Crown, while Baldwin would surely have chafed at the frustrations which had irked Munro Ferguson. In the event, the future British prime minister declined the offer and Milner submitted three other names for the Commonwealth government's consideration.

By allowing the Dominion ministers the final choice Milner was making a small concession, granting what Barton had first requested in 1902. Subsequently a similar procedure was followed in the appointment of Jellicoe as governor-general to New Zealand. For Hughes, it was to be the last change in status which he urged. By 1921 it was clear that opinion in his National Party was opposed to any further loosening of the Imperial links. At the Imperial Conference of 1921, despite his earlier enthusiasm for changes in the structure of Empire, he argued forcefully that such delicate machinery ought not to be further tampered with. But the Australian leader's initiative was soon to be followed up by ministers in other Dominions. The status of governors-general was still unsatisfactory to South African and Irish leaders.

The three names Milner submitted to Hughes in June 1920 were those of

Lord Forster and Lady
Forster, c.1920

General J.E. Seely, the Earl of Donoughmore and Lord Forster. Of the three
the two first-mentioned were the more distinguished. Seely (later created Baron
Mottistone) had been secretary of state for war in the Liberal government of
1913–14 until forced to resign over the 'Curragh incident'. After serving
gallantly and prominently in World War I, he was for some months under
secretary to the air ministry. R.W.J. Hely Hutchison, sixth Earl of Donoughmore, was the scion of an ancient Anglo-Irish family with long experience in the
House of Lords. He had been under secretary of state for war in the
Conservative government from 1903 to 1905 and chairman of committees in the
House of Lords since 1911. Though neither he nor Seely was an outstanding
public figure, both were men of some political importance.

But the Hughes government chose the third man — Sir Henry William, first
Baron Forster of Lepe. He was born on 31 January 1866 at Southend Hall,
Kent, son of Major John Forster, formerly of the Dragoon Guards, and his wife
Emily Jane, née Case. Educated at Eton and New College, Oxford, on 3 June

1890 he married a childhood friend, Rachel Cecily, daughter of the first Lord Montague of Beaulieu. He possessed neither the political significance of Seely nor the aristocratic antecedents of Donoughmore; Forster's chief distinction was that he had played cricket for Oxford, Kent and Hampshire, had twice represented the Gentlemen against the Players and was president of the Marylebone Cricket Club. He was over six feet tall, dignified, with the spare, typical sportsman's build. He had been a Conservative member of parliament for Sevenoaks from 1892 to 1918, and for Bromley from 1918 until his elevation to the peerage in 1919. During those long years in the House of Commons he had risen to only minor political office; he was a junior lord of the treasury from 1902 to 1905, and financial secretary to the War Office from 1915 to 1919.

The most likely reasons for the Australian cabinet's preference for Forster were his parliamentary experience and his association with cricket. The Colonial Office felt it was necessary to explain Forster to the press, correctly adding that 'a reference to his cricket would probably go down well in Australia'. He was not wealthy and was worried by the well-known disinclination of the Australian parliament to supply an adequate allowance. He accepted the post on the assurance that it would be for two years only and that a special allowance would be provided by the British government. A major personal factor in his decision to take the appointment was that it offered a distraction for Lady Forster, their only two sons having died for the Empire in the war. He arrived in Australia in October 1920. After briefly meeting Munro Ferguson in Kalgoorlie he was sworn in as Australia's seventh governor-general at a ceremony in Melbourne on 6 October.

The end of the Great War and the changing status of the Dominions meant that social leadership of the community, always a significant role for the governor-general, tended to become pre-eminent. Lord and Lady Forster devoted themselves zealously to these duties and succeeded in achieving a wide-ranging popularity. Less of the aristocratic grandees than their predecessors, they brought a more relaxed atmosphere to Government House. Forster was assisted in this by his natural interest in outdoor sport. Though he no longer played cricket he took special care to retain his association with the game, and was prominent in the members' enclosure at Melbourne Cricket Ground for matches against interstate and overseas touring teams. One pastime in which he did participate actively was yachting. He owned several boats and sailed them successfully in numerous regattas.

Nor did he neglect other popular Australian sporting preoccupations. He attended international lawn tennis tournaments and polo matches. He was also a regular observer of the GPS rowing championship in Sydney. But the outdoor activity which occupied the greatest part of His Excellency's time was horse-racing. A few years later, Forster's successor considered that a governor-general needed to be fond of racing, otherwise he would be 'hideously bored by the amount of attendance at race meetings which is compulsory'. He was expected to be seen at jockey or turf club meetings in cities throughout Australia, and the most important such occasion, not surprisingly, was the running of the Melbourne Cup each November.

Vice-regal patronage of this annual carnival helped perpetuate the anachronistic formality of the occasion; their top hats and British *éclat* added style. Before federation it had been customary for a large party of visiting dignitaries to accompany the Victorian governor to the meeting and Hopetoun as governor-general had continued the practice. Cup Week before the war was a time of vice-regal levees, garden parties, banquets and balls. During the war, though 'the cup' was still run, the vice-regal enclosure at Flemington was not used.

Forster revived the glamour of the Melbourne season. Federal Government House was an ideal venue for grand occasions, with spacious grounds and a grandiose ballroom. The *Argus* commented on the Cup Day ball in 1921: 'with the exception of the balls given in honour of the Prince of Wales, there has not been since the war a more brilliant function at Federal Government House than the ball given by ... the Governor-General and Lady Forster'. The *Bulletin*, a shadow of its former self, went through the motions of criticising the expense, but there was little other opposition on grounds of economy. The amount spent annually upon the governor-general had not risen significantly, though it was higher than Hopetoun could have hoped for.

The following table details in £s the cost of the governor-general's establishment, 1912–26, including the £10 000 statutory salary and expenses of the Executive Council Office. Figures are from *Commonwealth Year Books*.

1911–12	1912–13	1913–14	1914–15	1915–16
£23 951	£21 776	£17 967	£24 914	£23 672
1916–17	1917–18	1918–19	1919–20	1920–21
£25 449	£27 053	£24 052	£27 416	£30 957
1921–22	1922–23	1923–24	1924–25	1925–26
£28 063	£28 045	£27 845	£26 777	£29 928

Forster continued to complain that his allowance was still quite inadequate and that he was required to supplement it out of his own pocket.

In addition to making a show in Melbourne society, Forster kept in touch with country areas and with the less lofty elements of the Australian community. For example he was always willing to open agricultural shows away from the capital cities. He took seriously his duties as chief scout for the Commonwealth. The importance of the scouting movement in shaping Australians' ideals and attitudes ought not to be overlooked. Thousands of boys were inculcated with Christian virtues and Imperial and monarchical sentiment; Forster was proud that he had helped to establish the popularity of this movement after the war.

The representative of the Crown in the Commonwealth was expected to embody in himself all the Christian virtues. Attendence at divine service on Sunday became an important item on the vice-regal itinerary. This was a post-war development. With the exception of Tennyson earlier governors-general were irregular churchgoers. Tennyson noted in his diary on 14 August 1902 that Chermside, governor of Queensland, told him that Hopetoun 'would not go to church as no one had approached him on the subject'. Lord and Lady Forster regularly worshipped at St Paul's Cathedral Melbourne and St Andrew's Sydney. They were also generous with their time in supporting charitable causes. Forster was prominent in the establishment of a branch of Dr Barnado's Homes for Boys in New South Wales during 1921. Her Excellency, too, followed the pattern of public activity set by her predecessors. She was president of the Red Cross Society, patron of the National Council of Women and closely identified with the work of the Free Kindergarten Union of Victoria. Besides these formal and administrative functions, she was kept busy attending charity bazaars and school fetes. She was appointed Dame Grand Cross of the British Empire (Civil Division) in January 1926 for her public services in Australia.

Writing to his successor in May 1925 about the social duties of the role of governor-general, Forster commented that 'The incessant speech making is the only fly in the ointment. Where-ever you go, & whatever you do, you are expected to make a speech. The trouble is that one can't touch on anything which is the subject of political controversy and as most things are, one's choice of subjects is limited!' Forster was a cautious speaker, his orations often ponderous or jejune. In October 1923 a casual remark of his predicting that 'Government enterprise would not succeed' led to a call from the secretary of the federal Labor Party caucus, Arthur Blakeley, that he be recalled. But he was allowed one safe topic, namely, praise of the courage of Australian soldiers on the field of battle and the staunch Imperial spirit exhibited by the people of the Commonwealth during the Great War. It was a prolific subject for Forster because a large amount of his time was occupied in dedicating monuments to fallen AIF soldiers. As Australian pride in Anzac burgeoned, he laid innumerable foundation stones for memorial halls, and unveiled plaques, statues and columns. In countless towns through the Commonwealth these tributes to those Australians who had paid the supreme sacrifice in the Imperial cause became a prominent civic feature.

The governor-general's earnest attention to his public duties, whether social, athletic or ceremonial, was not limited to Sydney and Melbourne. Both he and his wife were tireless travellers. He was conscious of the governor-general's unifying role within the federation, recognising that his office not only linked Australia with Britain, but also the six States of the Commonwealth together. From the beginning he publicly emphasised a desire to 'draw closer the interstate ties'. During his first twelve months of office he covered no less than 20 000 miles within Australia, without the benefit of the internal aviation services which his successors were to enjoy. Not all of this travelling was repetitious. In 1924 he spent four weeks in Papua and the newly acquired mandated territory of New Guinea. But much of the governor-general's journeying was merely tiresome. In particular he was constantly required to motor or travel by train between Melbourne and Sydney.

In the New South Wales capital the governor-general's residence, Admiralty House, was too small for vice-regal entertainments. But Forster benefited from the efforts of Munro Ferguson who, shortly before leaving Australia, had

Lord Forster and Lady Forster dedicating a war memorial

persuaded Hughes to purchase in January 1920 the adjacent property, Kirribilli House, as staff quarters and so make available more space in the other house. After the manner of his predecessors, Forster spent an appropriate amount of time each year in Sydney, including Easter, when he was expected to open the Royal Agricultural Show. The winter months were ordinarily spent in the warmer climates of Queensland and northern New South Wales.

Forster's zeal in carrying out the arduous public duties of his office echoed the style in which George V was exercising the functions of monarch in Britain at the same time. The King, too, was a man of moral earnestness, assiduous in carrying out his ceremonial and charitable duties. The prestige of the royal family, consolidated by the war and given added dash by the Prince of Wales, was never higher. The devotion of countless loyal Australian citizens to the royal family reflected the role of the Crown as a unifying symbol in the Empire. As the international personality of the Dominions grew and the Empire's foreign policy began to suffer internal disunity, the idea of the monarchy linking otherwise separate parts of the British community became the essential element in the Imperial structure. Allegiance to the Crown was to be the formal link which signified membership of an organisation which was becoming distinguished as the British Commonwealth. Thus, while the formal powers of governors and governors-general diminished, their symbolic function as representatives of the

Crown increased. But the increased accessibility of the King tended to lower the prestige of British quasi monarchs in Australia.

There had always existed a persistent egalitarian strand for whom the retention of British governors was an unnecessary and demeaning reflection upon Australian self-esteem. The firm control of the Commonwealth government by conservative elements precluded this trend from becoming obvious in respect of the governor-general's office. But the 1920s saw a revival of attempts by various State governments to abolish Imperial State governors.

Agitation against Imperial governors had not been a prominent feature of public debate in Australia during the war. But there was an attempt made by the Western Australian government in 1915 to secure the appointment of Sir John Forrest as State governor. Though Hughes was eager to avail himself of this solution as a means of dislodging a troublesome colleague, when the post became vacant the secretary of state decided not to vary the existing practice. In January 1917 Long informed the governor-general that if the States were to manifest a strong desire for change then the British government would offer no objection. But his successors were reluctant to follow this line.

After the war, feeling in Australia favouring local appointments again surfaced. On Victoria's initiative the matter had been discussed at the 1918 Premiers' Conference. In July 1919 the Victorian treasurer, William McPherson, while visiting London, informed Milner that there existed in Victoria a strong and growing opinion, which his government shared, that in the future Australian lieutenant-governors should be appointed to the States. In October of the same year, when a vacancy arose in the governorship of Victoria, the State government urged the postponement of any appointment until after the matter had been discussed at a convention to consider the future relationship of Commonwealth and States. While an appointment was delayed for a few months, the Victorian government agreed in 1920 to the Colonial Office's selection of Lord Stradbroke.

The premier of Queensland, E.G. Theodore, was the next to raise the question. In July 1920 he urged that 'the time has arrived when self-governing states should be given the power ... to nominate Governor of their own choosing'. He suggested that former Labor minister William Lennon, who had become lieutenant-governor in January 1920, should be appointed governor. But the secretary of state decided that no change should be made without concerted action on behalf of all the Australian States. When a British governor of the traditional type, Sir Matthew Nathan, was nominated, Theodore acquiesced.

The continued reluctance of secretaries of state to grant individual State's requests for alteration in the procedure was, to some extent, contrary to the advice of some servants of the Colonial Office itself. In 1919 Munro Ferguson supported a change whereby State chief justices would become lieutenant-governors. Sir Arthur Stanley in Victoria and Sir Archibald Weigall in South Australia felt that their office was an anachronism. Forster, too, thought of dispensing with them. In a minute of 3 November 1922, one Colonial Office official argued that the appointment of Australian-born governors would localise the 'States' rights' conflicts; 'a local man would be less open to accusations of acting under instructions when taking unpopular decisions'.

The exercise of office as State governor was becoming an expensive privilege. Salaries remained at the level they had been earlier in the century and allowances were limited. In September 1921 Weigall resigned prematurely, giving financial difficulties as his reason. His successor's salary was raised from £4000 to £5000. In January 1922 Sir William Allardyce, governor of Tasmania, also resigned, complaining of his salary and allowance being insufficient to pay for maintenance of a large and expensive Government House. As the Tasmanian parliament declined to increase its governor's salary, no replacement was appointed until December 1924, when a 'democratic' governor, Sir J.J. O'Grady, formerly a British Labour parliamentarian, accepted the post. A smaller Government House was also provided. In other States there were similar complaints. Newdegate, governor of Western Australia, claimed he spent an extra £2500 a year. Governor Davidson of New South Wales complained that his position cost him £1000 a year.

The coincidence of Labor governments in all States except Victoria during 1925 led to a concerted attempt to change the system of appointing State governors. In August a memorial signed by all premiers except the Victorian (John Allan) asked that Australian citizens be selected for future appointments. In their memorial the premiers emphasised that the proposed change was not a new idea and the reasoning they advanced in support of their contention certainly had a familiar ring. The argument that by appointing a local citizen they would considerably lessen 'the expenditure from public funds in the maintenance of Vice-Regal establishments' dated from before federation. Again the premiers stressed that the governor-general was sufficient representation of Imperial interests in Australia, in so far as such an appointment 'automatically modified the status of State Governors'. It was pointed out that during the frequent absences of governors, local men of proven ability and administrative skill had discharged vice-regal duties with conspicuous success. Anticipating the charge that local appointments would lead to the identification of the governor with local party politics, the petitioners pointed out that the gentlemen then being appointed were themselves the nominees of the party in power for the time being in the British parliament. Forestalling the accusation of disloyalty to the King or the British Empire, they emphasised that their attitude was 'entirely consistent with the feeling of the greatest loyalty of His Majesty's Throne and Person and a desire to strengthen ... the bonds of Empire unity'.

The most significant opposition to this memorial came from Victoria, the one State which had declined to sign. There the attorney-general, F.W. Eggleston (later Sir Frederic), prepared a memorandum in November 1925 refuting the premiers' memorial and setting out the reasons for the Victorian government's attitude. In a skilful orchestration of judicial protest, Eggleston defended the continuation of existing practice. He pointed out the advantages to both States and Commonwealth which lay in a succession of returned governors in Britain, well informed on Australian questions, able to explain the local point of view. The most important advantage of the system, he claimed, was that it enabled 'responsible government as developed in the British parliamentary system to be operated with the same ease and efficiency as in Great Britain'.

Eggleston argued that a constitutional head of state should come to office by 'some legal means outside those political forces and attachments' of the community over which he presided. In the case of the British Crown this was effected by hereditary descent. In the case of other governments under the Crown it could be effected by the 'appointment of the Head of State on the advice of an outside Government'. In the opinion of the Victorian attorney-general a governor appointed from Great Britain had no association with local politics and would be completely neutral, with a mind unaffected by local bias. Behind the advocacy of a change in the system, Eggleston discerned the belief that the administrator of the government was a mere automaton. This he denied strongly. Under the system of responsible government, which he regarded with reverence, great powers resided in the head of state: a governor who was appointed by a political party and almost inevitably chosen from among the ranks of politicians or ex-politicians would threaten some of the greatest safeguards of that system. Eggleston concluded his argument by emphasising the symbolic value of the Crown as 'an element of permanence and unity' which was 'an essential foundation upon which the unity of the Empire must rest'.

A vast gulf separated the point of view expressed by the premiers and that held by the Victorian government. The latter presumed the British Empire and the British system of responsible government to be a delicate bloom which ought to be handled with care if it were to be handled at all. Links with the Empire ought to be retained. Any changes which might be considered to threaten those links were to be deprecated. This fear stimulated the often hysterical accusations which greeted apparently minor reforms such as the idea of selecting Australian citizens as State governors. On the other hand, the five premiers regarded the Imperial connection as an exercise in practical co-operation whose success depended upon spirit rather than form. They tended to emphasise this community of interest rather than structure. But at the same time they felt that the appointment of an officer of the State by an outside government was a slur on the competence of that State to manage its own affairs and a restriction upon national self-expression. It was an argument which could easily be extended to the Commonwealth.

The dissenting voice of the Victorian government reinforced the inclination of the British authorities to allow the situation to remain undisturbed. The premiers' memorial, for all its near unanimity, was but a request. If the King's British advisors chose to reject that request there was little that could be done. It is also likely that the premiers were less enthusiastic about their own proposal than was evident on the surface. In the State Labor Parties there were some who clung to an Imperial appointee because such an avenue to British government preserved their status against that of the Commonwealth. Nor was Eggleston's the only communication received in London which denied the premiers' conclusions. Petitions and letters protesting at the proposed change were forwarded to the Colonial Office from Legislative Councils and opposition parties in all the five States, and from a miscellany of conservative-minded bodies including the Graziers' Federal Council, the Council of Manufacturers of New South Wales and the Central Council of Employers of Australia. In this situation it was not difficult for L.S. Amery, who had become secretary of state for Dominions in 1925, to point to 'very strong opposition to the proposal'. His reply to the memorial was brief. Declining to enter into discussion of the issues, and claiming that opinion in Australia was so acutely divided that there could be no assurance that the proposed settlement would be accepted as definitive, he concluded that there was insufficient justification for the abandonment of existing procedures.

Although there was no comparable agitation for the selection of Australian citizens as governors-general, beneath the surface there was a considerable body of opinion to that effect. In June 1918 the Australian Natives' Association, at its annual conference in Brisbane, resolved that 'all appointees to the positions of Governor General and State Governors should be Australian born'. The following year at a conference of the Australian Labor Party in Sydney a motion was carried which demanded 'That the Governor-General be an Australian-born, and be elected by the people'.

Though these were isolated opinions they did reflect a significant trend, which the governor-general himself recognised. In January 1922 Forster drew Churchill's attention to the fact that the premature resignations of the governors of South Australia and Tasmania had provoked a certain amount of criticism. He considered that this criticism would be strengthened if he were to relinquish office after only two years, as had earlier been intended. He indicated his preparedness to carry on for the normal term of five years, if the British government provided additional financial assistance. Prime Minister Hughes, too, was anxious that Forster remain for a longer term. He pointed out that if Forster went 'sharp on the heels of Weigall and Allardyce it will have a most unfortunate effect upon public opinion'. Churchill minuted: 'I think it essential Lord Forster shd stay on'. As a result of these representations His Excellency's term was quietly extended to 1925.

In urging that Forster be enabled to remain for a full term of five years, Hughes praised Their Excellencies for having 'won their way into the hearts of the people'. But Forster seems never to have become particularly close to Hughes himself. The few letters from him in Hughes' papers are brief and impersonal compared with the frequent, friendly, often chiding messages from Munro Ferguson. He appears never to have approached the intimacy which his predecessor had succeeded in establishing with leading Australian public figures. Part of the reason for this was Forster's personality. One Australian newspaper proprietor, Sir Joynton Smith, described him in terms which suggest a certain aloofness. His own limited financial means and the Commonwealth government's insistence that he restrict his expenditure meant that the governor-general hosted fewer banquets and dinner parties than his predecessors before the war. In addition, his devotion to the public aspects of his role left him less time for the business of cultivating friendships with Australian politicians.

Indeed there was less reason for such close association from the point of view of diplomatic representation of the British government. During the latter years of Munro Ferguson's term of office, the governor-general tended to be pushed to the side in negotiations between the Imperial and Australian leaders. This trend continued during Forster's tour of duty. Apart from the Imperial Conferences, which were more frequent during the 1920s than at any time before the war, Australia was becoming increasingly involved in international affairs. Though its leaders never had particular faith in the League of Nations, Australian delegates did participate in the deliberations at Geneva. At first, communications between Australia and the League secretariat passed through the Colonial Office. But after January 1921 the Australian government requested that in future all correspondence should be forwarded to it directly. Pearce represented Australia at the international conference on a limitation of armaments held in Washington during 1921 and 1922. During Forster's term of office an Australian overseas Trade Commissioner Service was established. This direct Dominion involvement in external affairs during the 1920s tended to devalue the governor-general's role as representative of the British government.

After 1920 the confidential cabled reports from the Foreign Office, previously addressed to the governor-general and handed by him to the prime minister, were discontinued. The practice of forwarding occasional Foreign Office papers through the representative of the Crown ceased after the 1921 Imperial Conference, when Hughes began to receive, directly, confidential Foreign Office prints and summaries normally seen only by British cabinet ministers and heads of missions abroad. It is unlikely that the Australian prime minister kept His Excellency adequately informed. Even the forceful Munro Ferguson had constantly complained of being overlooked. In September 1921 Forster complained to Churchill that he was 'wretchedly . . . served in the matter of cabled news . . . we never know what is really doing at home'. A month later he renewed his predecessor's complaint that Hughes was communicating directly with the British prime minister.

In the early 1920s the traditional channel of communication between the Commonwealth and Great Britain showed increasing signs of strain. The Chanak crisis in late 1922 highlighted the deficiencies of the governor-general's office for the purpose of consultation. Among the consequences of this sudden crisis, during which Britain seemed on the verge of war with Turkey, was the shattering of the hopes expressed at the 1921 Imperial Conference that a unified British Imperial foreign policy could be sustained by full consultation with Dominions. The crisis had arisen as a result of a policy initiated without the knowledge of Dominion prime ministers. Yet the British government asked the latter for support and published the appeal before official notification reached the recipients. This action angered the Dominion governments, emphasising the unsatisfactory nature of the existing consultative channels. The delay occasioned by transmitting cables through the Colonial Office and the governor-general continued to frustrate Hughes. He complained that telegraphed situation reports forwarded through the governor-general reached him many hours and sometimes days after press cables had been published in local journals. With hindsight, it can now be seen that the intimate consultation to which

Hughes was aiming was impossible, just as an Imperial foreign policy was to prove unattainable. But at the time Australian leaders were committed to the pursuit of improved consultative devices.

'Consultation' proved to be equally elusive. Britain's failure to include the Dominions in the Lausanne conference called to settle the Chanak dispute provoked further complaints from Australian and other Dominion leaders. This dissatisfaction was shared by Stanley Melbourne Bruce, who in February 1923 succeeded Hughes as prime minister of Australia. In 1924, in an attempt to remedy the unsatisfactory machinery of Imperial communication, he appointed as liaison officer between Australia and Great Britain. Richard Gardiner Casey (later Lord Casey), who was stationed at the cabinet secretariat in Whitehall and communicated directly with the Australian prime minister. Moreover, from December 1926 copies of all dispatches from Forster, including those marked confidential and secret, were to be forwarded by the Colonial Office for Casey's perusal. The quasi-diplomatic role of the governor-general was, clearly, nearing its end.

Prime minister to prime minister correspondence had increased. The flow of defence information between Britain and Australia which by-passed the governor-general had become a 'torrent of documents'. The office of high commissioner continued to afford the Commonwealth quasi-diplomatic representation in London. In 1921 Fisher had been succeeded by Sir Joseph Cook. With channels of communication between Australia and Britain proliferating in this manner the official channel naturally declined in importance. This development was accentuated by Forster's inexperience. His official dispatches showed less insight and knowledge of men and affairs than those of Munro Ferguson. Lacking Steward's diligent research, Forster's reports were commonplace and uninformative, often consisting simply of newspaper clippings without accompanying comment. By contrast, Jellicoe, his contemporary as governor-general in New Zealand, was by no means a mere social figurehead, having a real influence on naval policy.

In 1919 Munro Ferguson had suggested to London that Britain should have 'agents ... of the secret service type' in Australia. There exists some evidence that during the term of his successor the British secret service began to show an interest in Australia. Forster had brought with him as his private-secretary his son-in-law, George Pitt-Rivers. Richard Hall in 1978 suggested that Pitt-Rivers was 'close to the British Secret Service (M.I.6)' and may have been doing work for it while in Australia. Hall has uncovered in Australian Archives a memorandum written by Pitt-Rivers for the reformation of Australian security operations.

Forster wrote of his duties as 'just like the work of looking after a big constituency'. Within the narrowing limits of the office he had been successful. He left Australia on 7 October 1925, and on returning to England lived quietly in his house overlooking the Solent, near Southampton. He died in London on 15 January 1936. While he lacked the zeal and active influence of his predecessor he had provided the type of social leadership that was becoming the most important practical role of the representative of the Crown. His term of

Lord Stonehaven with S.M. Bruce

office had witnessed the accelerated growth of Dominion status within the Empire. The climax of these developments, involving a fundamental change in the role of the governor-general, came during the term of office of Forster's successor.

The appointment of the eighth governor-general of the Commonwealth was made according to the practice upon which Hughes had insisted in 1920. By 1925 the Dominions' increasing status had emphasised the right of Dominion governments to a significant role in the selection of the individual who was to be local head of state. But as the representative of the Crown was still a servant of the British government that role fell short of Hughes' request for the right of nomination. In announcing that Forster's successor was to be Sir John Baird it was publicly stated that the new governor-general's name 'had been submitted, with others, to the Commonwealth ministry, who had selected him'.

I have not discovered the names presented to Bruce, but in the Baldwin papers in Cambridge there is a letter from Amery listing possible candidates. He mentions Seely (who had been passed over by Hughes in 1920) and Sir Evelyn Cecil, 'both of whom would be ready to be considered'. The others he suggests are the Marquis of Linlithgow ('the best of the lot, if he could afford the £6000 or so a year out of pocket involved'); the Earl of Ronaldshay (Amery doubted he had 'the drive and insight' for India 'but would be good in Australia');

Sutherland, probably the fifth Duke of Sutherland ('very eager to do something'); and 'Johnny Baird' ('ministerial experience and many of the right qualities ... may not like the expense and he has recently gone deep into business'). Certainly Seely was on the final list, for later Amery reminded Baldwin of 'the grievous distress created in poor Jack Seely's mind by the fact that after having been sounded as to his willingness to go he was not chosen by Bruce'.

John Lawrence Baird had been born on 27 April 1874 at Chelsea, son of Sir Alexander Baird, first Baronet of Urie, and his wife Annette Maria, daughter of Sir Lawrence Palk, first Baron Haldon. After education at Eton he attended Christ Church, Oxford, which he treated 'as a very convenient centre for fox hunting' and which he quit after two terms. In 1894 he became aide-de-camp to Governor Duff in New South Wales, before entering the Foreign Service, serving in Cairo, Paris, Vienna and elsewhere. He married on 16 February 1905 Ethel Keith-Falconer, daughter of the tenth Earl of Kintore, who had been governor of South Australia from 1889 to 1895. In 1910, as a Conservative, Baird entered the House of Commons, representing Rugby until 1922 and Ayr Burghs from 1922 to 1925. He was parliamentary private secretary to Bonar Law from 1911 to 1916, under secretary of state for the air ministry from 1916 to 1919 and for the home office from 1919 to 1922. He was minister for transport and first commissioner for public works from 1922 to 1924. A few days after the announcement of his appointment to Australia he was created Baron Stonehaven.

The new governor-general was sworn in at Melbourne on 8 October 1925. Stonehaven was short and dapper, smoked a pipe and wore a monacle. Like his old friend Forster, he was an active man, fond of yachting and golf. For the most part he set out to emulate the style of office established by his predecessor. He kept up the links with sporting bodies, was generous with his public time and journeyed extensively about the continent.

The governor-general's style of travelling changed during Stonehaven's term of office. Internal air services were introduced to Australia during the 1920s and Stonehaven did a good deal to encourage interest in their development. His experience in pioneering the use of aeroplanes was not without incident; in February 1926 he survived, uninjured, an air crash. But he did help to establish public confidence in the industry by extensive use of that form of transport for his visits to remote areas of Australia, despite the discomfort of air travel in its early days. After Stonehaven's death, the Australian government was asked to recognise his services to aviation by naming a town after him. The Commonwealth Department of Air acknowledged that he had fostered interest in air transport and supported the proposal but the Curtin government refused. The days of naming pubs or towns after British governors had finally gone.

His Excellency quickly established good relations with the prime minister, S.M. Bruce, whom he considered 'an outstanding example of what can be done by a combination of an Australian Public School and a British University'. The normal social contacts between the two men were supplemented by a shared predilection for gentlemanly pastimes. Writing to his predecessor in December

Lady Stonehaven

1925 Stonehaven expressed his high opinion of Bruce and commented: 'I keep in touch with him by riding in the morning, and am going out to Frankston next week for a game of golf'. It was understandable that, lacking such identity of interests with leading Labor Party members, Stonehaven's opinion of the opposition was less than sympathetic.

Notwithstanding Stonehaven's close relationship with the Nationalist government, his diplomatic experience and his administrative ability, his term of office signified the end of the governor-general's quasi-ambassadorial role as formal channel of communication with the British government. Twelve months after his arrival in Australia a formal definition of Dominion sovereignty was enunciated at the Imperial Conference in October 1926.

This conference confirmed the tendencies which had been evident in the British Empire since World War I, enabling the establishment of a framework which was to preserve that Empire, nominally transformed into the British Commonwealth, for another 25 years. The leading advocate of change at the conference was the South African prime minister, General J.B.M. Hertzog. A Nationalist with wide Afrikaner support, Hertzog had defeated the more moderate Smuts in 1924 and was determined to assert his radicalism by forcing a definition of equality out of the conference. To his surprise he found the groundwork already laid and the British leaders ready to acquiesce gracefully. His aims were satisfied by the Balfour report which declared that Britain and the Dominions were 'autonomous Communities within the British Empire, equal in status, in no way subordinate one to another in any aspect of their domestic or external affairs, though united by a common allegiance to the Crown, and freely associated as members of the British Commonwealth of Nations'. One of the corollaries of this declaration was a change in the role of the governor-general.

The first steps towards an alteration in the role of the representative of the Crown had been taken by Hughes as early as 1918. Thereafter Smuts had argued constantly that the vice-regal functions of the office ought to be separated from the duty of ambassadorial representation. Smuts had prepared a paper on the 'Status of Dominion Governors-General' which was circulated among Canadian, South African and British representatives in Paris on 16 January 1919. Ireland, too, was anxious to reduce the role of the representative of the Crown to that of a figurehead. But it was not until these ranks were joined by the Canadian prime minister, W.L. Mackenzie King, that any substantial readjustment was effected.

In mid-1926 King had become involved in a political dispute with the Dominion's governor-general, Lord Byng, over the right of the King's representative to refuse his prime minister's advice to dissolve parliament. Byng had declined to accept King's request that he should dissolve the Canadian House of Commons and when King reluctantly resigned, Arthur Meighen was commissioned to form a government. But the new prime minister was unable to control the business of the house and was himself forced to ask for a dissolution. On this occasion Byng agreed. Though Byng was legally and constitutionally justified in so doing, practically it was a major blunder. The election which followed was won by King with a comfortable majority. One of the results of this controversy was that the Canadian leader became convinced that it was time to remove from the office of governor-general the function of representing the British government. He arrived at the Imperial Conference of 1926 prepared to press this point.

King found little opposition in London. South Africa and Ireland supported his position. The secretary of state, Amery, had been convinced since 1920 of the necessity for a change such as King was urging. As a result of the consultations of the Inter-Imperial Relations Committee the conference resolved that the governor-general of a Dominion was 'no longer the representative of His Majesty's Government in Great Britain'. It was, therefore, 'no longer wholly in accordance with the constitutional position of the Governor-General' for him to remain as the formal official channel of communication. The conference resolved that the recognised channel in future should be directly between government and government, emphasising instead the governor-general's monarchical function. The report asserted that it was 'an essential consequence of the equality of status existing among the members of the British Commonwealth of Nations that the Governor-General . . . is the representative of the Crown, holding in all essential respects the same position in relation to the administration of public affairs in the Dominion as is held by . . . the King in Great Britain . . .' Finally, it was recognised that a governor-general should be supplied with copies of all documents of importance and should be kept as fully informed of cabinet business and public affairs as the King was.

In Australia there were several direct consequences of these changes. Consistent with the attitudes of Australian governments since the war, Bruce's cabinet decided to take advantage of the provisions regarding direct communication between government and government. Implementation of this decision was postponed until after the Commonwealth parliament had transferred from Melbourne to Canberra. From 31 December 1927 the governor-general ceased to be the official channel of communication between the Australian and British governments. The functions of coding, decoding and dispatching official correspondence, previously carried out by the governor-general's official secretary, were taken over by the cables section of the Prime Minister's Department. J.H. Starling, who had succeeded Steward as official secretary in 1919, was transferred to other duties and the post was abolished. Stonehaven no longer sent official dispatches to the Dominions Office, except in relation to honours.

Writing privately to the secretary of state, Lord Passfield (formerly Sidney Webb), in December 1929, Stonehaven suggested that, as a result of the 1926 Imperial Conference, the post of governor-general had become more important. He claimed that this was 'because the Crown is the sole remaining unifying factor which is an active element in the national life of the self-governing dominions. In every other respect the development of the Empire seems to be tending in the direction of disintigration'. In asserting that common loyalty to the Crown was to be a potent unifying factor in the new Imperial Structure, Stonehaven was correct. The symbolic significance of his post as visible link

'Yarralumla', Government House, Canberra before (above) and after (below) renovations in 1927

with Britain had been accentuated by the increased emphasis on the autonomy of Dominions such as Australia.

Stonehaven went on to suggest to Passfield that the assimilation of the post to that of the sovereign of Great Britain 'makes it harder for a subject of fill'. Though he did not spell out the nature of this difficulty, if he meant that a commoner lacked the aura of monarchy he was referring to a basic difficulty in the nature of the vice-regal role. In the same letter he warned Passfield that the post had become less attractive:

> The number of people to whom the prospect would appeal of pretending to be the King during five years' expensive exile at the opposite end of the Earth must necessarily be limited . . . The only people really qualified for the post are members of the Royal Family. Failing them . . . someone of the highest social position, provided it is combined with a reasonable amount of tact, intelligence and money.

He opposed any suggestion that an Australian be appointed. Such an appointment 'would completely alter the character of the office and deprive it of an element which I believe is greatly valued by the overwhelming majority of Australians, namely, that of a visible personal link with Great Britain'.

Stonehaven's advice that a member of the royal family be considered for the post was a pertinent enough suggestion. Certainly at the time there were eligible such candidates available, and Australia was to see more royal visits in the 1920s and 1930s than at any time in its previous history. During 1927 the governor-general was once again host to such a tour. The Duke and Duchess of York (later King George VI) arrived in Sydney on the 'Renown' on 28 March for a two-month progress around Australia. On 9 May 1927 the Duke ceremonially opened the first parliament to meet in the newly constructed Parliament House in Canberra.

The move of the seat of government to the Capital Territory at last provided a permanent official residence for the governor-general. Extensive renovations to the old homestead 'Yarralumla' had been carried out. This was partly justified by the fact that the Duke and Duchess of York were to stay there while they were in Canberra for the ceremonies in 1927. Government House Melbourne and Admiralty House Sydney continued to be used by the governor-general. An additional allowance of £2000 per year was granted to Stonehaven for the costs involved in his Canberra responsibilities.

In keeping with the expansive mood of Australia in the 1920s, Stonehaven carried out his role with a degree of ceremony. He believed that 'the Representative of the King should live on a different footing and in a different atmosphere from other people, as the King does at home'. But he found that the 'salary and emoluments are quite inadequate for that purpose', falling short of 'the expenditure involved in keeping up the dignity of the position by something in the region of £5000 a year'. The persistent misapprehension of so many of our early governors-general on this matter of the expense of their dignity is a curious feature of the early decades of the office, reflecting, undoubtedly, the difficulties of exercising a monarchical role when not assisted by the aura of royalty. While

Stonehaven did not come to so undignified an end as either Hopetoun or Dudley, he was criticised for the excessive expense he had incurred. One official British observer later wrote that he had seen enough of Stonehaven's regime to realise that 'a lot of the expenditure was simply stupid — and out of all proportion to the public satisfaction given by the results'.

Most of Stonehaven's entertaining was done in Melbourne; he wrote that Admiralty House, in Sydney, was 'too small for any entertaining on a large scale'. Something of the scale of his hospitality can be discovered from his monthly consumption of wine: 30 champagne (French), 40 port, 25 whiskey, 6 brandy, 15 white wine, 3 sherry, 15 claret. In Melbourne he entertained 'on a large scale in Cup Week, i.e. the first week in November, giving two big Dinner Parties of about 60 guests each. A ball for about 2000 and a Garden Party of some 3000 guests. For the rest of the year, we usually have a Dinner Party of about twenty once or twice a week.' It was to be expected that such expenditure would come under attack. In parliament on several occasions there were pointed questions about the governor-general's allowances. The published figures revealed the increasing cost of the office during Stonehaven's term.

In his last few years in Australia, Stonehaven was less keen about his post. Earlier, he had written enthusiastically to Baldwin, thanking him for finding such an enjoyable billet. But the change in functions wrought by the Imperial Conference had disappointed him. By November 1929, in private letters to Dominions Office staff, he was referring to 'the strain which is inseparable from an artificial existence such as one perforce leads'. He felt both a physical strain, due to the constant travelling, and 'a psychological strain which is hard to define but undeniable'. His feeling of isolation, no doubt, increased when, in October 1929, J.H. Scullin's Labor government came into office, and he could no longer enjoy the frequent company of Bruce (who had been defeated in his own electorate of Flinders). Stonehaven regarded Scullin as 'a very decent little fellow,' but they were not close.

The events leading to the defeat of Bruce's government had once again involved the governor-general's constitutional responsibilities. In September 1929 Stonehaven had accepted his prime minister's advice and dissolved the House of Representatives, though it was only 10 months old. The circumstances of the case had left the governor-general with little freedom to exercise his discretion. The motion on which the ministry had been defeated had declared that the proposed legislation (the Maritime Industries Bill) be submitted to a referendum or an election. The opposition leader, Scullin, was unlikely to have been able to carry on the government, and did not criticise Stonehaven's action in agreeing to Bruce's request. But in apparently seeking no advice apart from that of the prime minister, Stonehaven lost an opportunity to emphasise his independence of action.

In October 1925, shortly after his arrival, he had been interviewed by the *Labor Daily* in Sydney and had been 'particularly anxious to refute the suggestion that Conservative political bias' would affect his actions during his period of office. When the reporter showed the 'former Tory member for Ayr Burghs' his voting record and asked what his attitude would be if Labor reforms were brought to him to receive his official assent, he was quoted as replying that 'if a Socialist Government were in power, he would be bound to comply with all its wishes, and his private political opinions, which were not for publication, would have to be subordinated'. It was a classical statement of the political impartiality required in a constitutional monarch. And there never arose any difference between him and his Labor advisers. But his private farewell letter to J.G. Latham, leader of the opposition, was more than non-committal:

> I do hope the sound men, in all walks of life, will rally round you. I have met many such in all parts of the Commonwealth, but they don't give you the support which you deserve, and which, if they could only see it, their interests imperatively demand. I have strained the indulgence of many friendly audiences about to breaking point, by urging this view upon them during the past few months.

Presumably, his urging the merits of the opposition leader upon his audiences had been to selected sympathetic gatherings, for this kind of partisanship never became public.

In part his sympathy for the opposition's values can be linked to the difficulty which had arisen over the appointment of his successor as governor-general. Stonehaven left Australia on 2 October 1930 not knowing who was to be his permanent replacement. For the time being Lord Somers, the Victorian governor, took over under the Dormant Commission.

While the majority of the Australian press blandly praised Stonehaven for his term of office, there were predictable dissenting voices. The *Labor Daily* was critical and *Labor Call* published a contributor's comment that Stonehaven was 'the most expensive and least useful of all the Governors-General since 1901'. *Smith's Weekly* suggested that he had done 'everything possible to prove that an English Governor-General can be at once irritating, costly and useless'.

After Stonehaven's return to England he became chairman of the Conservative Party, in which capacity he was a partisan anti-Labour propagandist during the National coalition government. He was elevated in the peerage to Viscount in 1938. He died in Scotland on 20 August 1941.

6   'Visible link'

In February 1930 the Dominions Office began its search for a replacement for Stonehaven. The presence of a Labor government in Australia, and the need (since the 1926 conference) to involve the King in the negotiations at an earlier stage than previously, made the process more delicate than usual. Once the preliminary telegram to Stonehaven was drafted, a copy was sent to King George's private secretary, Lord Stamfordham. On 22 February the secretary of state was advised that 'His Majesty feels strongly that it would be a grave mistake to give the Prime Minister of the Commonwealth an opportunity of naming the next Governor-General'. The King was anxious to avoid the situation that had arisen in South Africa in 1927 when General Hertzog had insisted on nominating Lord Clarendon as governor-general.

The permanent officials at the Dominions Office knew that the King's attitude was anachronistic. A memorandum by Sir Charles Davis in 1928 had noted that as early as 1920 Lord Milner had invited a Dominion prime minister, Hughes, to propose a name. Where the British government had suggested a number of candidates, Davis pointed out, 'the Dominion Prime Minister has been as free to reject the whole list as he has been to reject a single name'. Moreover, he observed that 'names have been proposed by Dominion Ministers and that in at least three cases, Prince Arthur (1920) Sir Charles Ferguson (1920) Lord Willingdon (1926), the choice has fallen on a name so proposed'.

Despite these signs of change, the Dominions Office bowed to the King's wishes, and a carefully worded telegram was sent to Stonehaven on 28 February: 'If you could discuss with Prime Minister the type of candidate who would, in his view, be most suitable and let us know his views on the subject, it would be of material assistance.'

At about the same time Scullin had also begun to take action. On 27 February he sent a telegram to the Australian liaison officer in London, Casey, asking for details of the procedure that had been followed in selecting governors-general since 1926; in particular he sought to know 'the nature of the participation in such procedure by the Dominion Governments concerned'. He also asked 'whether any of the Dominion Governments submitted any names for the consideration of His Majesty, and, if so, at what stage and through what channel'. Casey replied that the general practice was for a name or names to be suggested by the British government to the Dominion prime minister 'who either agrees or disagrees or states his preference or asks for further names or suggests names himself'. This summary, possibly supplied to Casey by the

Dominions Office, set out the steps followed in previous Australian cases, that is before the 1926 conference. But, as Casey also pointed out, 'in connection with the last appointments of Governor General in the Irish Free State and South Africa the latter governments dissented from the above procedure and made every effort to insist on their right to direct approach to the King'.

As a result of Casey's advice, Scullin was forearmed when Stonehaven informed him by letter on 3 March of Passfield's telegram and suggested that they meet to discuss the subject personally. Owing to their respective engagements no opportunity arose for such a meeting for about three weeks. Before Stonehaven could convey his government's views, the *Morning Post* in London published on 25 March a rumour in 'Australian parliamentary lobbies that Scullin intends to recommend that an Australian, Sir Adrian Knox, Chief Justice of Australia, should be appointed as Governor-General'. On the previous day the Melbourne *Herald* had suggested that five names were in contention, and had tipped Knox. This report was quickly denied by London. On 28 March, Stonehaven forwarded the Australian government's official recommendation.

Through Stonehaven, Scullin advised Passfield that, while recognising 'His Majesty's personal wish must be the governing factor', both he and his cabinet felt 'strongly and unanimously that the Right Honorable Isaac Isaacs . . . would be by far the most suitable appointment', and they asked that Isaacs' name should be submitted to the King. Scullin had assured Stonehaven that the recommendation was 'not based primarily on a desire that an Australian should be given the position, but, . . . that the career and personal attainments of the man put forward qualify him in a very exceptional manner for this office'.

Despite Scullin's disclaimer, it is difficult to believe that the chief object of the Labor government was not to secure the appointment of an Australian. The names considered by cabinet were those of Isaacs and Sir John Monash. It is unlikely that Knox had been considered. Both Monash and Isaacs were Jews; both were from humble backgrounds. Monash was an engineer who had been the highest-ranking Australian soldier in World War I, and had then become chairman of the Victorian State Electricity Commission. But illness had marked his later years and he died in 1931.

Isaacs, though ten years older than Monash, was in remarkably excellent health. He was born in Melbourne on 6 August 1855, first child of Alfred Isaacs, a tailor, and his wife Rebecca, née Abrahams. He had become a pupil teacher in Beechworth, then a clerk in the Victorian Crown Law Department in Melbourne. After part-time study he graduated LLB in 1880. In 1888 he married Deborah Jacobs. A very successful barrister, he was elected to the colonial Legislative Assembly in April 1892. For the next fourteen years he combined a busy legal practice with an active political career. He was minister in several cabinets in Victoria, a member of the Federal Convention in 1897–98, federal parliamentarian from 1901 to 1906 and attorney-general in Deakin's second ministry in 1905–06. From 12 October 1906 Isaacs was a justice of the High Court of Australia, and eventually a powerful influence on that court's interpretation of the Commonwealth Constitution. In 1928 he was appointed

KCMG and on 2 April 1930 he became chief justice. He was undoubtedly a most distinguished Australian.

A copy of Stonehaven's telegram advising Scullin's recommendation was promptly forwarded by the Dominions Office to the King's private secretary. His Majesty was 'astonished' at the Australian attitude and 'strongly deprecated' Scullin's action. Stamfordham explained:

> The King feels that, with the change in the position of the Governor-General made at the Imperial Conference of 1926, which divested them of all political power and eliminated them from the administrative machinery of the respective Dominions, leaving them merely as the representative of the Sovereign, more than ever His Majesty should be consulted in the selection of candidates, and indeed, subject of course to the concurrence of the British Prime Minister, be left to make the choice himself.

George V was attempting to introduce a significant change in the practice of appointing governors, involving a personal role for the monarch which he had not possessed when the British government was responsible for these positions. Prime Minister Ramsay MacDonald telegraphed direct to Scullin on 8 April, suggesting that, on account of Isaacs' age and for other reasons, the Australian government's nomination seemed to present serious difficulties. He proposed that, since Scullin would be in London for the Imperial Conference later in the year, the appointment be postponed until they could discuss the matter personally. Scullin replied insisting on Isaacs' good health (indeed, Isaacs was to long outlive the King and his private secretary). An opinion from the British attorney-general, Sir William Jowitt, supported the King's position and the British government again suggested postponement. Still Scullin attempted to have the recommendation put before the King quickly, pointing out that delay increased the likelihood of unseemly public controversy, but MacDonald continued to stall, insisting that nothing be done formally until Scullin arrived in London. Unable to communicate with the King directly, and with Stonehaven adding his voice to those urging delay, the prime minister reluctantly agreed on 30 June to wait until he reached London.

As early as 1 April rumours of a local appointment were raised in parliament. Reports naming Isaacs were published in Australian newspapers on 23 April. Scullin's position was difficult. He had telegraphed a definite recommendation to London a month previously, but he could neither confirm nor deny the report, since the British government declined to place his nomination officially before the King. In these circumstances the press and the parliamentary opposition were able to canvass the proposal widely, while the government could not defend itself.

It was predictable that the reported selection would be objected to by the federal opposition: its leader, John Latham, described the appointment as 'a gratuitously unfriendly gesture' displaying 'narrow Australian jingoism'. The conservative press was opposed to what the *Argus*, for example, saw as 'a preposterous and impudent attempt to alter a system which has lasted since the institution of responsible government in Australia'. Bodies such as the Royal

ANOTHER THREATENED FALL IN BRITISH EXPORTS.

'ANOTHER THREATENED FALL IN BRITISH EXPORTS' *Evening Standard*,
London, cartoon by David Low, 29 April 1930

Empire Society and the Australian Women's National League were also quick to
condemn the rumoured recommendation.

Not all the public opposition to the rumour was hysterical. The *Sydney
Morning Herald* conceded that to be an Australian was not necessarily a
disqualification for the position. Its leader writer believed that the policy of
filling gubernatorial posts from the old country had 'helped to keep the spirit of
Imperial unity alive'. Cautiously he asked: 'Is it wise to sever a link which is, at
any rate, a symbol of our association?'

If the conservative reaction was predictable, so too was that of the government's supporters. Labor newspapers praised Scullin's choice. So did more
independent newspapers, such as the *Canberra Times* and the *Age*. The latter
objected to the 'hysterical outbursts by the Government's political enemies'.
The *Mail* in Adelaide considered that 'if the Scullin Government has actually
recommended the appointment of an Australian then it is to be congratulated'.

There was some discussion in legal circles about the right of Australian
ministers to tender advice to the King. Much of this was premature, since at this
stage the British government was still the intermediary in the appointment. As
former prime minister Billy Hughes pointed out, 'the right of the Commonwealth to nominate whomsoever it pleases cannot be challenged', but he warned
that the British government need not necessarily advise the King 'to appoint
anyone so nominated'.

In the absence of any official comment on the subject of Stonehaven's successor, the matter dropped out of public view. With the Victorian governor, Lord Somers, administering the office after Stonehaven left Australia, the situation resembled that which had occurred in several States when Labor ministries had declined to recommend a British governor. Somers was administrator from 3 October 1930 to 23 January 1931. In the Dominions Office there was discussion about issuing another Dormant Commission to the acting governor of New South Wales, in case Somers were incapacitated. But no action was taken, lest it give Scullin the opportunity to have the Dormant Commission made out to Isaacs, and let him thereby get into Government House by the back door.

Scullin had no intention of allowing the situation of stalemate to continue. He arrived in England in October determined to press his advice. On 2 October he formally raised at the Imperial Conference the question of the rights of Dominion governments to deal directly with the King in the appointments of governors-general. While the conference was proceeding a concerted British attempt was made to dissuade him from insisting on Isaacs. First MacDonald, anxious to prevent a direct confrontation with the King, tried to alter Scullin's mind. This having failed, an interview was arranged with the King's private secretary on 30 October. Stamfordham told Scullin that the King did not object to the fact of Isaacs being an Australian

> but upon the principle that any local man, whether in politics or not, must have local political predilections, political friends and political opponents — whereas a nominee from England had no local politics and would therefore, as the King's representative, stand aloof from all politics as much as the Sovereign does at home. If this appointment were made and another Party was in office when a vacancy occurred as Governor-General, the same procedure would follow, and the selection would be made from the friends of the Party in office.

Whether or not this was the chief reason for the King's opposition to Isaacs cannot be determined, certainly not until the policy of the Royal Archives is altered to allow inspection of the relevant documents, and perhaps not even then. The impression gained from other files is that the King was opposed to Isaacs not only on this point of principle but also on personal grounds. At an interview with MacDonald in April, the King had shown himself 'very adverse to approval of Sir Isaacs's appointment, mainly on the ground that he had no personal knowledge of him whatever'. While personal objections to Isaacs may have been uppermost in the King's mind, the contention that Stamfordham presented to Scullin went to the heart of the matter.

It cannot be argued that the appointments of all governors-general from Hopetoun to Stonehaven were not political. Of the eight who had been sent out before 1930, two had been previously Liberal politicians (Denman and Munro Ferguson) and four were former Conservative politicians (Hopetoun, North-cote, Forster and Stonehaven). Given the rough similarity of political divisions in Britain and Australia, a former-Tory politician was an uncomfortable 'impartial umpire' in Australian political controversies. Several governors-general had privately expressed misgivings about Labor cabinets. Northcote had attracted no accusations of political bias, but Dudley was so accused, and Munro Ferguson had consistently supported the Hughes non-Labor government. The time when a British governor-general could be seen as an impartial arbiter in Australian political controversies had passed. Disputes in the 1920s between Labor governments and the governor of New South Wales over appointments to the Upper House had emphasised this, and had consolidated the opinion among Labor politicians that British governors were another arm of their conservative opponents. To a man of Scullin's experience in Australian politics the political impartiality argument was a thin one.

But Australia's was a monarchical constitution upon the Westminster model. While monarchs in such a system might possess private political opinions, there existed a convention that these opinions would not influence the Crown in the exercise of its discretionary functions. Such occasions became rare in Britain. But for the King's men in Australia, where the monarchical functions had been constitutionally fixed according to the theoretical position at the end of the nineteenth century, occasions which drew attention to the monarchical function had not been rare since 1901. Moreover, the existence in Australia of no less than seven such mini-Westminster systems, in some of which the governor had the additional role of appointing members of the Upper House, multiplied the occasions for exercise and criticism of gubernatorial authority.

For the British monarchy in the twentieth century the illusion of impartiality was preserved by the royal family. For the first 30 years of the Commonwealth of Australia a partial immunity to accusations of partisanship had been provided by leaving the power of appointing (and removing) governors-general in outside hands. The reasons for this were historical rather than prudent or theoretical. The political impartiality of British appointees became one of the most significant arguments, however, second only to the fear of cutting all links with Britain.

To successive Australian leaders, allowing another government the exclusive right to nominate the governor-general became an increasingly unacceptable form of subordination. Scullin, after all, merely strove to achieve what Barton had asked for 30 years, and Hughes ten years, before. The problem was, as Stamfordham pointed out, if governors were no longer appointed by the British ministry, and if the King himself could not select his representative, then they would indeed become the nominees of one party in power in Australia. When such a man was called on to exercise his prerogatives then his political impartiality was likely to be impugned, particularly if he chose not to follow his ministry's advice.

According to Scullin's account of his interview with Stamfordham, Stamfordham asked whether he would be prepared to take a referendum on the subject. Scullin replied: 'Yes and would, if necessary be prepared to fight an election'. He concluded the interview by warning of the dangers of subjecting the appointment of the King's personal representative to public propaganda and controversy.

Since the Isaacs appointment was a cabinet decision he could hardly have done otherwise than stand firm. On 4 November the Imperial Conference returned to the question of appointments of Dominion governors-general, and resolved that in making such appointments the King 'should' act on the advice of His Majesty's Ministers in the Dominion concerned'. But it also asserted that a formal submission should be made by Dominion ministers after informal consultation with the King. Neither the meaning of 'consultation' nor the practicality of informal consultation in the case of a distant Dominion was clarified by this resolution.

Having established both the right of the Scullin government to submit a name to the King, and the right of the King to be consulted, the Imperial Conference set the scene for a direct confrontation. On 17 November Stamfordham wrote to the veteran former Liberal secretary of state for colonies, Lord Crewe:

> The question of the appointment of a GG to Australia is still unsettled. The King has consulted Lord Macmillan, who holds that, in virtue of the resolutions of the 1926 Imperial Conference, the Prime Minister of Australia is the constitutional adviser in this instance. Whether His Majesty should accept that advice is a question of policy and as to this point we are still considering.

A few days later, on 20 November, Stamfordham called in Casey and asked him to pass on to Scullin, who was visiting Ireland, the King's views on the appointment. Casey did this in a letter the following day. As this document has not previously been published and contains new information, it merits quotation in full:

Office of the High Commissioner
London S.W.1.
21 November 1930

Personal and Confidential

The Rt Hon. J.H. Scullin, M.P.
Prime Minister of the Commonwealth of Australia.

My dear Prime Minister,

Lord Stamfordham, Private Secretary to the King, asked me to go and see him yesterday in order to ask me to transmit to you the King's view with regard to the appointment of Governor General of the Commonwealth.

Lord Stamfordham asked me to let you know at the earliest possible moment that the King would be glad for you to consider the name of Field Marshal Sir William Birdwood as Governor-General. By reason of his intimate and prolonged association with Australians during the War, the King has long had in mind the peculiar suitability of General Birdwood for this appointment, but owing to the necessity, that has prevailed up to the present, for a Governor General to have considerable private means, it has not been appropriate to put forward General Birdwood's name. The King now understands, however, by reason of the economic conditions that obtain at present in Australia, that it has been decided to do away with the Government Houses in Melbourne and Sydney as residences for the Governor General, and to confine the official residence of the Governor General to Canberra. In addition to this, the King would imagine that the temporary economic depression in Australia renders it inappropriate to entertain on any considerable scale. In these circumstances, the King thinks it probable that General Birdwood would be able to maintain a suitable establishment on the official salary, or at least without any considerable encroachment on such limited private means as he understands General Birdwood to possess.

General Birdwood, as you know, has just vacated the appointment of Commander-in-Chief in India, and is either on his way home to England or is about to embark. Should the Commonwealth Government favour this proposal, immediate steps would be taken to ascertain if it would be agreeable to General Birdwood. It is the King's impression that such would be the case.

Lord Stamfordham asks me to say that the reason why General Birdwood's name has not been brought forward on an earlier occasion is that it has only quite recently come to the notice of the King that the establishments to be maintained by the Governor General were in course of being reduced, which at once made the King anxious that General Birdwood's name should be most seriously considered, as it is his impression that such an appointment would be particularly acceptable to a wide range of people in Australia.

The King is anxious to discuss the matter with you as soon as possible, and I am asked to enquire if you would be so good as to let me know, for the King's information, when you expect to be back in London. The King will be at Buckingham Palace from Monday, 24 November, to Monday, 1st December.

If you would like him to do so, Lord Stamfordham would be ready to telegraph confidentially and without commitment to discover General Birdwood's views before you arrive back in London.

In putting forward the above proposal, Lord Stamfordham asks me to say that the King is aware that it runs counter to the suggestion that the name of Sir Isaac Isaacs should be considered. The King has now had time to give the whole matter his full consideration and his views on the former proposal are as follows. He appreciates the desire of the Commonwealth Government to put forward the name of a prominent Australian and he fully recognizes the high qualities and distinguished services of Sir Isaac Isaacs. He wishes it to be clearly understood that his reluctance to agree is on quite other grounds. The King makes no distinction in his mind between any of his subjects wherever situated. He does, however, sincerely believe that it is not in the best interests of the Crown or of the British Commonwealth for a citizen of a Dominion to be appointed the personal representative of the Crown in *that* Dominion.

The King is, of course, fully aware that the Irish Free State has so far been an exception to this principle — but the conditions there, as you know, are quite special.

The King is moved to his opinion, not so much by the Australian case in itself, as by the precedent that it would inevitably create in respect of other Dominions, in some of which the situation is not so straightforward. The King has in mind the probability that, following an Australian precedent, he would similarly be asked sooner or later to agree to a South African citizen being appointed Governor General of South Africa and a Canadian citizen in Canada. The fact of the existence of the two races in South Africa (British and Dutch) and to a lesser extent in Canada (British and French-Canadian) would make the selection of an appropriate and generally acceptable citizen of either of these Dominions almost an impossibility, if the inhabitants generally of these Dominions were to be satisfied. The racial cleavage is so distinct and the political and social outlook of the two sections of the community so marked in both these Dominions, that it is difficult to imagine that general satisfaction would result from the appointment of a native-born individual. But if a precedent existed in Australia, such a proposal would inevitably be made, sooner or later, by pressure from one or other of the sections of the community in South Africa or Canada, should one racial group be prominently represented in the Government of the day.

Lord Stamfordham went on to say that the above does not in any way militate against a citizen of one Dominion being appointed Governor or Governor General of another part of the British Commonwealth, and the King looks forward to the day when such an appointment eventuates, as it would, in his mind, signally mark both the unity and autonomy of the component parts of the British Commonwealth.

Lord Stamfordham considered the question of addressing a letter to you personally on this matter, but he thought it preferable that he should explain the King's views to me personally and at some length and that I should condense the matter in my own language to you. I listened carefully to what he said and I believe that I have reproduced almost textually the gist of what Lord Stamfordham wanted to convey.

I am,
Yours sincerely,
R.G. Casey

In accordance with this request, the Australian prime minister and the King met on 29 November. Scullin recorded that the interview lasted about 45 minutes and that the King 'traversed much of the ground which had been covered by Lord Stamfordham'. But he assured Scullin that the last thing he desired was a referendum or public controversy, and that 'they had the highest regard, personally, for Sir Isaac Isaacs'. Although Scullin's account does not mention the Palace's counter-proposal of Birdwood, it is evident that the suggestion was rejected. Scullin insisted on Isaacs. At the conclusion of the interview the King agreed to accept Scullin's advice, which Scullin formally tendered on 1 December. Next day the news was released.

The official announcement of Isaacs' appointment reflected the King's pique at having been forced to follow the Australian government's advice. Previously such bulletins had come from Buckingham Palace and the form of words was that His Majesty was 'graciously pleased to appoint ...' In this case the announcement was made at Australia House and the wording was 'The King, on the recommendation of the Rt. Hon. J.H. Scullin, Prime Minister of Australia, has appointed ...' Sir Robert Garran, solicitor-general, had even been summoned to Lord Stamfordham's presence and informed of the changed procedure to ensure that the snub did not go unnoticed, and the London press drew public attention to it.

In his diary the King forecast that the selection of Isaacs 'would be very unpopular in Australia', but, perhaps because it had been common speculation for so long, the news, when it finally came officially, did not really cause a furore. Two lawyers, Sir Edward Mitchell and Wilfred Fullagar (later to become Sir Wilfred and a High Court judge) argued learnedly and abstrusely that Isaacs' appointment was invalid because it had not been recommended by a

Sir Isaac Isaacs at Victoria Barracks, Sydney

British minister. Mitchell's argument was the more ingenious, as it was based on the provision in the Constitution that 'there shall be an executive council to advise the Governor-General in the government of the Commonwealth'. He claimed that there was no right, therefore, to directly advise the King. Such reasoning, however, ignored the Imperial Conference as a policy-making body and reminds us of the curious period of Dominion status before the Statute of Westminster (enacted in 1931, but not adopted in Australia until 1942) attempted to regularise the constitutional situation.

Conservative newspapers and the opposition were constrained from further criticism by the fact that the new governor-general represented the Crown and had been appointed by the King. *Labor Call* hoped that 'many more like appointments will be made, and thus show the world that Australians are equal, if not superior to, any imported pooh-bahs'. It observed: 'Had the Labor Government's choice fallen upon an Australian military swashbuckler of the fire-low-and-lay-'em out type, instead of upon a learned judge, there would probably have been much less opposition'. The *Canberra Times* editorial on 8 December presented a rational, non-partisan view: 'The present appointment is one, therefore, which should be regarded by constitutionalists as a constitutional triumph rather than a matter for petty political differences and party standpoints', and it accused critics of basing their opposition 'on political bias rather than constitutional wisdom'.

Isaacs was sworn in on 22 January 1931 at Melbourne. The ceremony in the Victorian Legislative Council chamber was witnessed by 400 people, but a crowd of several thousands waited outside and cheered the new vice-regal pair enthusiastically. After the swearing-in Sir Isaac received official calls at the Commonwealth offices. He made a courtesy call on acting-governor Sir William Irvine at State Government House, Stonnington, then returned to his own home at Macedon.

For the first time since federation, the governor-general had no official residence in Victoria. In December 1930 the federal Labor government had cancelled its lease of Government House, Melbourne, which for a time became a girls' school. In 1934 the State governor moved back in. The lease of Admiralty House, in Sydney, was also terminated by the Scullin government. So for Sir Isaacs' term the governor-general's only official residence was in Canberra. On 26 February he and Lady Isaacs left Melbourne for the Federal Capital Territory.

Though it had been Stonehaven who had first occupied 'Yarralumla', Isaacs was the first governor-general to reside there exclusively. The frictions over the governor-generals' residences, which had dogged the office since federation, were thereby finally resolved. At the same time, the opportunity for jealousy which had on occasion surfaced over the respective duties of governors and governors-general was largely removed. In Canberra, the governor-general was unquestionably monarch of all he surveyed. When on 3 May 1931 Isaacs opened the Australian Rules football season at Manuka Oval and Her Excellency unfurled the premiership pennant, no State governor could feel slighted. Canberra in 1931 might have been a small kingdom, but it was all theirs, and the Isaacs enjoyed it and were popular there.

The State governors naturally regarded Isaacs' appointment without enthusiasm. Sir John Goodwin, in Queensland, believed that 'a *lamentable* error' had been made. In a letter to Stonehaven he wrote that he could not imagine 'that any British gentleman of ability, ambition or devotion to Empire service will be content to be banished to Canberra for 5 years' and he forecast that the post would 'become a political job for any worn out party politician'. Remembering Stonehaven's own previous political career, he hurriedly changed this forecast to read 'worn-out Australian party politician'. In February the governor of South Australia, Sir Alexander Hore-Ruthven, also wrote to Stonehaven describing an official call he had made on the new governor-general: 'He seemed very nervous and jumpy ... I am told he is very much afraid of doing the wrong thing ... He is rather a pathetic figure, poor little man, and appears to be wondering who is going to kick him next'. Governor Sir Philip Game of New South Wales, on the other hand, seems to have been well-disposed towards the governor-general and was a guest at Yarralumla in 1932.

State governors continued to provide confidential reports to the Dominions Office about affairs in the Australian States as they had done since before federation. However, after 1927 such intelligence was lacking in respect of federal government affairs. In that year, on the recommendation of Amery, the British government had resolved that what was needed in Canberra was a British high commissioner. But implementation of this decision was delayed during the remainder of Stonehaven's term, partly because of Stonehaven's fear that if such a post existed Australian public opinion would press that the governor-general's post should be filled by an Australian. He informed Amery that Bruce's opinion was also unfavourable.

Once Isaacs had been appointed, the Dominions Office was able to implement the change. Indeed Stonehaven himself now urged this. Though Scullin, like Bruce, lacked enthusiasm for the proposal when put to him in January, he finally agreed. On 22 May 1931 Ernest Tristram Crutchley, formerly stationed in Melbourne from 1928 as British migration representative, moved to Canberra to begin duty as 'representative of His Majesty's government in the United Kingdom' in Australia. His tasks were: to supplement information supplied directly by the Australian government; to make representations to the Australian government on matters not dealt with directly; and to supplement the official communications by informal representations when instructed to do so. It was announced that a high commissioner was to be appointed in the near future. Delayed by economic constraints, it was not until 1935 that Sir Geoffrey Whiskard took up the post.

Crutchley, who had been on the staff of the chief secretary for Ireland, Dublin castle, from 1920 to 1921, was certainly in the mould of the 'secret service type' suggested by Munro Ferguson. In the following years, as the government of Scullin tottered and fell and State ministries disintegrated the Dominions Office received regular secret reports of affairs for the first time since 1927 from a British official close to the centre of State and Commonwealth politics. In mid 1931 Crutchley reported the formation of a vigilante organization to ensure civil order in the event of a break-down of authority in New South Wales. Probably this was the so-called 'Old Guard'. Indeed, not only was he aware of its existence, he was himself involved in it!

The appointment of Crutchley, and later Whiskard, can be seen as a significant result of the 1926 Imperial Conference, emphasizing the loss of the dual roles possessed by Isaacs, predecessors. No longer an agent of the British government, the governor-general was in theory solely a local constitutional monarch, with his permanent base in the federal capital.

Canberra was, in the 1930s, a very modest capital. In March 1932 Crutchley described it as 'a good sheep station spoilt'. He observed that 'the bulk of Australians regard it as a great joke with a tragic side to it'. He had met 'very few people in any class who share with its founders the conception of a great national capital with monumental buildings' but he conceded that 'physically the place is one of great beauty'. The opening and closing of the croquet season were, he remarked, two of the main social functions.

The pace of life in Canberra, slow though it might have been for Crutchley, suited the governor-general. Frugal by nature, set in his habits, careful of his health and conscious that public extravagance was inappropriate in a time of economic depression, Isaacs eschewed elaborate functions such as Stonehaven had given. Small dinner parties or luncheons at Government House in Canberra were the preferred form of entertainment. In July 1931 he voluntarily reduced his official salary of £10 000 by £1100 per year. He also agreed to the discontinuance of the £2000 Canberra allowance and relinquished his judicial pension of £1750. State governors quickly followed his example.

Much of the economising was made possible by the changed residential arrangements. Whereas Stonehaven had been at 'Yarralumla' for about three months of each year, Isaacs resided for the whole time in Canberra, making brief visits to Melbourne, for such events as the Melbourne Cup, and to Sydney, at Easter. In Sydney the governor, Sir Philip Game, was able to offer the governor-general accommodation at State Government House. But in Melbourne the State Labor government led by E. J. Hogan had relinquished its lease of 'Stonnington' so the lieutenant-governor, Sir William Irvine, reduced to a temporary home in Toorak, was unable to act as host, and Isaacs stayed usually at the Menzies Hotel. At first he was provided with offices at Victoria Barracks. Later a suite in the Commonwealth Offices was made available.

Isaacs travelled around Australia as much as his predecessors. As a High Court judge he had been accustomed to moving around Australia, and this aspect of his role caused him no difficulties. Unlike Stonehaven, he did not take advantage of the new aerial services. Sir Isaac and Lady Isaacs preferred trains.

The chief member of Isaacs' staff was Captain (later Sir) Leighton Bracegirdle, his military and official secretary. Formerly a naval officer who had served at Gallipoli and in Palestine, 'Brace' had an appropriately commanding manner and an imposing presence. He was to retain his post as official secretary until 1947.

Isaacs appeared to find no difficulties in the incessant speech-making, which Forster had found one of the chief drawbacks of the office. The *Argus* reported that 'Sir Isaac Isaacs steps warily at all public gatherings' and was 'one of the most guarded speakers Sydney had known'. In a typical speech in May 1931 to the Millions Club in Sydney on the problems facing Australia, he pledged 'whatever is in my power or duty to do I shall be happy to do. But remember I neither think nor act politically. It is not my job and I have to keep clear of these things'. According to the *Canberra Times* he had a 'ringing inspiring voice' that with 'dignified precision never failed to find the sincere and apt word — the sculptured phrase — that made every utterance of the little white-haired man a very jewel'.

On several occasions in his term of office Isaacs was called upon to exercise constitutional functions. The first, in mid-1931, concerned regulations under the Transport Workers Act, giving members of the Waterside Workers Federation preference in employment in certain ports. The regulations were an attempt to reverse the policy towards the W.W.F. of Bruce's Nationalist administration. A situation resembling farce had arisen. Regulations disallowed by the Senate, controlled by anti-Labor parties, were re-issued by the government after the Upper House adjourned. The Senate petitioned the governor-general to refuse to approve such regulations as had already been disallowed during the current session. In a lengthy reply Isaacs declined, arguing after careful consideration of the legal issues, that his duty was to follow the advice of his ministers. Both contemporary opinion and later assessment by constitutional experts have found his refusal sound, though Evatt pointed out that not every governor-general was entitled to determine, as Isaacs had, issues which are essentially matters of law.

The question of potential illegality was a persistent problem for governors-general. It was to be expected, perhaps, that with his long judicial experience Isaacs would handle the constitutional duties of his office in a judicial manner. There are dangers in such a practice, however, since it implies that he might judge his advisers to be legally in error, whereas this was a matter not for him but for the courts to determine. As (Sir)Zelman Cowen has written, the sound constitutional practice is for a governor-general 'to assent to the action proposed by his ministers, leaving questions of legality to be determined by the courts'.

The second occasion on which Isaacs was called on to exercise constitutional judgement was in November 1931. Defeated in the House of Representatives on a motion which Scullin had warned he would treat as one of confidence, the Labor cabinet requested a dissolution. Scullin's written request that the House of Representatives be dissolved twelve months prematurely was brief, setting out no reasons but merely noting that, the Appropriation Bill having been passed, financial provision had been made for the public services. Isaacs' reply was again a lengthy one. Citing the works of Professor Berriedale Keith, he asserted that only in extreme or exceptional cases should ministers' advice to dissolve be declined. He mentioned considerations such as the strength and relation of various parties in the House of Representatives and the probability in any case of an early election being necessary. Although Evatt considered that the position may not have been as straightforward as Isaacs stated, it cannot be said that he was in error in accepting his government's advice.

At the Dominions Office one internal memorandum questioned whether it was wise for a governor-general 'to set out in such detail the reasons for his action, and whether it would not be preferable for him merely to inform his Prime Minister that he accepts the advice tendered to him without assigning reason'. But this comment seems to have little merit. There had been numerous precedents for a governor-general setting out the reasons for his constitutional action. By doing so, moreover, Isaacs emphasised the fact that he was exercising an independent discretion.

In the resulting election the United Australia Party, led by former Labor minister Joseph Lyons, swept into office. The accession to power of an opposition which had so strongly opposed his appointment might be thought to have caused some difficulty for Isaacs. There was some press speculation in 1932 that two ministers had snubbed him, but this seems doubtful. His scrupulous avoidance of political comment, the convention that the Crown was above criticism, and the fact that Lyons had been a member of the cabinet which had recommended him lessened the danger of any undignified wrangle. Nevertheless, on one occasion there was evidence that not all the members of the new government were well disposed.

Former prime minister Bruce, who had won back his seat of Flinders in the House of Representatives, was assigned in June 1932 the post of Australian minister resident in London. In September 1933 he became high commissioner, and next month finally resigned from parliament. In October he proposed to Lyons the appointment of a royal governor-general in succession to Isaacs, 'the appointment being timed to take effect just before' the Victorian centenary celebrations due in 1934. Both the King and the Dominions Office believed that, whatever had occurred before his appointment, Isaacs was the properly constituted representative of the Crown, and they were anxious to give no impression that he was being treated discourteously. When Bruce put his suggestion before Sir Edward Harding, permanent under secretary for Dominion affairs, he was warned that 'the King was averse to any action being taken which would lead to Sir Isaacs's ceasing to hold office as Governor-General before his term was up'. Bruce replied that he realised this but that Isaacs 'was not in very good health, and that he did not anticipate that there would be any great difficulty in arranging for a change to take place'. However, Bruce admitted that he had 'no knowledge whatever' of Lyons' opinion on the idea, and there was no further official suggestion that Isaacs' term be shortened.

The government did unsuccessfully attempt to persuade first a member of the royal family, and then several high-ranking British peers, to succeed Isaacs. The King agreed, however, with the suggestion of the Victorian government, supported by Lyons, that a member of the royal family preside at the centenary celebrations in Melbourne. Crutchley reported to London that the arrangements for this visit by the Duke of Gloucester caused 'a certain amount of friction between the governor-general and the authorities in Melbourne' over the respective roles of State governor and governor-general. Following the defeat of the Hogan ministry, in May 1932 the government of Sir Stanley Argyle had come to office in Victoria. In May 1934 it reverted to the practice of appointing British governors, but the selection of Lord Huntingfield for the post was a shrewd gesture towards Australian sentiment, since he had been born and spent his early childhood in Queensland. The Victorian government had taken back the former federal Government House as an official residence for Huntingfield. He was thus well placed to entertain the royal guest. Isaacs, with an official residence only in Canberra, was forced to agree that his responsibilities in Melbourne should be limited to receiving the visitor on 18 October and presiding at the formal ceremony at which the Duke declared the centenary celebrations open. Huntingfield graciously accommodated Isaacs on this occasion. He and Lady Isaacs returned to Canberra on 20 October, leaving Huntingfield to act as official host for the rest of the centenary festivities. Isaacs welcomed the royal guest to Yarralumla later in the month. But on 6 November the Duke of Gloucester presented the Melbourne Cup (to the owner of the winning horse, Peter Pan) while Isaacs remained in Canberra.

Shortly before his term expired, Isaacs was called on again to exercise his constitutional power to dissolve parliament. In July 1935 Lyons had accepted a challenge from Scullin to hold an early election in September. As this was only a few months early, Isaacs' granting of the request was not a matter of controversy. On 18 August 1935 it was announced that at the conclusion of Isaacs' term he would be succeeded by Sir Alexander Hore-Ruthven (later elevated to the peerage as Lord Gowrie), who had been governor of South

Australia from 1928 to 1934 and had recently been appointed to New South Wales.

On 5 December 1935 Isaacs was accorded both an official farewell by the Commonwealth parliament and a citizens' farewell by the residents of Canberra. The *Canberra Times*, in a rather florid tribute on 3 January 1936, the day Isaacs left Canberra for the last time, drew attention to his 'association with every good work in the capital and the earnest co-operation of his wife in all those activities'. Isaacs relinquished office as governor-general on 23 January 1936, the ceremony of swearing in his successor, Gowrie, having been postponed for a day because of the death of King George V. Aged 82, he travelled to England later that year to kiss the hands of the new King, Edward VIII, and then retired to private life. After a very active and controversial retirement, he died at South Yarra on 11 February 1948.

Isaacs' term had ended rather quietly. With the United Australia Party in government, pledged to a system of non-Australian governors-general, the conservative press dwelt on the maintenance of the link with Britain embodied in his successor rather than on the achievements of Isaacs. Yet the term of the first Australian to occupy the post was one of the most important in its history. It was important in a symbolic as much as a practical way. Following upon the 1926 Imperial Conference, it was a tentative step in the process of disconnection of Australia from Britain. As Hopetoun had been the model for Isaacs' predecessors, Isaacs was to set the pattern for subsequent Australian-born governors-general.

There were to be about 30 more years during which British governors-general continued to be appointed. In this period the symbolic role of the representative of the Crown as 'visible link' with Britain was paramount. Isaacs' was the fore-runner of a series of appointments of Australians which significantly altered the nature of the institution. Prior to Stonehaven the monarchical element in the Australian Constitution, exercised by British officials, was overtly linked with the protection of British interests. The 1926 Imperial Conference removed from the formal structure the justification for this supposition, and the term of office of Isaacs completed the process. When Isaacs passed constitutional judgement in areas of political discretion, he was acting as a local constitutional monarch, not because of any inclination to further the interests of the British government.

Scullin's insistence that the responsibility for selecting the governor-general lay with the Australian prime minister was a most important development. One effect of this, however, was to leave a vacuum. For it could hardly be argued that a constitutional monarch owed responsibility to the ministry that selected him, yet he no longer owed responsibility to the British government. The constitution makers had not anticipated the situation where a governor-general was to have responsibility to no-one apart from himself.

The history of the office of governor-general in Australia has been one of adapting existing political and administrative institutions rather than inventing new ones. For the first quarter-century of its existence Australia conducted its relations with the external world through the office of governor-general. In the

Sir Isaac Isaacs and Lady Isaacs leaving Canberra by train, 1936.

limited independence which Australia possessed internationally in 1901, few regarded it as inappropriate that this should be so. On the contrary, the most commonly held opinion was that Australia would benefit by such a 'Connecting link'. Part of the reason for this attitude was fear of external threat, and the belief that Australia's best prospects for safety lay within the British Empire. The appointment and arrival of Hopetoun and the military demonstrations at the inauguration of the Commonwealth reflected a conviction that the governor-general's presence safe-guarded Australia's connection with the might of the Empire. The most significant role of the representative of the Crown was symbolic. His presence as head of state was a guarantee of Imperial solidarity. In July 1906 the mayor of Cootamundra referred to Lord Northcote as 'the visible link between this young Commonwealth and the Motherland, securing to us the right to work out our own destiny, without fear of invasion from foreign powers'. Twenty-four years later, the *Argus* still saw the office in these terms. 'Links of Empire', it editorialised, 'require outward expression as well as inward consciousness ... the Governor-General is almost the sole outward link remaining to bind a distant Dominion to its allegiance to the Crown and the Throne'.

The governor-general was one of the most important of what might be called 'Britishness devices'. To many Australians, who regarded their British ancestry as a birthright and England as 'home', the institution of Government House, with its ersatz monarchical trappings and colourful ceremony, was a symbol of their Britishness. The minority who rejected these trappings made the mistake of regarding the office as a mere rubber stamp. Symbol of the British connection it might have been, but the office was also a cog in the system of Imperial management: a part of the technique of Empire.

At first there was little doubt that the governor-general's primary responsibility was not to Australia, but to the central Imperial authority. During the first decades of the twentieth century the Kings' men in Australia, appointed by the British government, were the guardians of Imperial interests. Although the power to reserve legislation for the Royal Assent withered within ten years, the important duty remained for the governor-general of scrutinising legislation and informing the secretary of state of any matters which might be likely to conflict with the policy of the British government. In such cases the governor-general was required to convey representations from Britain to his Australian ministers, and was expected to use his personal and private influence in the direction of British interests. To this purpose his role as channel of communication between the two governments was crucial. As the sole agent by which the Australian government communicated with Britain and thence with other nations, he was uniquely able to supervise those relations.

In the exercise of his Imperial responsibilities the governor-general was required to avoid public exposition of his connection with Australian government policy. The reaction to Hopetoun's speech to the Australian Natives' Association in January 1902 indicated that his influence upon Australian ministers must be private. The most important avenue for this influence was in the close relationship of governor-general with his chief minister. The personal element was crucial. Tennyson's frequent private advice to his cabinet probably carried little weight. Dudley's personal failings lessened the likelihood of his achieving a close and constructive role in Australian affairs, particularly in view of his disputes with the Labor ministers. There had also been some dissatisfaction with Denman on the ground that he had tended to be too ready to take the Australian side on certain issues, notably the establishment of an Australian navy. But Northcote and Munro Ferguson were particularly successful in the exercise of their role as diplomatic representative of the British government. The Colonial Office comment in 1919 that able governors-general 'had often had a very real influence' reflected general satisfaction in London with the way the system had worked. This aspect of the role of governor-general had necessarily to cease when an Australian was appointed. A Dominions Office bureaucrat minuted in 1936: 'from the point of view of closer relations between this country and Australia, it is useful that a Governor-General from this country should be appointed'. It was useful, too, to protect British investment in Australia. As King George V, no doubt, recognised, this was an unspoken role which Isaacs could never fill.

In addition to their responsibilities to Britain, governors-general had an important role as local constitutional monarch. Writing in 1897, Professor Harrison Moore considered that the representative of the Crown would be 'not merely the guardian of Imperial interests, but also the guardian of the

Constitution and the Law' and that in the exercise of these functions he would have 'a large amount of personal discretion'. In the early years of the Australian Commonwealth, before a stable two-party system had developed, his most significant constitutional duty concerned the dissolution of parliament. On the three occasions before 1910 when the Kings' men exercised these discretionary powers there was no significant dissatisfaction with their role. It was generally accepted that experienced British officials provided an impartial authority, who could be trusted to avoid local bias. By 1920 the political stability of the parliament had greatly reduced the discretionary role of the representative of the Crown in this sphere of activity, while the close identification of Munro Ferguson with Hughes rendered less persuasive, at least to Labor Party members, the argument that British governors-general would be more impartial than Australian citizens. This was an important element in Scullin's insistence upon the appointment of Isaacs.

Despite general acceptance of the necessity for the office, Australian politicians were unwilling to sanction excessive vice-regal ostentation or expense. Extravagant display was only appropriate for special celebrations, such as the inauguration of the Commonwealth or during royal visits. On the occasions when governors-general asked for more than this they were rebuffed.

Though ostentatious and expensive entertainment was out of place, the role of governor-general in community activities was important. Speech-making without venturing onto forbidden ground presented difficulties, but it was a vital aspect of the vice-regal role. In this social role the governor-general's wife was an important element. Her presence was as much a symbol of the British connection in society as was her husband's in politics.

Most governors-general were aware of the need to travel extensively around Australia. They recognised that their office represented the federal union of the separate States as perhaps no other institution could do while the Commonwealth parliament met in Melbourne and lacked prestige as a national institution. Until the Australian capital, Canberra, was established, the occasional glimpses of the governor-general represented all that many citizens recognised as the Commonwealth government. Once Canberra had been built the governor-general became quickly identified as its chief resident.

It had been hoped that the practice of selecting British officials for the post would be of practical advantage for Australia. Many considered that this would establish in the mother country a lobby of influential and sympathetic patrons. In practice this expectation was rarely fulfilled. In the first place the appointees were seldom as distinguished as had been hoped. The British government generally found it difficult to persuade ambitious men to interrupt their political career for a tour of duty in the colonies, and the governor-generalship of Australia was less attractive than other vice-regal posts in the Empire. South Africa offered more scope for an active pro-consul, while Canada, less geographically isolated, was also more generous in the provision of salary and allowances. Consequently, representatives of the Crown in Australia were seldom as influential as was hoped and on their return were rarely consulted by the Imperial government on matters concerning Australia. Forster informed

Stonehaven in 1929: 'of course no one ever consults an ex-Governor-General about anything connected with Australia, and they always seem rather to resent any offer of help or suggestion'.

One problem which had from the beginning involved a restriction of the prestige of the governor-general had been the survival of State governors. These officials, appointed from Britain, and with their own vice-regal establishments, hindered the indentification of the governor-general as the Imperial figurehead in Australia. Jealousy of their local spheres of influence often led to friction between them and the principal representative of the Crown in Australia. More often than not, State governors encouraged their State governments to protest against the encroaching authority of the central government. Prior to federation it had been frequently thought that Imperial State governors would be abolished after the establishment of the Commonwealth. But, chiefly because they provided a useful guarantee of State's sovereignty against Commonwealth interference, British officials continued to occupy Government Houses in all State capital cities.

State antagonism towards the federal government was also a contributing factor in the persistent problem of the governor-general's residence. Rivalry between Sydney and Melbourne, and the Commonwealth parliament's reluctance to approve extra vice-regal expenditure, added to a difficulty which was not resolved until the national parliament moved to Canberra in 1927 and 'Yarralumla' became the governor-general's principal residence.

Despite difficulties, the office of governor-general operated to general satisfaction in both Australia and Britain up to and during World War I. The war wrought far-reaching changes upon the British Empire. There had been previous tendencies towards fragmentation, but war accelerated the process. The Dominions' increased autonomy and their growing participation in international affairs meant that an Imperial relationship which had been appropriate in 1901 was less so twenty years later. Further development of the Imperial Conference system as an organ of intra-Imperial co-operation meant that Australian politicians were able to negotiate directly with British ministers. The growth of alternative avenues for correspondence between the Commonwealth and British governments diminished the usefulness of the official channel of communication through the Kings' men. Signs of a change emerged during the term of the most successful and resourceful governor-general, Munro Ferguson. Despite his active interpretation of his functions, the office was, by 1920, suffering a lessening of status and a diminution in responsibilities. A new structure for the British Empire, thereafter to be known as the British Commonwealth of Nations, emerged at the 1926 Imperial Conference. Changes formally enunciated at this conference, and effected in succeeding years, eliminated the governor-general as diplomatic representative of the British government. The altered nature of the office was highlighted by the selection of the Australian, Isaacs, to succeed Stonehaven in 1931, and the subsequent appointment of a British high commissioner to Australia.

The appointment of Isaacs marked a temporary halt to the high Imperial period of the office. With an Australian installed, no matter how loyal to the

Crown or the British connection, the post could not remain an active element in the structure of the Empire. Had Isaacs not been followed by a series of British appointments, the development into a purely Australian constitutional monarchy would have continued at a much faster pace.

A significant change had been wrought by Scullin. The appointment of the governor-general had always been in theory the act of the King. But the character of that act had been altered when the advice upon which the King acted was that of the Australian political party in power at the time. The makers of the Constitution had not envisaged such a situation. One effect of this change was to emphasize the strength of the elected government at the expense of the monarch in the Australian system. Being seen to be the creatures of the party in power, Isaacs and his successors seemed to have degenerated to the 'political dummy' role forecast by liberals in making the constitution. As this was a period of growth in the central power in the Australian government, both politically and economically, such a development was logical.

This seeming innocuousness was emphasized by the policy of continuing to appoint British governors-general. By so doing conservative governments were emphasizing the British connection; but they were also strengthening the arguments of those who thought that the governor-general's power ought to be minimal. Curtin's appointment of the Duke of Gloucester shrewdly continued the trend. But this interpretation of the role of governor-general in the constitution was at variance with the actual constitutional position, and with the activities of the first twenty years of Kings' men in Australia. The second stage of revived activity for governors-general was to begin when conservative governments in Australia began to abandon British appointments and allow the office of governor-general to continue the development of its Australian character begun in the term of Isaacs.

His predecessors were by no means mere cyphers. It is true that the effectiveness of a governor-general depended greatly upon his personal qualities. The relatively undistinguished men who were sent out from Britain helped to mask the strong constitutional position of the governor-general in the machinery of government. But the more successful terms of able and experienced men such as Northcote, Munro Ferguson and Isaacs showed the true position. Under the Australian constitution the Crown, through the Kings' men, from Hopetoun to Isaacs, had played a real part as a residual institution of government in the political and social life of Australia, and as 'visible link' with Britain.

Notes

Publication details for works referred to here are provided in the bibliography. The full title of each work is used for the first reference only, as is the place of publication of newspapers. The following abbreviations are used:

AA	Australian Archives, Canberra
ADB	*Australian Dictionary of Biography*
ANU	Australian National University
CO	Colonial Office
CPD	*Commonwealth Parliamentary Debates*
CPP	*Commonwealth Parliamentary Papers*
DAB	*Dictionary of Australian Biography*, P. Serle
DNB	*Dictionary of National Biography*
HS	*Historical Studies*
JRAHS	*Journal of the Royal Australian Historical Society*
MA	Master of Arts
ML	Mitchell Library, Sydney
NL	National Library of Australia, Canberra
NSWPD	*New South Wales Parliamentary Debates*
NSWPP	*New South Wales Parliamentary Papers*
PhD	Doctor of Philosophy
SMH	*Sydney Morning Herald*
VPD	*Victorian Parliamentary Debates*

Numbers in the margin relate to page numbers.

p. 1   Preparation, procession and swearing in: *Age* (Melbourne) and *SMH*, 1 and 2 January 1901; *NSWPD* 1900, CVII, 5036–5099; J.J. Keenan, *The inaugural celebrations of the Commonwealth of Australia* ('eclat', 52); and W.M. Hughes, *Policies and potentates*, 42–45. Booth: *ADB*, vol. 7. Reid: *DAB*, vol. 2. Hughes: *ADB*, vol. 9.

p. 2   'Khaki clad centaurs': J.A. Cockburn, *Australian federation*, 71. Composition of the Imperial force: CO/418/7/37184, 494. *SMH*, 2 January 1901, is the source for quotes referring to 'unity with mother country', 'newest born of nations' and for the estimated crowd size at Centennial Park. Use of Hopetoun colours: *Australasian* (Melbourne), 5 January 1901. Re-enactment with tall Aborigines: *SMH*, 5 January 1901. Barton: *ADB*, vol. 7. Cricket match: *SMH*, 9 January 1901. Trumper: J.H. Fingleton, *The immortal Victor Trumper*.

p. 3   Hopetoun: *DNB* 1901–1911, and *ADB*, vol. 9. Hopetoun described his childhood, education and 'affairs of the family estate' in T.P. O'Connor, ed., *In the days of my youth*. Broken bones: *ADB*, vol. 9. 'Willowy stoop' is reported in *Bulletin*, Sydney, 16 November 1901.

p. 4 'Ex Governor' described the 'juvenile noblemen' in *National Review*, XV (1890), 614–624.

p. 5 Robertson: *ADB*, vol. 6; 'boys now': B.R. Wise, *The making of the Australian Commonwealth 1889–1900*, 46. For Carrington see *ADB*, vol. 3. E.H. Collis, *Lost years: a backward glance at Australian life and manners*, described 1890s government house functions. Julian Ashton (*ADB*, vol. 7) reported champagne boast in *Now came still evening on*, 38.

p. 6 *Argus* (Melbourne), 29 November 1889, described Hopetoun's arrival. Carrington remarked on astonishment at hair powder in letter to Rosebery, 8 September 1890, Rosebery papers, Ms 10008/115, National Library of Scotland. Jersey: *ADB*, vol. 9. Salisbury's belief that Jersey had found 'less individual power': letter of 21 February 1893, Hopetoun House papers, microfilm, reel M936, NL. For powers of governors and discussion at the constitutional conventions see C. Cunneen, The role of governor-general in Australia, 1901–1927, PhD, ANU, 1973, chapter 1. *Mercury*, Hobart, remark is on 16 April 1891. For Parkes see A.W. Martin, *Henry Parkes: a biography* (391 for 'crimson thread' speech). The *Age* reported the banquet on 7 February 1890. Offer of Canada: Chamberlain to Hopetoun, 2 and 9 May 1898, Hopetoun House papers, microfilm, reel M936, NL.

p. 7 For Barton's letter asking for appointment of governor-general see undated draft to Cox, in Barton papers, MS 51/272, NL. Draft of notice to the press, and copy of the submission to the Queen is in CO 323/459/22523, 103–7. Chamberlain: *DNB* 1912–21. Barton's knowledge of selection before submission to Queen: Hopetoun's letter, 21 June 1900, which mentions 'nothing to prevent my going out', Barton Papers MS 51/326, NL. For intention of remaining less than full term see Salisbury's letter of 27 September 1900, Hopetoun House papers, microfilm, reel M936, NL. *Truth*, Sydney, mentioned 'Victorian intrigues' on 15 July 1900. For Lyne see *DAB*, vol. 2. Lyne's preference for 'statesman of Cabinet rank' noted by Tennyson, diary, 21 July 1900, Tennyson papers, MS 479/2, NL. Knutsford was secretary of state in 1888–92, Ripon in 1892–95, see *DNB* 1912–21, and 1901–10. Salisbury: *DNB* 1901–10. *SMH*'s preference for a stranger is reported on 16 July 1900. 'Max O'Rell' [Paul Blouet] described the 'Grand Seigneur' in *John Bull & Co*, 193. For correspondence between Hopetoun and CO officials in August and September 1900 see CO 418/8, 458–84.

p. 8 Lyne's wishes for Sydney arrival are in letter from NSW agent-general to CO, 9 July 1900, CO 201/629/22087, 120–3. 'Rejoicings': Beauchamp (*ADB*, vol. 7) to Chamberlain, 17 July 1900, CO 201/627/22390. Chamberlain's urging of postponement: 4/1401, NSW Archives. Beauchamp informed Chamberlain on 17 August 1900 of wish to return, CO 201/628/26929, 166. Conveyance details: agent-general's letters 18 and 20 July 1900, CO 201/629/2319 and 23562, 126 and 134, and Hopetoun's letter 23 September 1900, CO 418/8/31141, 430. 'Sallow face': *Age*, 11 December 1900.

p. 9 *SMH* reports plans for welcome: 12 December 1900. 'Cadaverous earl': *Truth*, 16 December 1900. Norton: M. Cannon, *That damned democrat*. Coningham: *ADB*, vol. 8. *Sydney Mail* quote is on 22 December 1900. Hopetoun told Barton of conditions imposed on Lyne on 8 May 1902, Barton papers, MS 51/503, NL. A vivid account of Hopetoun's first official task, upon which I draw heavily, though not in interpretation, is J.A. La Nauze's *The Hopetoun blunder*. CO 'false step' comment, 20 December 1900: CO 418/8/41418, 518. For Chamberlain's cable see CP 78/21/58/26, AA. Explanations for Hopetoun's actions: Wise, *The making of the Australian Commonwealth*, 326, suggests Lyne was commissioned by Hopetoun in anticipation of failing; C.C. Kingston, writing to Barton on 20 December 1900, blamed Hopetoun's health and influence of New South Wales ministers, Barton papers MS 51/373, NL; La Nauze, op. cit., suspects Reid's influence. Monck's commissioning of Macdonald: D. Creighton, *John A. Macdonald: the young politician*, 470.

p. 10   For an occasion when the prime minister of the senior colony was not selected to lead a united government see N.G. Garson, *Louis Botha or John X. Merriman: the choice of South Africa's first prime minister*. J. Mordecai, *The West Indies: the federal negotiations*, shows how failure of premier of the senior colony to lead a united government weakened the federal hold on that colony. Deakin: J.A. La Nauze, *Alfred Deakin: a biography*. Hopetoun's cable and CO minute is at CO 418/8/42280, 521. Madden: *DAB*, vol. 2. *Age* report was on 14 December 1900.

p. 11   Draft of Tennyson's wire is in Tennyson papers, diary entry 20 August 1900, MS 479/2, NL. J. Quick and R.R. Garran, *The annotated constitution of the Commonwealth of Australia*, 705, for Executive Council. For a colonial governor's use of such a body see N.B. Nairn, 'A new look at an old master', in *ANU Historical Journal*, 4, October 1967, 14; also see N.I. Graham, The role of the governor of New South Wales under responsible government, 1861–1890, PhD, Macquarie University, 1972. G. Neuendorff, *Studies in the evolution of Dominion status*, 144, reports Canadian practice. Hopetoun's request for guidance is in list of questions to Lord Ampthill, 30 August 1900, CO 418/8/28560, 462. The first Federal Executive Council minute book is in CP 451/1,1, AA.

p. 12   Hopetoun's speech to naval architects is in *The Times*, 2 October 1900. Hopetoun informed Barton of Lyne's complaint about the 'Victorian combination'; see undated letter endorsed 8 May '02 in Barton papers, MS 51/503, NL. G. Cockerill, *Scribblers and statesmen*, 97, reports Barton's notorious fondness for high living. For his friendship with Hopetoun see Hopetoun's letter to Chamberlain, 14 May 1902, Chamberlain papers, JC 14/1/1/41, University of Birmingham. Hopetoun wrote to Barton about need for 'sound stomach' on 27 July 1901, Barton papers, MS 51/414, NL. For daily discussions see Atlee Hunt's 'Federal memoirs' in *Argus*, 5 December 1931, and J. Reynolds, *Edmund Barton*, 173.

p. 13   For Wallington see *Who was who* 1929–40. Brassey: *ADB*, vol. 7. *Daily Telegraph*, Sydney, reported the Carrington quote on 13 May 1901. A.I. Diamond, History of the office of the Governor-General and of the Federal Executive Council, Inventory number 4, AA, is an excellent brief account on which I have drawn generally.

p. 14   I draw on D.I. Wright, Commonwealth and States 1901–1910, PhD thesis, ANU, 1968, for the dispute over channels of communication. Dr Wright has published a shorter version, *Shadow of dispute*, but I use the more detailed, earlier source. For draft of instruction to Australian governors see CO 418/8/31717, 289. Hopetoun's 9 February 1901 letter is in Tennyson papers, MS 1963/14, NL. The reply of 19 February 1901 and Hopetoun's cable to Chamberlain, 26 February 1901, are in CO 418/9/12336, 267ff.

p. 15   Election of governors: National Australasian Convention *Debates*, Sydney, 1891, 877. Chamberlain's circular, 27 October 1899, is reprinted in CO 881/10/172, 2–3. Compromise over copies: Wright, Commonwealth and States, 20–22. Deakin's 'one governor among many': National Australasian Convention *Debates*, Sydney, 1891, 857. When the tour was announced he was Duke of York, by his arrival he was Duke of Cornwall and York, in November 1901 he was created Prince of Wales, later he became King George V. For convenience, in this chapter he is described as Duke of York.

p. 16   'Hopie': letter from Prince of Wales, 29 August 1902, in Hopetoun House papers, microfilm, reel M936, NL. Hopetoun complained about campaigning on 21 March 1901, Tennyson papers, MS 1963/36, NL. For 1867 tour see B. McKinlay, *The first royal tour, 1867–68*. *Bacchante* cruise: *Argus*, 19 September 1890. *SMH*, 6 April 1891, mentions royal presence in Australia. The colonies' invitation is reported in *Age*, 28 & 29 December 1893. Queen's announcement: CO 418/8/30438, 283 and *Argus*, 19 September 1900. Chamberlain and Imperial federation: J. Kendle, *The Colonial and Imperial Conferences*, 33–40. 'Coming crawl': *Bulletin*, 29 September 1900. Death of Queen: *SMH*, 24 January 1901. King Edward's attitude: P. Magnus, *King Edward VII*, 291–2. For an account of the tour see J. Watson *The Queen's wish*. Loyal addresses: CO 418/9/10711, 187 ff.

p. 17   'Sob of heartbreak': J.M. Templeton, *The consolidation of the British Empire*, a pamphlet dedicated to Hopetoun. For appropriate ceremonies see CO 418/9/5089, 151. Correspondence about precedence and procedure at opening of parliament: CO 323/460/39113, 103–116; CO 418/8/5710, 398–417; and Barton papers, MS 51/390, NL. Objection to Sydney landing: *SMH*, 14 February 1901. Landing: *Daily Telegraph*, 7 May 1901.

p. 18   Timing of Queensland visit: CO 418/9/5927, 177. 'Acclamation of thousands': *SMH*, 28 May 1901. 'Loyal enthusiasm' and 'In times like these': *SMH*, 8 May 1901. 'Possible menaces': *Argus*, 10 May 1901. *Bulletin*, 4, 18 May & 1 June 1901 discusses royal tour. *Tocsin*, Melbourne, 'foul libel': 20 June 1901. For Findley see *ADB*, vol. 8.

p. 19   'Three fourths': *Bulletin*, 18 May 1901. 'Polluting fingermarks': *Tocsin*, 2 May 1901. *Tocsin* approved of governors and denounced levees on 16 May 1901. Royal levee described: *Age*, 8 May 1901. Hopetoun's exhaustion: *Bulletin*, 18 May 1901. Cancellation functions: *Argus*, 11 July 1901.

p. 20   Brisbane speech: *Telegraph* (Brisbane), 25 September 1901. Hopetoun estimated his mileage on 23 May 1902, CP 78/9, vol. 1, 145, AA. Luxurious railway carriage: *SMH*, 18 May 1901. Wright, Commonwealth and States, 219–225, describes disagreement over vice-regal expenses and travel. Hopetoun's dislike of speeches: his letter to Barton 22 February 1902, Barton papers, MS 51/485, NL.

p. 22   For a governor's indiscrete speech see Beauchamp, *ADB*, vol. 7. Hopetoun promised Barton to be careful on 12 September 1901: Barton papers, MS 51/422, NL. Speeches reported in *Age*, 19 June & 12 November 1901 and *Argus*, 22 June 1901. Opposition complaint: *CPD*, VII, 9487. For report of A.N.A. speech and Barton's reply see *SMH*, 28 January 1902. *Punch* commented on 6 February 1902. For parliamentary debate see *CPD*, VII, 9476–9502.

p. 23   Hopetoun reported to Chamberlain, 3 February 1902: CO 418/8/9858, 126–9. *Brisbane Courier*: 1 February 1902; *Bulletin*: 8 February 1902. Cook: *ADB*, vol. 8.

p. 24   Barton's speech is in *CPD*, VII, 9481. Watson: *DAB*, vol. 2. I draw generally on L. Atkinson, Australian defence policy: a study of Empire and nation 1897–1910, PhD, ANU, 1964, 115–127. Chamberlain's secret cable of 9 December 1901 is in CP 78, series 1, bundle 45a. Hopetoun's reply, 15 December 1901, is in CO 418/10/44234, 557, and his cable of 17 December 1901 in CO 418/10/44450, 559. The suggestion of Heaton's influence is in Atkinson, op. cit., 115. For Heaton see *ADB*, vol. 4. *Daily Telegraph* commented on 31 January 1901.

p. 25   For correspondence about appointment of commandant see Barton papers MS 51/405, NL; and CP 78, series 9, 67, 78, 89, AA. 'Utmost endeavours': CO

418/9/13322, 479. Hopetoun pressed Barton on 22 April 1901, Barton papers, MS 51/399A, NL. Proposed court of Colonial Appeal: *Parliamentary Papers*, Great Britain, 1902, LXVI, Cd. 846 [hereafter paper number only will be shown for British parliamentary papers]. D.B. Swinfen, *Imperial control of colonial legislation 1813–1865*, discusses use of power to reserve Royal Assent. Chamberlain's view on disallowance is quoted in A.F. Madden, 'Changing attitudes and widening responsibilities, 1895–1914', in *Cambridge History of the British Empire*, III, 337–405.

p. 26   Instruction to Lamington (*ADB*, vol. 9), 14 May 1901: copy in CP 78, series 1, item 65, AA. Correspondence on Immigration Restriction Bill is in CO 418/10/29263, (81–86 for Hopetoun's secret cable 19 August 1901, and Chamberlain's draft reply 9 September). See, too, CP 78, series 9, 69, AA. The 12 November 1901 dispatch is in CO 418/10/44750, 394–6.

p. 27   For cable 12 December 1901 see CO 418/10/43872, 538. The 18 October dispatch had contained correspondence on Japanese objections to Australian legislation. This reported that Chamberlain did not think that the British government was in a position 'to suggest a modification of the Australian immigration test'. See CP 78, series 1, item 65, AA. Hopetoun asked Barton for 'any shadow of reason' on 8 August 1901, Barton papers, MS 51/419, NL. Barton had informed Deakin of the width of the Instructions on 5 November 1900: Deakin papers, MS 1540/435, NL. For discussion of Barton and the Labor Party see R. Norris, The emergent Commonwealth, PhD, ANU, 1970. Crouch's question is in *CPD*, III, 2807. For Crouch see *ADB*, vol. 8. Hopetoun's 11 November 1901 letter to Barton is in Barton papers, MS 51/440, NL. 'Most anxious': Hopetoun to Barton, 11 December 1901, Barton papers, MS 51/453, NL. For Queensland appeal to reserve see CO 418/10/3604, 583–9.

p. 28   For assent in the train see Norris, op. cit., 178–9. Japanese intervention: ibid. Chamberlain's instruction to defer assent was on 30 January 1902: CP 78, series 1, item 65, AA. 'Much anxiety': Hopetoun to Chamberlain, 24 February 1902, Chamberlain papers, JC 14/1/1/32, University of Birmingham. For salary of governor-general see National Australasian Convention *Debates* Adelaide, 1897, 629, and Sydney, 1897, 254. For Canadian figures see *Statistical yearbook of Canada for 1901* (Ottawa, 1902), 36, and *Dominion of Canada, Sessional Papers*, 1902, vol XXXVI, vol 1, part 1 (pages I-2 to I-4) and part 2 (pages V-100 to V-103 and W-52). For Chamberlain's 1899 dispatch see CO 418/6/21202, 367. The correspondence was published: *CPP*   1905, II, 1101–1118, 'Papers Relating to the Residence of the Governor-General in New South Wales'.

p. 29   Victorian reply, 25 September 1899, is in CO 309/148/29916, 366. For Turner see *DAB*, vol. 2. Lyne's reply, also dated 25 September, is in *CPP* 1905, II, 1103. For Lyne's attempt to combine both posts see cable 26 July 1900, CO 201/628/24221, 95–103. Lord Ampthill commented on Lyne's 'lack of consideration' on CO 201/628/27748, 188. For correspondence between Sydney and London on residence see Barton papers, MS 51/260, 264 and 267, NL; also *CPP* 1905, II, 1104–5, 1109, 'Must be subject': ibid. For Chamberlain's suggestion of allowance of £10,000 see ibid., 1110. For allowance legislation see *NSWPD* 1900, CVIII, 6227–8, and *VPD* 1900, 481–497. Bent's statement is ibid., 491–2, Reay's ibid., 493. For Bent see *ADB*, vol. 3. For Reay see G. Browne, A biographical register of the Victorian parliament, MA thesis, Monash University, 1982, 152.

p. 30   Chamberlain's dispatch, 30 November 1900, is in CP 78, series 21 bundle 13, AA. An endorsement states that a copy went to Barton on 7 January 1900. The reminding dispatch, 11 January 1901, is in ibid. It was initialled by Hopetoun on 15 February and a copy sent to Barton on 19 February. A copy of Barton's minute of 21 February and of the two dispatches are in *CPP* 1901, II, Governor-General's Establishment (Despatches with Regard to), 827–30. Hopetoun informed Chamberlain of Barton's private assurance on 29 March 1901, copy in Deakin papers, MS 1540/2465, NL. Dispatch of 27 March about exceptional expenses is in CP 78, series 63, folder 1, item 1, AA. A copy of Hopetoun's reply, dated 29 March, is in Deakin papers, MS 1540/2465. For questions about the allowance see *CPD*, III, 3333, and IV, 4295. For the retrenchment campaign see H.L. Nielsen, *The voice of the people or the history of the Kyabram reform movement*. House of Representatives debate: *CPD*, IX, 12213–42.

p. 31   'In the lurch': *Daily Telegraph*, 16 May 1902. Hopetoun's secret cable of 5 May 1902 is in CO 418/18/17447, 527. 'All the gas lamps': *Argus*, 17 May 1902.

p. 32   'It must be brought home': CO 418/18/17447, 525–32. The official was Sir John Anderson. The tabled papers were printed in *CPP* 1901–02, II, 833. 'A veritable cyclone': Deakin to Barton, 20 May 1902, Barton papers, MS 51/505, NL. 'The public regret': Hunt to Barton, 21 May 1902, ibid. MS 51/507. For Hunt see *ADB*, vol. 9. I quote *Daily Telegraph*, *Argus*, *Brisbane Courier* and *SMH*, 16 May, *Truth*, 25 May, *Melbourne Punch*, 15 May, *West Australian*, 20 May, and *Bulletin*, 24 May 1902.

p. 33   The *Mercury*'s hard words are on 19 May 1902. Labor critics were Gregor McGregor (Senate) and Charles McDonald (House of Representatives): *CPD*, X, 13042, 13446. 'Able and excellent': *Register*, Adelaide, 15 May 1902. 'Disappointment': *Bulletin*, 16 May 1902. Deakin described Hopetoun's demeanour on 10 June 1902, Barton papers, MS 51/515, NL. 'Lunatic asylums': Hopetoun to Tennyson, 19 May 1902, Tennyson papers, MS 479/2/201, NL. 'Procrastination and delay' and 'in any way responsible': Hopetoun to Chamberlain, 14 and 24 May 1902, Chamberlain papers, JC 14/1/1/41 and 42, University of Birmingham. For *The Times* comment see 16 May 1902. Hopetoun mentioned it to Deakin on 20 June and to Barton on 7 July 1902; see Deakin papers, MS 1540/2486, and Barton papers, MS 51/527, NL. For the farewell letter of 1 July 1902 see Deakin papers, MS 1540/2494, NL, and *SMH*, 16 July 1902. 'A love letter': *Table Talk*, Melbourne, 24 July 1902. Tennyson's comment appears in draft of letter to Chamberlain, diary entry for 12 May 1902, Tennyson papers, MS 479/2. The *Argus* conclusion was on 16 May 1902. O'Connor: *DAB*, vol. 2. His announcement: *CPD*, X, 13229. Parliamentary authorization of expenditure is in ibid., 13440–54. Hopetoun's personal extravagance resulted in financial difficulties for his son, see J. Glendevon, *The viceroy at bay: Lord Linlithgow in India, 1936–43*, 10. Crouch suggested election, *CPD* XI, 14583. McMillan's speech is in ibid., 12944.

p. 35   For tearful farewell see *Argus* and *Age*, 18 July 1902. Balfour: *DNB* 1922–30. Deakin's summary is in *Morning Post* (London), 2 September 1902.

p. 36   Deakin's letter to Barton, 10 June 1902, is in Barton papers, MS 51/515, NL.

p. 37   Biographical details on Tennyson are generally from *DAB*, vol. 2, and from obituary, *The Times*, 3 December 1928. His book of children's poetry was *Jack and the Beanstalk*. Gout: Tennyson papers, MS 479/41/157, 190, NL. See J. Richardson, *The pre-eminent Victorian*, for details of his parents. Hallam Tennyson's biography of his father is *Tennyson: a memoir by his son*. Verse is from 'The Opening of the Indian and Colonial Exhibition by the Queen', published 1886; see C. Ricks (ed.), *The poems of Lord Tennyson*, 1357–8.

p. 38   Imperial Federation League membership: T. Brassey, *Papers and addresses*, 284. For the cricketing son see L. Tennyson, *From verse to worse*. 'Terrible twang':

Tennyson papers MS 479/41/192, NL. Lady Tennyson's letters have been published, edited by Lady Hasluck, *Audrey Tennyson's vice-regal days*. For Way see A.J. Hannan, *The life of Chief Justice Way*. For Holder's accusation see Tennyson papers, diary entry for 5 October 1900, MS 479/2, NL. Holder: *ADB*, vol. 9. Deakin forecast 'trouble' on 24 June 1902, Barton papers, MS 51/520, NL. Reluctance of Colonial Office to issue dormant commission: CO 418/9/21909, 613–9.

p. 39   A copy of Chamberlain's 4 July 1902 telegram is in Deakin papers, MS 1540/2493, NL.

p. 40   Melbourne *Punch* comments were on 27 November 1902, *Bulletin*'s on 29 December 1900 and 19 April 1902. Tennyson reported meeting with Turner and Deakin on 5 August 1902: CO 418/19/37459, 91–100. For parliament's approval see *CPD*, XII, 15356–15405. Deakin's explanation of role of official secretary is in ibid., 15177–9.

p. 41   'Society favourite' gibe: ibid., 16180. Comments by Anderson and Ommanney are in CO 418/19/42161, 336–9. Ommanney was permanent under secretary from 1900–07. For Steward see Melbourne *Punch*, 29 August 1907 and obituary *SMH*, 12 May 1920. Norris, op. cit., 170–1 and 410–6, refers to Steward's secret mission to Brisbane. 'Too big': Tennyson to Barton, draft in diary entry for 26 December 1902, Tennyson papers, MS 479/2. As I have not found the letter in the Barton papers, it may not have been sent. J. La Nauze, *Alfred Deakin*, I, 255–7, describes the dispute between Barton and Tennyson, emphasizing Deakin's peacemaker role. For Steward's complaint to Hunt, 23 December 1902, see CP 78, series 1, bundle 50, secret file 'Conduct of governor-general's correspondence', AA. An undated copy of Wallington's rules is in Barton papers, MS 51/574a, NL. Lord Richard Plantagenet Nevill was the youngest son of the Marquis of Abergavenny.

p. 42   Copies of Barton's letter to Tennyson, 8 January 1903, and Hunt's to Nevill, 23 December 1902, are in CP 78/21, bundle 50, AA. Copies of Tennyson's reply, 16 January 1903, and Barton's rejoinder, 31 January 1903, are in CO 418/26/9107, 51–65. Barton asked for Deakin's help on 24 January and Tennyson wrote to Deakin on 31 January 1903; see Deakin papers, MS 1540/457 and 4716, NL. Compromise is set out in Tennyson's letter of 6 February 1903 and attached minute, Barton papers, MS 51/573–4, NL. For Salmond's definition and correspondence see Tennyson's dispatch of 25 February 1903 and enclosures, CO 418/26/12824, 115–122.

p. 43   Anderson's minute is in ibid., as is Chamberlain's rebuttal, 24 April 1903. *Advertiser*, Adelaide, 27 August 1901 reports Tennyson's support for Aborigines. For his urging of Commonwealth responsibility see Tennyson papers, MS 479/2/77 and 192. Removal of Moran: Tennyson to Chamberlain, 6 April 1903, CO 418/26/16921, 296–301. Anderson's minute is in ibid.

p. 44   Tennyson's comment on Deakin's policy was in his dispatch of 30 September 1902; a copy is in CP 78/9, vol. 1, 167–8, AA. Deakin's letter of 22 June 1903 is in Tennyson papers, MS 1963/176, NL. The *Daily Telegraph*, 23 June 1903, reported the disagreement. See *CPD*, XIV, 1402, 1435, for parliamentary question. For lessons of South African war I use D.C. Gordon, *The dominion partnership in Imperial defence*. 1887 Naval agreement: M. Hooper, 'The Naval Defence Agreement of 1887', *AJPH*, April 1968, XIV, no 1, 52–74. Selborne: *DNB* 1941–50. Atkinson, op. cit., 205–6 discusses the 1902 conference. Hopes of an Imperial council: Kendle, op. cit., 50.

p. 45   Atkinson, op. cit., 208–9, describes the Australasian response to the 1902 conference. Tennyson advised of Reid's support in a cable of 24 April 1903, CO

418/26/15044, 331–4. Selborne complimented Tennyson on 14 August and 15 September 1903: Tennyson papers, MS 479/2/317 and MS 1963/233, NL. For career of Clarke, later Lord Sydenham of Combe, see his autobiography, *My working life*. Reid conveyed his request to Lord Northcote, 23 November 1904: CP 78, series 21, bundle 59, item 8, AA. Hopetoun's memorandum to Barton of 29 April 1902 is in Barton papers, MS 51/497, NL. For admirals' advice see Atkinson, op. cit., 199–203 and 216–8. Tennyson's assertion about his fleet role is in his cable to Department of External Affairs, 18 November 1914, in Tennyson papers A5011, part 1, 19, ML. For Creswell see *ADB*, vol. 8. Latter's correspondence with Tennyson is in Tennyson papers, MS 479/5/37, 38 and 77, NL.

p. 46   Hutton: *ADB*, vol. 9. His frequent visits were reported by Lady Tennyson to her mother, 12 October 1902, Tennyson papers, MS 479/41/191, NL. Tennyson explained his reasons for withholding the document in a cable of 17 February and was rebuffed by cable on 27 February 1903: CO 418/26/6494, 82–6. Tennyson's personal letter, 11 March 1903, is in CO 418/26/13563, 145–159, in which he also forecasts Australia's unstinting support. The *Daily Telegraph* article was on 21 January 1904.

p. 47   Hopetoun's delegation of authority, 7 August 1901, is in CP 290, series 12, bundle 1, AA. Tennyson discussed the practice of Executive Council meetings in a cable of 5 September 1903: CP 290, series 12, bundle 1, AA. See also Deakin to Tennyson, 19 October 1903, in CP 78, series 19A, AA, where can be found Tennyson's delegation of 30 November 1903 and those of his successors. *Australian Magazine*, 2 August 1909, no 8, vol. 10 (new series), 667, commented on Tennyson's unobtrusive departure. Lyttelton: *DNB* 1912–21. Offer of Madras post: Tennyson papers, MS 479/21, vol. 2, 70–1. 'To cross the threshold': *The Times*, 3 December 1928.

p. 48   'High honour' and 'stable era': *Australasian*, 23 January 1904. *West Australian* drew attention to average term on 14 January 1904. Copy of Barton's 25 October 1902 letter to Tennyson is in CP 78, series 21, bundle 50, AA. Tennyson forwarded it to London on 26 October 1903: CO 418/19/44392, 361–2. Inquiry about suitability of Northcote: Tennyson to Barton, 27 July 1903, Barton papers, MS 51/646, NL. Cabinet's consideration is indicated by a note in Barton's diary, 3 August 1903: 'Northcote — yes'; see Barton papers, MS 51/646, NL. 'Spare little man': *Australian Magazine*, 1 February 1908, 439. For Northcote see *DNB* 1901–11, and *DAB*, vol. 2.

p. 50   Northcote described his wife's wish to be out of England to Selborne, 18 August 1902: Selborne papers, vol. 33, 207–8, Bodleian Library, Oxford. I quote the *Age* of 22 January 1901 and *Argus*, 8 February 1904. 'Slow': Forrest to Tennyson, 25 May 1904, Tennyson papers, A5011, part 2, 104, ML. 'Not showy': Way to Tennyson, 12 October 1904, Tennyson papers, MS 1963/281, NL. Paderewski visited Australia in 1904; for Northcote's comment see Selborne papers, vol. 197, 119–124, Bodleian Library, Oxford. 'Tactful, patient': Deakin's note in minute book, 3 pages from end; Deakin papers, MS 1540/19/275, NL. La Nauze, *Deakin*, II, 362, also refers to this note.

p. 52   For Deakin's *Morning Post* articles see J.A. La Nauze, 'Alfred Deakin and the *Morning Post*', *HS*, vol. 6, May 1955, 361–75, and A. Deakin, *Federated Australia*, J.A. La Nauze, ed. The remark to Jebb (*DNB* 1901–10) is quoted in La Nauze, *Deakin*, II, 353. 'Growing number of ex-Australians': *SMH*, 21 January 1904. 'Chivalrous gentleman' and 'nice fellow': Northcote to Balfour, 21 August and 22 November 1904, Balfour papers, vol. XV, Add. Mss. 49697, 46–50, British Library; La Nauze, *Deakin*, II, 363, also quotes this. 'Respect for blue books': *Punch* (Melbourne), 17 September 1908. 'Three elevens' speech is reported in *Age*, 2 February 1904. For parliamentary vote see *CPD*, XIX, 1243.

p. 53   'Considerable weight': *Argus*, 22 April 1904. For formation of the Labor government see H.S. Broadhead, The Australian Federal Labour Party 1900– 1905, M.A., University of Melbourne, 1959. Northcote's 7 March 1904 letter to Lyttelton is in Chandos papers, vol. 1, 2/27, Churchill College Archives, Cambridge. For Tennyson's criticism of Barton's reliance on Labor see his diary entry, 1 January 1903, Tennyson papers, MS 479/2, NL. Reid interview: *Argus*, 30 April 1904. 'Fair trial': Northcote to secretary of state, 23 April 1904, CO 418/31/19140, 239–42. 'Honey & butter': Northcote to Balfour, 9 May 1904, Balfour papers, Add. Mss. 49697, vol. XV, 43–4 British Library. He asked Deakin about visiting Tasmania on 19 June 1904, Deakin papers, MS 1540/3903, NL. Tour of Northern Territory: *Review of Reviews for Australasia*, XXXI, no. 3, 1 September 1907, 232–40.

p. 54   'Ponderous style': *Australian Magazine*, 2 August 1909, 670. Response to his sympathy for Melanesians: *Argus*, 11 July 1904. Debate on the Higgs (*ADB* vol. 9) motion: *CPD*, XXVII, 3438–53. Pearce: P. Heydon, *Quiet decision: A study of George Foster Pearce*.

p. 55   Northcote's undated defence of his speech is in Deakin papers, MS 1540/3918, NL. Higgs' compliment: *CPD*, XXVII, 3439. Defeat of Labor government: *CPD*, XXI, 4264. Griffith's 'calmer authority': [C. 5091], vol. 1, 557. Griffith: *ADB*, vol. 9.

p. 56   Carrington precedent: *NSWPD*, 1888–89, XXXVI, 1644–59. Dibbs: *ADB*, vol. 4. I use E. Forsey, *The royal power of dissolution of parliament in the British Commonwealth* as the definitive source on dissolutions. For the three refusals of dissolutions in 1899 see ibid., 285. The second edition of Todd's *Parliamentary government* was published in 1894; Northcote refers to it in his dispatch of 15 August 1904, CP 78, series 9, vol. 1, 337, AA. *Age, Argus* and other newspaper comment was on 13 August 1904. A copy of Northcote's letter to Watson rejecting a general election, 15 August 1904, is in CP 78, series 9, vol. 1, AA; his letter to Balfour, 21 August 1904, is in Balfour papers, Add. Mss. 49697, vol. XV, 46–7, British Library. Keith: *DNB* 1941–50. I quote his *Responsible government in the Dominions*, 191.

p. 57   Evatt: K. Tennant, *Evatt: politics and justice*. I draw on his, *The King and his Dominion governors*, 50, and Forsey, op. cit., 36. Northcote's cable expressing disquiet, 2 December 1904, and Colonial Office comments, are in CO 418/31/ 40895, 672–4. For past Colonial Office guidance of colonial legislators see Swinfen, op. cit., 5–6. Copies of Lyttelton's cable of 6 December and Northcote's letter to Symon (*DAB*, vol. 2) of 10 December are in CP 78, series 1, item 1/828, AA.

p. 58   Symon's memorandum, 14 December 1904, Northcote's letter to Reid of same date, and Reid's note: 'Ministers advise Your Excellency to give your assent to the Bill as passed by Parliament', are all in ibid. Northcote wrote to Deakin on 1 December 1904, Deakin papers, MS 1540/3908, NL. Questions in the House of Lords: Deakin papers MS 1540/3910, NL. The incident is referred to in La Nauze, *Deakin*, II, 380. Copies of Northcote's dispatch, 15 December 1904, explaining his action and asking for British government's views, and of Lyttelton's reply, 2 February 1905, are in CP 78, series 1, item 1/828, AA.

p. 59   Northcote refers to Findley's advice in a letter to Deakin, 24 March 1905, Deakin papers, MS 1540/3910, NL. The official, H.B. Cox, minuted his opinion on Northcote's cable, 2 December 1904, CO 418/3/40895, 673. For a close examination of the attempt to ensure that States recommended honours through the governor-general see Wright, Commonwealth and States, 90–98. Chamberlain's dispatch to Hopetoun, 14 March 1902, accepting Tennyson's compromise, is in CP 78, series 4, vol. 1, AA.

p. 60 Lyttelton's reproof of Northcote is referred to in Northcote to Deakin, 18 April 1904, Deakin papers, MS 1540/3900, NL. Lyttelton warned Northcote that State lists were for his personal observations on 8 July 1904, CP 78, series 4, vol. 1, AA. The circular sent by Northcote to all State governors, 2 December 1904, is reproduced in CO 881/11/189, 22–3. Rules in Lyttelton's circular dispatch of 17 April 1905: ibid., 28–9. For Talbot see obituary, *SMH*, 17 January 1929. His objection: CO 881/11/189, 31–2. For Bent's dinner behaviour see Northcote to Selborne, 9 March 1904, Selborne papers, vol. 197, 103–5, Bodleian Library, Oxford.

p. 61 Talbot's 'tantamount to the abandonment' dispatch, 21 January 1906, is reproduced in CO 881/11/189, 47–8. For resignation thoughts see Elgin to Northcote, 9 August 1906, Northcote papers, CO gifts and deposits, PRO 30/56/1, 97–100. For Northcote's own seeking after honours, see November 1903 correspondence, Mss Eng Hist C747, 24–30, Bodleian Library, Oxford. 'Make Australians realize': Northcote to Elgin, 28 May 1906, copy in Northcote papers, PRO 30/56/1, 62. Wright, Commonwealth and States, 28–31, accuses Northcote of not understanding 'the business in which he was meddling'. 'Best interests of Australia': Northcote's dispatch 28 May 1906, copy in CO 881/11/189, 63. For agreement of governors to the procedure see minute by Sir Harry Rawson, to Elgin, 29 May 1906, copy in ibid., 64–5. Crewe (*DNB* 1941–50) declined to disturb compromise: dispatch, 18 August 1908: CP 78, series 4, vol. 1. 'Primus inter pares': Tennyson to Northcote, 16 September 1903, Tennyson papers, MS 479/2/320, NL. I rely on la Nauze, *Deakin*, II, 381–404 for the fall of Reid's ministry.

p. 62 *Argus* and *Register*, 3 July 1905, comment on anxiety among Protectionists. *SMH* and *Daily Telegraph*, 30 June, 1 July, and *Argus*, 4 July 1905, urge dissolution. *Age*, 3 July 1905, warns that a dissolution would be an 'outrage'. *Advertiser* and *Register* commented on 3 July, *West Australian* on 1 July 1905. Deakin's letter assuring Northcote of Watson's support, and Northcote's memorandum, both dated 3 July 1905, are enclosures in Northcote's dispatch of 4 July 1905, CO 418/36/28156, 274–84. *SMH*, 5 July 1905, accepts Northcote's decision. Reid's private displeasure: Selborne papers, vol. 197, Bodleian Library, Oxford. *Advertiser* letter: 4 July 1905.

p. 63 Northcote complained of not receiving the States' correspondence on 8 February 1904, CO 418/31/9044, 82–7. He raised the issue again on 30 June 1905, CO 418/36/28154, 251–62. Elgin (*DNB* 1912–21) declines to disturb compromise: dispatch, 11 January 1906, CO 418/40/44464, 568–75. Deakin's memorandum, quoted, is dated 7 March 1906; CO 418/44/12371, 196–210.

p. 64 Elgin's suggestion of consultation with governors is referred to by Wright, Commonwealth and States, 34. A copy of Deakin's advice to let the matter rest is in CP 78, series 21, bundle 50, folder 1, file P.M. 06/440, AA.

p. 65 Correspondence over Australia's discriminatory legislation: CO 886/1/3. The 28 September 1905 letter from India Office and the CO circular dispatch advising reservation is in ibid., 224–7. Seddon: *DNB* 1901–11. Suggested withdrawal of CO dispatch on 15 February 1906: CO 418/44/5392, 134–5. Deakin's memorandum is enclosed in Northcote's dispatch of 7 March 1906, CO 418/44/12370, 188–95. Resolution of Premiers Conference: Rawson's dispatch, 26 April 1906, CO 418/46/21664, 76–7.

p. 66   A Copy of Elgin's dispatch, 9 May 1906, withdrawing hs earlier circular, is in CO 886/1/3, 234. For Indian and CO correspondence over 1906 amendments to Immigration Act, see CO 418/50/11904, 17500 & 25125, 44–9, 54–73, and 84. Elgin's cable of 4 October 1906 about the preference bill is in CO 418/45/36425, 291–7.

p. 67   Isaacs' and Deakin's advice to reserve assent is in Northcote's dispatch of 17 October 1906, CO 418/45/42460, 353–65. Kendle, op. cit., 83–106, has an excellent account of the 1907 conference. La Nauze, *Deakin*, II, 493–514, and 488–9, discusses Deakin's role at the conference and the Judiciary Bill dispute. I rely on G. Sawer, *Australian federal politics and law, 1901–1929*, 56–7 and 69 for my summary of the object of the Judiciary Bill. 'Perhaps you will consider': Elgin to Northcote, 2 October 1907, CO 418/56/33318, 300–3. Northcote's reply is in ibid. My account of Deakin's second thoughts is based on Northcote's dispatch, 14 October 1906, CO 418/52/40578, 589–93.

p. 68   Northcote explained Deakin's position in ibid. Northcote's telegram of 9 October 1906 is in CO 418/52/35967, 564–75. I quote Keith's and other CO minutes, ibid. The 11 October telegram against reservation is in CO 418/56/33118, 306.

p. 69   Reservation of assent is mandatory under section 74 of the Australian Constitution. Legislation affecting merchant shipping also required the Royal Assent to be reserved. A copy of Keith's memorandum summary, 29 June 1908, is in CO 886/1/4. 'Alarm and regret': Deakin to secretary of state, 4 February 1908, CO 418/68/9951, 196. W. Bagehot, *The English Constitution*, R.H.S. Crossman, ed., 225, discusses colonial governorships. Northcote reported his inability to alter plans despite pressure on 12 February 1908, CO 418/60/5307, 70.

p. 70   Agreement over governor-general's use of railway: Wright, Commonwealth and States, 219–26. Hopes for Northcote's future influence; *SMH*, 7 September 1908. Farewell banquet and Deakin's speech: *Age*, 15 July 1908. 'Diehard' attitude: G. Phillips, *The Diehards*. Obituary: *The Times*, 30 September 1911.

p. 71   For Lady Northcote's death see *Argus*, 3 June 1934.

p. 72   Dudley: *DNB* 1931–40, and *ADB*, vol. 8. 'Like the hero': *SMH*, 7 September 1908. For scandalized Queen Victoria see Magnus, op. cit., 74, 89, 101. Dudley's marriage: *The Times*, 15 September 1891. The hothouse atmosphere is captured marvellously in V. Sackville West's *The Edwardians*. For pride in women see J.B. Priestley, *The Edwardians*, 69. *SMH*, 7 September 1908, quoted Lady Randolph's description of Georgiana Dudley. For the prince's lady friends see A. Leslie, *Edwardians in love*.

p. 73   'Aristocracy in working condition': B. Tuchman, *The proud tower*, 3. Extravagance in Ireland: Magnus, op. cit., 318, states that Dudley spent £30,000 more than his salary on his social duties. Support of devolution: M.V. Brett, ed., *Journals and letters of Reginald, Viscount Esher*, vol. 2, 78–81. Correspondence on Dudley's selection: Campbell-Bannerman (*DNB* 1901–11) papers, Add Mss. 41225, vol. XX, 230–37; Ripon papers, Add. Mss. 43518, vol. XXVII, 157–61 and Add. Mss. 43552, vol. LXII, 44–52, British Library. Dudley's ambitions for India or Canada are expressed in his letter to Elgin, 15 March 1908, CO 418/68/9477, 229–44. For notification to Australia of appointment see Northcote's cable, 17 March 1908, CO 418/60/9645, 126. Dudley's hope to save money: Dudley to Lyttelton, 9 May 1907, Chandos papers, Chan 1, 2/5, Churchill College Archives, Cambridge. *The Times*, 7 and 9 November 1918, reported marriage difficulties. 'Gorgeous affair': *Labor Call*, 10 September 1908.

p. 75   'Recalled the splendour': *Australasian*, 12 September 1908. 'Most successful': *Daily Telegraph*, 9 September 1908. 'Sham Australian court': *Worker* (Sydney),

17 September 1908. Sufficiently wealthy peer: Elgin to Ripon, 2 March 1908, Ripon papers, Add. Mss. 43552, vol. LXII, 44–7, British Library. See I.M. Poore, *Recollections of an admiral's wife*, for an account of Government House in Dudley's time.

p. 76 Deakin ministry's defeat: *CPD*, XLVIII, 2137–41. *Argus*, 12 November 1908 reports Deakin's visit to Government House. Dudley's scheme to visit Adelaide: 18 April 1909, CO 418/70/17665, 276. Rising expenditure on the governor-general was quoted by Higgs in parliament on 23 November 1910, *CPD*, LIX, 6675–86. For a Labor protest at vice-regal expense in 1908 see *CPD*, XLV, 9882.

p. 77 For State Labor platforms calling for abolition of governors see W.G. Spence, *Australia's awakening*, 597–628. For support of Australian-born governors see *Age*, 5 August 1908; *VPD*, vol. 103, 2797, vol. 105, 610, vol. 107, 349, vol. 110, 725, vol. 116, 1137; *Herald* (Melbourne), 9 February 1905. Report of 1907 premiers discussion on governors: *NSWPP*, 1907 (second session), I, 1115–24. Price: *DAB*, vol. 2. His discussions in London: Whiting to CO, 11 April 1908, CO 418/65/13318, 226–7; and Elgin to Northcote, 20 March 1908, Northcote papers, CO gifts and deposits, PRO 30/56/1, 123–4. Price's dispatch, 13 August 1908: CO 418/63/35269, 367–81. Menzies' comment on appointment of McKell: L.F. Crisp, *Ben Chifley*, 279. Criticism in Adelaide of Price's dispatch: South Australia, *Parliamentary Debates*, Legislative Council, 1908, 146–9, 158–62, 175–87. Press reaction: *Age*, 23 September 1908.

p. 78 *Register* and *Advertiser*, 16 September, *Argus*, 26 September, *Mercury*, 30 September, and *SMH*, 17 September 1908. Crewe's rejection of Price's request: 9 October 1908, CO 418/63/35269, 375–81. Selection of Bosanquet (*ADB*, vol. 7), 20 November, and Price's acquiescence, 26 November 1908, are in CO 418/68/42685, 500 and CO 418/63/43268, 482–3. Later State debates: *VPD*, 1910, vol. 124, 375–84; Western Australia, *Parliamentary Debates*, 1908–09, XXXV (new series), 1138–46; and Queensland *Parliamentary Debates*, 1908, CII, 209–222. Forrest's suggestion: *West Australian*, 25 February 1913. Strickland: *DNB* 1931–40. His reaction, 1 March 1913, is in CO 418/116/10565, 363–81. Scaddan resolution, sent to CO on 25 July: CO 418/116/29547, 406–17. Scaddan: *DAB*, vol. 2. Previous discussion in parliament: Western Australia, *Parliamentary Debates*, 1912, XLV (new series), 3921–47. Harcourt: *DNB* 1922–30.

p. 79 The authoritative account of the naval scare is A.J. Marder, *From the Dread-nought to Scapa Flow*, vol. 1. Effect of controversy on Dominions: Gordon, op. cit., 215–41. La Nauze, *Deakin*, II, 553–7, discusses the reaction in Australia. *Age* proposed offer of dreadnought on 19 March 1909. The Empire Day quote is from Poore, op. cit., 85. Dudley reported his conversation with Fisher on 18 April 1909, CO 418/70/17665, 274–7. I draw details of naval expenditure etc. from La Nauze, *Deakin*, II, 517–30. Fisher's policy speech: *Argus*, 31 March 1909.

p. 80 Fisher's letter, 22 March 1909, assuring Dudley of support for Mother Country is published in *CPP*, 1909, II, 147. For Deakin's concern for Australian control of its navy see Gordon, op. cit., 211, and La Nauze, *Deakin*, II, 525. Dudley's redrafting of Fisher's memorandum on control of naval vessels: Dudley to Crewe, 18 April 1909, CO 418/70/17665, 279–88. Formation of Fusion Party: La Nauze, *Deakin*, II, 534–75. See too J.R.M. Murdoch, Joseph Cook: a political biography, PhD, University of New South Wales, 1969. Uproarious parliamentary debate: *CPD*, XLIX, 114–227.

p. 81 Hughes' memorandum: *CPP*, 1914–17, vol. 2, 1223–35; Hughes' authorship: L.F. Fitzhardinge, *William Morris Hughes: a political biography*, I, 218–9.

Tamworth Observer's warning: 1 June 1909. Press expectations: Mercury, 31 May 1909. 'If two opposition parties': Forsey, op. cit., 117. A draft of Griffith's memorandum is in Griffith papers, MSS 363, 8X, 36–9, ML. See Fitzhardinge, op. cit., I, 219, for report that Dudley did not even read Labor's memorandum. In accord: Evatt, op. cit., 54. 'Prima facie': Keith, op. cit., 165. The Melbourne Punch letter is on 3 June 1909.

p. 82   Dudley's dispatch reporting refusal of dissolution, 12 July 1909: CO 418/71/27594, 31–6. 'Uncompromising foe': Melbourne Punch, 10 June 1909. Chelmsford: ADB, vol. 7. Lady Hopetoun's unsociability: Bulletin, 30 March 1895, and Freemans Journal (Sydney), 22 December 1901.

p. 84   Draft of Lady Tennyson's advice to Lady Northcote is in Tennyson papers, MS 479/37/4, NL.

p. 85   Dudley commented on Lady Northcote's public reticence in letter to Denman, 5 March 1911, Denman papers, MS 769/7, NL. Irish visitor's description of Lady Dudley is expressed in F. Ponsonby, Recollections of three reigns, 205. 'Reserved': The Times, 28 June 1920. Lady Dudley at dinner: A. Holman, Memoirs of a premier's wife, 41. For Ada and W.A. Holman see ADB, vol. 9. 'Cultivated' and 'singularly beautiful': A.B. Paterson, Happy dispatches, 150–64.

p. 86   'Steel': ibid. 'In solemn truth': Melbourne Punch, 3 June 1909. Lady Dudley's presence in public gallery in parliament is reported by Sir J. Smith, My life story, 103. The speech in Brisbane: Brisbane Courier, 23 August 1909. For Lady Dudley's attempt to attract English support and the federal constitution see Argus, 24 May and 21 July 1910. Lone Hand, 1 August 1911, 293–301, is Lady Dudley's own account of her nursing scheme. Deakin and Fisher's support: Argus, 31 May 1910. Preference for statue of the king: Argus, 1 July 1910. Paterson, op. cit., 150–5, reports opposition from medical profession. 'Not wholly acceptable': Argus, 7 September 1910. Holman, op. cit., 41, cites 'common knowledge'. 'Concupiscent capers': Truth, 18 September 1910. Deterioration in marriage and terms of settlement: The Times, 7 November 1918. 'Trouble with the Ministry': Sun, Sydney, 5 September 1910. 'Superseded': Dudley to Fisher, 19 June 1910, copy in M.L. Shepherd, Memoirs, CRS A1632, AA. Denials of friction: SMH, 6 September, and Argus, 10 September 1910. Higgs' motion: CPD, LIX, 6675–86 (Scullin's comment: 6684; Hughes' intervention: 6685). Scullin: J. Robertson, J.H. Scullin: a political biography. Copies of Dudley's circumnavigation proposal of 19 June 1910 and of Fisher's replies of 5 and 8 July, are in M.L. Shepherd, Memoirs, CRS A1632, AA. 'Even a Governor-General': Melbourne Punch, 22 December 1910. Request to be relieved: Dudley to Crewe, 7 October 1910, Crewe papers, C/13, Cambridge University Library.

p. 88   Announcement of retirement: Argus, 3 March 1911. Rumours: Sun, 8 September 1910. Dudley's vexation at levee is reported by Deakin, see foolscap minute book, three pages from end, elaborating a note in rough diary for 1911, Deakin papers, MS 1540/19/275. Hughes' apology for oversight: Argus, 26 June 1911. Dudley's departure: Argus, 10 August 1911. For reaction to speech see Argus, 23, 24 October 1911. Higgs' renewed attack: CPD, LXI, 1975–7. Lady Dudley's death: The Times, 28 June 1920. 'His ambition was high': note in minute book, previously cited, Deakin papers, MS 1540/19/275, NL. 'It puts the clock back': Northcote to Deakin, 7 September 1911, Deakin papers, MS 1540/3999, NL. 'Thankless task': Co 418/88/24751, 349–54.

p. 89   'Not a pleasant position': Melbourne Punch, 3 August 1911. Quotes of Grey, Munro (ADB, vols. 1, 5) and Deakin: National Australasian Convention Debates, Sydney 1891, 563, 579 & 571. Gladstone: DNB 1922–30. His appointment: Magnus, op. cit., 542–3. Connaught: *DNB* 1941–50. Canadian appointment: Neuendorff, op. cit., 212–3. Denman: *ADB*, vol. 8. 'It might be a good thing': Ripon to Crewe, 12 February 1908, Crewe papers, C/43, Cambridge University Library. 'Pleasantly narrow': Dudley's remark to Deakin, minute book (three pages from end), Deakin papers, MS 1540/19/275, NL. 'As regards the new G.G.': Northcote to Deakin, 31 March 1911, Deakin papers, MS 1540/3996, NL.

p. 90   Lady Denman: *ADB*, vol. 8, and G. Huxley, *Lady Denman G.B.E.* Cowdray: R.K. Middlemas, *The master builders*, 161–247.

p. 91   Unhappy marriage and Denman's hay fever: Huxley, op. cit. 'Keen to work hard': Northcote to Deakin, 7 June 1911, Deakin papers MS 1540/3998, NL. 'Prosperity': *Age*, 3 July 1911. Population figures are from *Official Yearbook of the Commonwealth of Australia*, vol. 54 (1968).

p. 92   O'Malley: A.R Hoyle, *King O'Malley: the American bounder*. Batchelor: *ADB*, vol. 7. 'Singularly destitute': Rider Haggard (*DNB* 1922–30) to CO, 27 May 1913, copy in CO 881/14/217. Irvine: *ADB*, vol. 9. Millen: *SMH*, 15 September 1923. 'The people I like': Huxley, op. cit., 44. Cordial relations with Labor: *SMH*, 18 April 1914. Cowdray's financial support: Huxley, op. cit., 39. 'Money like water': ibid., 45. 'Joyous Denmans': *Bulletin*, 7 November 1912. More relaxed: Melbourne *Punch*, 23 November 1911. Refusing 'to adopt that pose': ibid., 3 August 1911. Enthusiasm for bush: Huxley, op. cit., 48–9. 'Travelling about': Dudley to Denman, 5 March 1911, Denman papers, MS 769/4–5, NL.

p. 94   'Often difficult': Denman to Munro Ferguson, 11 May 1914, Novar papers, MS 696/7393–7400, NL. Asquith: *DNB* 1922–30. 1911 Imperial Conference: I.R. Hancock, 'The 1911 Imperial Conference', *HS*, vol. 12, no. 47, October 1966, 306–72. See also J.P. Mackintosh, 'The role of the Committee of Imperial Defence before 1914', *English Historical Review*, LXXVII, July 1962, 490. Deakin at 1907 conference: La Nauze, *Deakin*, II, 484–92.

p. 95   Australian high commissioner: J.R. Thompson, The Australian High Commission in London, MA, ANU, 1972. See J.A. Cross, *Whitehall and the Commonwealth*, 37, for CO insistence on controlling correspondence with Dominions. Problem persisted: dispatch to Denman, 6 October 1911, MP 84/1, item 1850/1/93, AA. 'Exercise the personal influence': Harcourt to Churchill, 31 August 1912, CO 418/106/26651, 176–9.

p. 96   Churchill's reply to Harcourt, 9 September 1912, is in ibid., 105–7. 'Transfer portion': Steward to Shepherd, Prime Ministers Department correspondence, CRS A461, item E334/1/2, part 1, AA. Irregularities continued: see Denman to Harcourt, 22 February 1913, CO 418/110/11617, 129. The *Round Table* article, 'Downing Street', is in volume III, 1912–13, 590. On this question of correspondence and the CO see Cross, op. cit., 38.

p. 97   Consternation of CO: see minutes on CO 418/100/510, 324–43. Denman's speech welcoming 'Melbourne': *Argus*, 27 March 1913. Churchill in particular wanted 'one Imperial navy', see CO 418/106/26651, 106, and *CPP*, 1914, II, 'Naval defence . . .', 205–9. 'Most ill timed': CO 418/100/510, 343. 'Personal influence': see above, p. 95. Denman and the Navigation Bill: CO 418/100/33518, 232–7, and CO 418/109/31011, 175–6. Lyne's offer of Government House: Beauchamp cable, 29 March 1900, CO 201/627/9918, 253–5. Wright, Commonwealth and States, 209–219, discusses the Government House controversy, emphasising the element of antipathy between the Commonwealth and the States. A.C. Child, *Cranbrook*, gives a history of the former residence of the State governor. I am grateful to Allan Lawson for drawing my attention to this source.

p. 98   Melbourne Government house was 'bitter cold', Lady Tennyson complained to

Barton, 20 May 1903, Barton papers, MS 51/617, NL. She found the Sydney residence 'very comfortable'; see her letter to lady Northcote, 25 September 1903, copy in Tennyson papers, MS 479/37/4, NL. Barton's advice to Tennyson about visiting Sydney, 11 December 1902, is in Tennyson papers, MS 1963/99, NL. 'Spend at least': Tennyson to Northcote, 16 September 1903, Tennyson papers, MS 479/2/320, NL. A copy of Carruthers' 12 July 1905 letter to Deakin is in 'Papers relating to the Residence of the Governor-General in New South Wales' *CPP*, 1905, II, 1101–1118. Carruthers: *ADB*, vol. 7. Deakin's reply, 24 July 1905, is in *CPP*, 1905, II, 1117. Bent requested payment for Melbourne residence on 28 May 1906, CRS A2, 06/3881, AA.

p. 99   Arrangements for occupation of both Government Houses: *CPD*, 1906, XXXI, 876–92. McGowen: *DAB*, vol. 2. Holman's letter, 23 May 1911, about resuming Government House, Sydney, is reproduced in 'The Residence of the Governor-General in New South Wales', *NSWPP*, 1912, I, 683–694. Possible use as hospital: *Argus*, 8 June 1911. Other suggested uses: *Bulletin*, 16 May 1912. 'To find the appliances': quoted in Wright, Commonwealth and States, 216–7. McGowen's offer of temporary rent: *NSWPP*, 1912, I, 691. Departure of Denman: *SMH*, 8 October 1912. *SMH*'s fears: 2 June 1911. 'Boorish' and 'shabby': *Daily Telegraph*, 16, 25 October 1912. 'Inhospitable': *Worker* (Sydney), 10 October 1912.

p. 100   Mayor's speech: *Daily Telegraph*, 9 October 1912. Censure motion: *NSWPD*, 1912, vol. 48, 2326–79.

p. 101   McMillan's committee: *Daily Telegraph*, 6,22 November 1912. McMillan: A.W. Martin, 'William McMillan', *JRAHS*, XL, part iv, March 1955, 197–224. 'Tory uproar': *Bulletin*, 15 June 1911. Outraged editorial on Fisher's speech: *SMH*, 24 July 1911. Fisher's repudiation: *Argus*, 31 July 1911. For an account of the controversy over Fisher's speech see C. Grimshaw, 'Some aspects of Australian attitudes to the Imperial connection 1900–19', MA, University of Queensland, 1957, 28–30. 'There is a body of opinion' and 'popular cry': *SMH*, 3 and 18 July 1911. 'At a time like the present': *Daily Telegraph*, 9 October 1912. 'Petty': *Advertiser*, 17 December 1912. Smug *Argus*: 14 October 1912. 'False position' and 'Never any reason': *Age*, 8 June 1911 and 10 October 1912.

p. 102   'Downing Street officials': ibid. Uproarious scenes: *Age*, 16 December 1912. Legal battle over Government House: Attorney General (NSW) Vs Williams, 16 *CLR* 404 and 19 *CLR* 343. Strickland's occupation of Government House is reported in his telegram of 21 October 1915, CO 418/136/48651. 'Seriously to impair': Denman to CO, 17 June 1912, CO 418/99/2287, 323.

p. 103   'Should not have meddled': minute on ibid. Warning from secretary of state: Harcourt to Denman, 20 August 1913, Denman papers, MS 769/57–8, NL. Humiliation over furniture: *Daily Telegraph*, 23 December 1912, and CO 418/112/4870, 43–4. Dispute with Millen: conversation reported by Munro Ferguson, 1 June 1914, Novar papers, MS 696/543, NL. Report on military forces: Denman to CO 23 April 1912, CO 418/99/16296, 209–17. 'Extraordinary deterioration': minutes on Denman's dispatch of 28 February 1912, CO 418/99/10240, 134–8. Dissatisfaction with official secretary: ibid. (Keith's memorandum), and CO/418/88/23154, 253.

p. 104   Governors-general 'not of much assistance': minutes by Keith on CO 418/122/4580, 101–37. Instructions to Denman's successor: CO 418/122/4580, 137. Harcourt urged Denman to stay on 20 August 1913, Denman papers, MS 769/57–8. A copy of cable of resignation of 11 November 1913 is in Denman papers, MS 769/102, NL. 'Moody' and unhappy marriage: Huxley, op. cit., 58–9. I am grateful to Professor La Nauze for drawing my attention to Helen Simpson's novel *Boomerang*, 374–5, for a description of a governor-general's wattle-induced hay fever. *Argus*, 27 January 1914, has announcement of resignation. For obituaries of Lord and Lady Denman see *The Times*, 3 and 25 June 1954. 'Justified his selection': *SMH*, 18 April 1914. 'Satisfaction': *Advertiser*, 15 May 1914. 'Most successful': *Bulletin*, 9 April 1914.

p. 105   'Neither irritated nor scandalised': ibid. *Westralian Worker* comment was on 30 January 1914. 'Two horses in a circus': C.W. de Kiewiet and F.H. Underhill, *Dufferin-Carnarvon correspondence 1874–1878*, 74.

p. 106   'Five years in so remote a country': *Argus*, 2 February 1914. Lyne's reaction in 1900 is recorded by Tennyson in his diary, 21 July 1900, Tennyson papers, MS 479/2, NL. 'One rubber stamp': *Westralian Worker*, 13 February 1914. 'Although the wide ocean': *SMH*, 9 February 1914.

p. 107   Qualities necessary: Melbourne *Punch*, 23 July 1914. Munro Ferguson: *The Times*, 31 March 1934, *DNB* 1931–40. Rosebery: *DNB* 1922–30. Imperial Federation League membership: Brassey, op. cit., 284. H.C.G. Matthew, *The Liberal Imperialists: the ideas and politics of a post Gladstonian elite*, describes Munro Ferguson's political role and attitudes.

p. 108   Opponent of Campbell Bannerman: R.R. James, *Rosebery*, 420, and Mathew, op. cit. Intimacy with Rosebery: Lord Crewe, *Lord Rosebery*, vol. 1, 282. Marconi vote: *The Times*, 30 June 1913. Independence: *The Times*, 7 February 1914. 'Office is being hawked about': *Argus*, 2 February 1914.

p. 109   Correspondence with Harcourt over appointment is in Harcourt papers, dep 463, 24–30, Bodleian Library, Oxford. 'Rabid politician': *Worker* (Brisbane), 9 February 1914. 'The days have passed': *Brisbane Courier*, 9 February 1914. Quarrel with Rosebery: Rosebery papers, MSS 10020, 67–74, National Library of Scotland. Disillusioned with politics: ibid. 78. 'Splendid presence': E. Scott, *Australia during the war*, 19–20.

p. 110   B. Clifford, *Proconsul*, 37–47, describes Munro Ferguson. The two bills in dispute between the Houses were the Government Preference Prohibition Bill and the Postal Voting Restoration Bill; see *CPD*, LXXI, 2834–5. Reid's comment on differing practice in Australia is in his *My reminiscences*, 246. Intention of section 57: Quick and Garran, op. cit., 683–8. J.A. La Nauze, *The making of the Australian Constitution*, 188–91, for failure to anticipate party groupings.

p. 111   Speculation of CO instruction: *Advertiser*, 6 June 1914. CO declines to advise: Novar papers, MS 696/5089, NL. Keith's memorandum, of 27 February 1914, is in Novar papers, MS 696/4648, 4650–54, NL. A pencilled account of the interview with Reid is in Novar papers, MS 696/3985–92, NL. Denman's letter, 11 May 1914, is in ibid., MS 696/7393–400.

p. 112   I have constructed the sequence of events from several dispatches, 9 June 1914, Novar papers, MS 696/556–60, NL, and CO 418/123/25528 and 25972, 13–14. The three memoranda which were 'put aside' are in Novar papers, MS 696/4441–4493, NL.

p. 113   'Head and shoulders above': Munro Ferguson to Harcourt, 24 March 1915, Novar papers, MS 696/674, NL. Memorandum from Griffith, 5 October 1914, embodying the 'views which I expressed ... on 3rd June', and covering letter: Novar papers, MS 696/4508, NL. Pencilled memo is in Novar papers, MS 696/4513, NL. Murdoch, op. cit., 267–9, reveals lack of caucus approval. The correspondence with Cook is in Novar papers, MS 696/4521–8, NL. It was later published, though in incorrect order, in *CPP* 1914–17, V, 127–136.

p. 114   Announcement of decision to dissolve is in *CPD*, LXXIV, 1917. Munro Ferguson forecast 'ebullitions' in letter to Harcourt, 21 June 1914, Novar papers, MS 696/574, NL. For Hughes' reaction see *Age*, 9 June 1914 and *Worker* (Brisbane), 18 June 1914. 'Peevishness': *Daily Telegraph*, 10 June 1914.

Harcourt's letter, 11 July 1914, expressed the view that the governor-general was 'free to use his discretion as to seeing the leader of the Opposition': Novar papers, MS 696/1298, NL. 'Utterly wrong': *Bulletin*, 11 June 1914. 'The imported viceroy': *Westralian Worker*, 12 June 1914. 'Ludicrous': *Australian Worker* (Sydney), 11 June 1914. 'Partisanship': *Labor Call*, 25 June 1914. 'Lack of knowledge': *Worker* (Brisbane), 11 June 1914. *Age*, 3 June 1914, and Melbourne *Punch*, 7 May 1914, supported dissolution of lower House only. 'Landmark': A.B. Kieth, *Imperial unity and the Dominions*, 110.

p. 115   'Serious responsibility': Keith, *Responsible government*, 209. See Quick and Garran, op. cit., 685, for comment on power in respect of simultaneous dissolution. 'Little if any discretion': Quick, *Legislative powers of the Commonwealth and States of Australia*, 639–41. Quick's letter of 9 September 1916 in in Novar papers, MS 696/8560, NL. Griffith's memorandum, 4 September 1916, is in Novar papers, MS 696/4703–16, NL. Moore wrote on 9 March 1919: Novar papers, MS 696/4500–1, NL. Evatt, op. cit., 37–39, and Forsey, op. cit., 38–9, disagree with Keith and support Munro Ferguson's view.

p. 116   'Constitutionally correct': G. Sawer, op. cit., 124. Regretful glance: Munro Ferguson to Harcourt, 12 July 1914, Novar papers, MS 696/582, NL. A decoded copy of the cable of 30 July 1914 is in CP 78, series 23, vol. 1, first paper, numbered 14/89/1/11, AA. 'Adopt' was decyphered as 'adoption', destroying the sense. My narrative of these events is largely drawn from Scott, op. cit., 6–15.

p. 117   For conference on 2 August see C.E.W. Bean, *The story of Anzac*, vol. 1, 25. Munro Ferguson's letter to Harcourt, 2 August 1914, described Millen as 'extremely business-like' and the cypher episode, Novar papers, MS 696/589–90. Draft of telegram to Cook suggesting cabinet meeting: 31 July 1914, CP 78, series 23, vol. 1, second paper, numbered 14/89/1/2, AA. A copy of his letter of the same date is in Novar papers, MS 696/4003, NL.

p. 118   For pledges of support see various newspapers, 1 August 1914. *Age*, 3 August 1914, reported prominence of Millen's 'no fair weather partner' speech in London, Executive Council meeting and Cook's announcement: *SMH*, 4 August 1914. 'Enthusiasm': telegram, 3 August 1914, CO 418/132/28514, 143. 'But a fraction' is from dispatch of 8 August 1914, Novar papers, MS 696/1588–90, NL. Munro Ferguson anticipated work as commander-in-chief in letter to Harcourt, 18 August 1914, Novar papers, MS 696/594, NL.

p. 119   'Influence and example': A.T. Paterson, *The Thirty Ninth, the history of the 39th Battalion Australian imperial Force*, 32. Camp inspection: Pearce papers, 10027, file 419/80/2, bundle 1, items 80 and 105, Australian War Memorial. Friendship with Maxwell and Hamilton, see letter to Legge, 22 August 1915, and Hamilton to Munro Ferguson, 7 February 1915, Novar papers, MS 696/3616 and 3650–53, NL. Forecasts of conflict of interests: *Bulletin*, 1 August 1891, and W.H. Traill, *NSWPD* 1892, LXI, 2498–9. 'At least as important': A.B. Keith, 'Recent changes in Canada's constitutional status', in *Canadian Historical Review*, IX, no. 2, June 1928, 111. 'Nothing could be more disturbing': Munro Ferguson's letter of 1 June 1914, Novar papers, MS 696/544, NL. Visit to Garden Island: *Age*, 3 August 1914. Interview with Patey is reported in letter of 4 August 1914, Novar papers, MS 696/591, NL.

p. 120   German cruiser sightings: A.W. Jose, *The Royal Australian Navy*, 153–5. I base my account of the recalling of the convoy on Munro Ferguson's dispatch of 29 September 1914, CO 418/123/43671, 293–319. British approval: cable of 28 September 1914, Novar papers, MS 696/1305, NL. 'Sir Ronald had in this matter': Jose, op. cit., 154. 'Assumption made by the Admiralty': Munro Ferguson to Harcourt, 29 September 1914, Novar papers, MS 696/604, NL. 'A loss of confidence': dispatch of 29 September 1914, CO 418/123/43671, 293–6.

p. 121   Authority to expend £500,000: dispatch of 25 August 1914, Novar papers, MS 696/1594–6, NL. 'With the exception of Mr Fisher': Munro Ferguson to Harcourt, 20 January 1915, Novar papers, MS 696/650–3, NL. For instrument setting up the royal commission see Federal Executive Council, Minute Papers Approved, 1915, Prime Ministers Department Correspondence, A 1573, minute no. 16, AA. Hughes had been absent from the cabinet meeting which had decided to send it. Decode of Hughes' cable to Fisher, 2 March 1915, is in Fisher papers, MS 2919/1/4, NL; so is Fisher's reply, sent on 26 March 1915. Munro Ferguson referred to the report of the royal commission in dispatch of 5 September 1916, Novar papers, MS 696/1729, NL. Fisher's 16 September 1915 letter about correct channels is in CRS A1, item 15/16430, AA.

p. 122   Munro Ferguson's description of Cook is in his letter to Walter Long, 24 October 1918, 'touching exchange' is in letter to Harcourt, 18 September 1914, and description of Fisher in letter to Bonar Law, 24 August 1915: Novar papers, MS 696/1085, 602 and 738, NL. Fisher's rule about communication with ministers, and later relaxation: dispatch of 28 December 1915, Novar papers, MS 696/1674–5, NL. Complaint about ministers, 31 August 1915, and Fisher's apology, 16 September, are in CRS A2/18/3313, AA. For an account of the discussions over occupation of Yap see L. F. Fitzhardinge, 'Australia, Japan and Great Britain: a study in triangular diplomacy', in *HS*, 14, no. 54, April 1970, 250–9. 'For your eye only': Harcourt to Munro Ferguson 6 December 1914, Novar papers, MS 696/1306–9, NL. 'Fool's paradise': Munro Ferguson to Harcourt, 6 April 1915, Novar papers, MS 696/676–7, NL. C.A. Hicks, The impossible alliance: Australia, the United States and the post war settlement, MA thesis, ANU, 1970, also discusses the diplomacy over Japanese retention of the Pacific Islands.

p. 123   Burns: *ADB*, vol. 7. Attempt to convince Fisher of Legge's view: Munro Ferguson to Harcourt, 13 May 1915, Novar papers, MS 696/687, NL. Legge: obituary *SMH*, 26 September 1947. For Eliot's attachment to staff see cable of 10 June 1916, CO 418/145/27549, 63–9. Munro Ferguson suggests drawing together of Pacific colonies in dispatches of 31 August and 8 September 1916, CO 418/145/49683 and 50695, 369–405 and 432–40.

p. 124   Bridges: *ADB*, vol. 7. Details of Legge's appointment: Munro Ferguson's dispatch of 28 May 1915, Novar papers, MS 696/1652–4, NL.

p. 125   Hamilton's objection is referred to in ibid. Monash's and McCay's reaction: Bean, op. cit., 423. Monash: G. Serle, *John Monash: a biography*. McCay: *DAB*, vol. 2. Legge's departure and Pearce's announcement of the appointment: *CPD*, LXXVI, 362. 'Fine character': Hamilton to Munro Ferguson, 6 October 1915, Novar papers, MS 696/3658–63, NL. Report of interview with Fisher and Pearce: dispatch of 28 May 1915, Novar papers, MS 696/1652, NL.

p.126   'Inured to Trade Unions' and 'disposed to make light': ibid. For Birdwood, see *ADB*, vol. 7. Cabinet's ignorance of Hamilton's communication: dispatch of 14 June 1915, CO 418/133/33751, 39A. Correspondence with Stanley over channel of communication: Novar papers, MS 696/5137–58, NL. Stanley, later 5th Baron Stanley of Alderley: *Who was who* 1929–40. Davidson and Newdegate disputes: CO/418/176/26467, 147–50, and CO 418/203/41936, 56. Davidson: *ADB*, vol. 8. Newdegate, *Who was who* 1929–40. Strickland: *DNB* 1931–40, and *The Times*, 23 August 1940. Annoyance of Northcote (7 October 1907) and Dudley (24 August 1909) with Strickland: CO 418/52/39688, 555–63, and CO 418/71/28434, 18. For dormant commission difficulties see Strickland's dispatch of 24 February 1914, CO 418/124/11545, 65–73. Not invited to levee: correspondence in July 1914 in Novar papers, MS 696/1580–7, NL. Strickland's sanity: Munro Ferguson to Harcourt, 8 August 1914, Novar papers, MS 696/15889, NL. Occupation of Government House: Strickland's dispatch, 21 October 1915, CO 418/136/4865, 280.

p. 127   Refusal to conduct business: Munro Ferguson's dispatch of 12 November 1916, CO 418/146/62214, 150–1. Strickland's recall is discussed in Evatt, op. cit., 146–52. Strickland complained about Munro Ferguson's forestry conference on 30 June 1916, CO 418/147/39679, 350–96. *Australian Forestry Journal*, III, no. 8, August 1920, 299, has tribute to Munro Ferguson. Stanley's report of the dispute between Lady Helen and Lady Madden is in his dispatch of 29 March 1916, CO 418/150/21740, 238–47. The description of Lady Helen is from Clifford, op. cit., 45. I am grateful to Dick Hall for this reference. A letter from Lady Helen to Holman, published in *SMH*, 1 September 1915, set out the history of the establishment of the Red Cross in Australia in August 1914. 'I had to make recommendations': Denman to Munro Ferguson, 11 May 1914, Novar papers, MS 696/7393–7400, NL. Munro Ferguson's opinion of honours is expressed in his letter to Harcourt, 7 October 1914, Novar papers, MS 696/606–7, NL. His attempt to persuade Fisher: Munro Ferguson to Harcourt, 29 September 1914, Novar papers, MS 696/604, NL. Attempt to honour Millen: dispatch, 15 December 1914, CO 418/123/4141, 499–506.

p. 128   Munro Ferguson reported his opinion of Hughes as 'above his whole party' and need to be on his guard with him in letter to Bonar Law (*DNB* 1922–30), 8 November 1915, Novar papers, MS 696/768–9, NL.

p. 129   'Go and grit': Munro Ferguson to Bonar Law, 11 January 1916, Novar papers, MS 696/793–5, NL. 'Though stone deaf': Munro Ferguson to Asquith, 5 December 1915, Novar papers, MS 696/699–700, NL. For a vivid account of Hughes' 1916 tour see his *The splendid adventure*. Failure to inform about price fixing, and follow up letter about rights of heads of state: Munro Ferguson to Pearce, 8 and 13 March 1916, Pearce papers, MS 213/5/15 and 18, NL. Pearce's apology, 8 March 1916, and his promise to do his best, are in Novar papers, MS 696/3134 and 3143, NL. Munro Ferguson's third letter to Pearce, 14 March 1916, is in Pearce papers, MS 213/2/20, NL. Memo of the 'frank exchange': 15 March 1916, Novar papers, MS 696/3142, NL. The reference to Queen Victoria is in his letter of 13 March, already quoted.

p. 130   'But a fraction': see above, p. 118. 'Might easily lead': Munro Ferguson to Harcourt, 6 December 1914, Novar papers, MS 696/632, NL. Suggestion about recruiting drives was cabled to Fisher on 15 October 1915. Draft is in CP 78, series 21, bundle 59, file 19, AA. Not impressive orator: see Melbourne *Punch*, 28 May 1914, and A. Holman, op. cit., 31. For example of recruiting speech see *Argus*, 10 November 1914. Fisher's letter of 16 October 1915 about ministers' recruiting is in Novar papers, MS 696/3973, NL.

p. 131   For accounts of the conscription crisis see L.C. Jauncey, *The story of conscription in Australia*; Scott, op. cit., 320–430; F.B. Smith, *The conscription plebiscites in Australia 1916–17* and L.L. Robson, *The First A.I.F.* Conscription not practicable: Munro Ferguson to Bonar Law 3 November 1915, CO 418/134/50801, 107a. 'Not going as well': Munro Ferguson to Bonar Law, 22 December 1919, Novar papers, MS 696/789, NL. 'In a war like this': Munro Ferguson to Cook, 5 April 1916, MS 696/4024–5, NL. 'We would certainly raise': Munro Ferguson to Birdwood, 12 July 1916, Birdwood papers, Australian War Memorial. Increased anxiety about shortage of recruits: Munro Ferguson to Hughes, 28 April 1916, Novar papers, MS 696/2480, NL. Commonwealth Bank opening: *SMH*, 23 August 1916. Details of conversation about promise of dissolution: Munro Ferguson to Bonar Law, 26 August 1916 (postscript dated 30 August), Novar papers MS 696/820–4, NL. 'Sword in the scabbard': ibid.

p. 132   'A memorable day': Munro Ferguson's dispatch of 31 August 1916, CP 78, series 23, file 1914–16/89/385, AA. Hughes influenced by sombre news: Fitzhardinge, *Hughes*, II, 182–5. Midnight rendezvous: ibid., 212. 'Poor little man': Munro Ferguson to Bonar Law, 29 October 1916 and 2 March 1917, Novar papers, MS 696/834–6 and 886, NL.

p. 133   Full facts not placed before him: Munro Ferguson to Hughes, 1 November 1915, Novar papers, MS 696/2513, NL. Munro Ferguson's letters to Bonar Law described 'touching simplicity' on 13 December 1915, 'general acquiescence' on 25 July 1916, 'serious blow' and 'anarchist ... section' on 29 October 1916, selfish class motives of Hughes' opponents on 20 September 1916 and thought the campaign 'discreditable' on 3 November 1916: Novar papers, MS 696/785, 818, 835, 825 and 1741, NL. Mannix: obituary, *SMH*, 7 November 1963. Munro Ferguson criticized Mannix in letter to Long (*DNB* 1922–30), 2 February 1916, Novar papers, MS 696/877, NL. 'Much below': Munro Ferguson to Long, 24 December 1916, Novar papers, MS 696/850, NL. 'Disgraceful': Cook's reaction described by Murdoch, op. cit., 314. 'Luke-warm to the War': *All for Australia*, no. 3, 18 April 1917, copy in Hughes papers, MS 1538, box 51, folder 6, NL.

p. 134   'Secret Trade Union Junta' and Labor revolutionary: Munro Ferguson to Long, 4 January and 4 April 1917, Novar papers MS 696/869 and 895, NL. Forecast reconstruction: dispatch of 3 November 1916, Novar papers, MS 696/1743, NL. Hughes' attempt to obtain promise of dissolution: memo by Munro Ferguson, 5 November 1916, Novar papers, MS 696/2342, NL. Mahon: obituary, *SMH*, 29 August 1931. Events after defeat of plebiscite: Scott, op. cit., 363–9, and Fitzhardinge, *Hughes*, II, 220–8. Neither of these sources refers to Hughes' 4 November 1916 request for a promise of a dissolution. Hughes' written assurance of Liberal support is in Novar papers, MS 696/2337, NL.

p. 135   'The one man': dispatch, 14 November 1916, Novar papers, MS 696/1754, NL. Munro Ferguson replied to Hughes' repeated request for promise of dissolution on 6 January 1917, Novar papers, MS 696/2583, NL. Hughes had secured concurrence of the British government with his proposal to extend the life of parliament, see CO 418/155/32081, 447–63. For charges of bribery in the Senate see *CPD*, LXXI, 10847–9. Fitzhardinge, *Hughes*, II, 256–60, describes the Senate manouvres. Earle: *ADB*, vol. 8. For Munro Ferguson's involvement see his letter to Long, 2 March 1917, Novar papers, MS 696/888, NL. Decline in enlistments: Scott, op. cit., 871–2. Munro Ferguson's continued support of compulsion: letter to Long, 13 December 1916, Novar papers, MS 696/848, NL. Hughes' belief conscription impracticable: dispatch, 14 October 1917, CO 418/159/57809, 144–53.

p. 136   Munro Ferguson reported a suggestion of a dissolution which he had made to Hughes, in a letter to Long, 30 November 1917, Novar papers, MS 696/976–82, NL. 'Eggs and road metal': dispatch, 8 January 1918, CO 418/169/9251, 8–10. The 'Warwick egg' incident: Scott, op. cit., 415–6, and Fitzhardinge, *Hughes*, II, 291–4. Hughes' pledges and other Nationalists' reactions: Evatt, op. cit., 153–4. Official secretary's interviews with Hughes and Munro Ferguson's response: Steward's 'most secret memorandum' and cable of 26 December 1917, memorandum of 27 December and Munro Ferguson's reply of 28 December, Novar papers, MS 696/2364–70, NL. Tudor: obituary, *SMH*, 11 January 1922. The aide memoire is in Novar papers, MS 696/2381–8, NL.

p. 137   'Averse to the relinquishment': dispatch of 9 December 1916, CO 418/146/4701, 370. *SMH*, 5 January 1918, reported the Nationalist support for Hughes. Munro Ferguson's account of Hughes' 8 January resignation and subsequent

interviews: dispatch, 15 January 1918, CO 418/169/13551, 47–62. Watt:
obituary, *SMH*, 14 September 1946. Poynton: obituary, *SMH*, 10 January
1935. Wise: obituary, *SMH*, 1 August 1950.

p. 138   Munro Ferguson's interviews with Tudor and Hughes on 8 January: CO
418/169/13551, 47–62. For the recommissioning of Hughes see also Fitzhardinge, *Hughes*, II. 303–4. Correspondence with Hughes about announcement,
and Steward's memorandum: Novar papers, MS 696/2693 and 2363, NL. 'Plot'
involving Irvine: *SMH*, 19 January 1918. Chapman: *ADB*, vol. 7. Announcement in party caucus: *SMH*, 10 January 1918. Consultation with Moore: *Age*,
10 January 1918. Moore's draft memorandum, 9 January 1918, is in Novar
papers, MS 696/2373–7, NL. For published memorandum see *CPD* LXXXIII,
2895–6.

p. 139   Toorak branch letter, which finally reached Long, is in CO 418/168/57188,
18–23. House of Representatives and Senate criticism of Munro Ferguson:
CPD, LXXXIII, 2992 and 3031, and LXXXIV, 339. 'Farce' and 'comic opera':
Labor Call, 17 and 24 January 1918. Anstey's meeting: poster in Hughes papers,
MS 1538, box 118, folder 2, NL. Anstey: *ADB*, vol. 7. Maloney: obituary,
SMH, 29 August 1940. His comments: *CPD*, LXXXIV, 4223–4. Labor
motion: *Official report of the eighth Commonwealth conference of the Australian Labor
Party ... 1919*, 80–1. 'You have been': Hughes to Munro Ferguson, 25 April
1918, Novar papers, MS 696/2718, NL. 'Make smooth the path': Munro Ferguson
to Hughes, 9 May 1918, Hughes papers, MS 1538, box 118, folder 5, NL.

p. 140   'Great advantage to the Empire': Long's minute on Munro Ferguson's cable of
17 February 1917, CO 418/157/8994, 285–7. The doggerel is from *Onlooker*
[n.d. probably October-December 1918]: I am grateful to Humphrey
McQueen, who found this source in the ML, for drawing my attention to it.
'The better kind of people': Munro Ferguson to Long, 27 December 1917,
Novar papers, MS 696/985–8, NL; the last two sentences have been censored,
probably by Munro Ferguson himself, but the original comments are decipher-
able. Carmichael, *ADB*, vol. 7. For recruiting figures see Scott, op. cit., 872.
Proceedings of the conference: *CPP*, 1917–19, IV, 448, 651–814.

p. 141   'Sums paid for maintenance': Munro Ferguson memo, 5 August 1914, Novar
papers, MS 696/1633, NL; a note dated 6 August 1915 admitting impracticabil-
ity of the proposal is also in ibid. Zeal controlling expenditure: CRS A571, file
08/6223, AA. A copy of Bonar Law's memo about espionage, 5 August 1915, is
in Novar papers, MS 696/797, NL. The loss was reported by Munro Ferguson
on 20 January 1916, ibid. For Steward's intelligence career see C.D. Coulthard-
Clark, *The citizen general staff: the Australian Intelligence Corps, 1907–1914*.
Setting up of Counter Espionage Bureau: Hughes to minister for the navy, 14
January 1916, Department of the Navy correspondence, MP 1049/1, file 16/014,
AA. The bureau's functions are from 'Most Secret Circular No. 1–1916' in ibid.
For Steward's 'unravelling' of schemes, see Munro Ferguson to Long, 20 April
1917, Novar papers, MS 696/901–2. 'Subsoil activities': Munro Ferguson to
Milner, 16 June 1919, Novar papers, MS 696/1126–7. 'Prejudicial to work':
Munro Ferguson to Pearce, 7 March 1916, Pearce papers, bundle 1, item 173,
Australian War Memorial. Other 'usages': Munro Ferguson to Long, 25 June
1917, Novar papers, MS 696/931–2, NL. Steward's death: *Argus*, 12 May 1920.

p. 142   'Strange mortal': Munro Ferguson to Harcourt, 28 May 1914, Novar papers,
MS 696/538, NL. 'Delicate position': dispatch, 25 February 1919, CP 78, series
25, vol. 2, file 1919/15/27, AA. For Steward's K.B.E. see *Argus*, 16 March 1918.
Steward mentioned need of 'small Federal Police Force' in letter to Pearce, 23
January 1917, Hughes papers, MS 1538, box 117, folder 1, NL. Munro
Ferguson supported suggestion of Federal Police in letter to Long of 30

November 1917, Novar papers, MS 696/976–82, NL. Warwick egg: see above, p. 136. Munro Ferguson urged expanding sphere of Commonwealth police in letter to Hughes, 8 December 1917, Hughes papers, MS 1538, box 117, folder 1, NL. Delegations to vice-presidents of the Executive Council: CP 78, series 19A, AA. Munro Ferguson's interest in Executive Council: conversation with Fisher, December 1915, quoted above, p. 122. Reversion to meetings in Government House: Munro Ferguson to prime minister, 20 November 1916, CP 290, series 12, bundle 1, AA, where can be also found a copy of Hughes' reply, 21 November 1916. Munro Ferguson objected to rushing business in letter to Hughes, 3 March 1917, Novar papers, MS 696/2619, NL. Complaint that important matters dealt with in absence: memorandum, 3 November 1916, Novar papers, MS 696/4751–2, NL. Memorandum of 22 January 1918: Hughes papers, MS 1538, box 118, folder 5, NL.

p. 143   'Hell of a talking to': undated note signed 'B.E.H.C[lifford]', Novar papers, MS 696/4765, NL. Agreed to discuss weekly: memo of conversation 29 August 1917, and Munro Ferguson to Long, 29 August 1917, Novar papers, MS 696/4761–3 and 957, NL. Hughes' lesson on the right to delay, 8 February [1918] (wrongly dated 1917): Novar papers, MS 696/2604, NL. Subsequent delegations are in CP 78, series 19a, AA. For alteration of credentials see dispatch, 1 May 1919, CO 418/176/35897, 259. Delayed proclamation: dispatch 27 November 1919, CO 418/178/955, 432–51. Hughes' open mind on honours: dispatch of 18 January 1916, CO 418/144/9028, 47–51. Labor cabinet's continued opposition: Pearce to Munro Ferguson, 15 March 1916, Pearce papers, bundle 1, item 103, Australian War Memorial.

p. 144   Protest of State governors: Munro Ferguson's dispatch, 1 March 1917, and Long's reply, 30 May 1917, CO 881/15/231, 119 and 122. Commonwealth responsibility for British Empire awards: telegram 17 April 1918, and Long's dispatch to Western Australia, 4 June 1918, ibid., 131, 145. Premiers conference criticism: *NSWPP*, 1918, I, 637–854. Naval correspondence: 21 July 1917, CP 78, series 21, bundle 50, file G.G. 1917/342; 4 October 1917, CRS A 461, item E334/1/2, part 1, file 1917/1999/4, AA. See also Munro Ferguson letters, 5 October 1917 and 18 February 1918, MS 696/964, NL, and CO 418/169/16834, 160–70. Objections to Hughes' corresponding directly with Lloyd George (*DNB* 1941–50): Long to Munro Ferguson, 15 February and 7 March 1917, Novar papers, MS 696/1397–415, NL. Hughes' complaint of lack of detailed reports: Munro Ferguson to Long, 14 August 1917, CO 418/158/40485, 519–20. Munro Ferguson reported irregular correspondence via Murdoch on 2 March 1917, Novar papers, MS 696/886, NL. For Murdoch see Fitzhardinge, *Hughes*, II, 74–5. Resolution of 1917 Imperial War Conference: [Cd. 8566], 5.

p. 145   Hughes' cable via Fiji, 6 May 1918, and Munro Ferguson's attempt to obtain details: CP 78, series 23, file 1918/1004, AA. See [Cd. 9177] for proceedings of 1918 Imperial War Conference. Munro Ferguson's fears of results of altered channel of communication, 21 July 1918, and dispatch of 25 July: Novar papers, MS 696/497 and 5197, NL. Correspondence with other governors-general: Novar papers, MS 696/5160, 5186 and 5197, NL. Borden: *DNB* 1931–40. Conference resolution: [Cd. 9177], 155–65. For British Commonwealth see S.R. Mehrota, 'On the use of the term "Commonwealth"', *Journal of Commonwealth Studies*, II (1963–64), 1–16. Lloyd George proposal of direct communication: Long to Munro Ferguson, 25 July 1918, Novar papers, MS 696/5294, NL.

p. 146   *The Times*, 14 September 1918, carried a public denial of dissatisfaction with CO. See [Cd. 9177], 156, for Hughes' reference to 'tortuous channel'. 'Crusted, procrastinating': *Herald* (Melbourne), 7 September 1918. 'The opinion that the

Colonial Office': Munro Ferguson to Long, 13 September 1918, and memorandum, Novar papers, MS 696/1080–2, NL. Hopes of increased functions: Munro Ferguson to Bonar Law, 3 October 1916, Novar papers, MS 696/829, NL. Munro Ferguson's letter to Long, 16 November 1918, lists the dispatches in which he had suggested acquiring responsibilities for the Pacific: Novar papers, MS 696/1095, NL. Dispatch of 28 October 1918, CO 886/7/61, 232, discussed new developments in Imperial affairs, federal affairs and Commonwealth administration. Game: *ADB*, vol. 8. Dismisses Lang: Evatt, op. cit., 157. Kerr dismisses Whitlam: P. Kelly, *The unmaking of Gough*.

p. 147   Distrust of trade with Japan: Munro Ferguson's dispatch, 1 May 1919, CO 418/176/35897, 258–66. 'Growing orientation': Munro Ferguson to Long, 5 June 1918, Novar papers, MS 696/1040, NL. Retrograde step: dispatch, 17 January 1917, Novar papers, MS 696/1774–6, NL. 'The formation of the League': Munro Ferguson to Milner, 22 March 1920, Novar papers, MS 696/1248, NL. Milner: *DNB* 1922–30. Hughes in Paris: Fitzhardinge, *Hughes*, II, 370–418. Suggested British commercial agents: dispatches, 1 May and 15 December 1919, CO 418/176/35897, 258–66, and 418/178/4997, 535–40.

p. 148   Secret service 'agents': Munro Ferguson to Milner, 16 June 1919, Novar papers, MS 696/1126–7, NL. Complaint about mandates: dispatch, 27 November 1919, CO 418/178/955, 447–50. Protest at U.S. fleet visit: dispatch, 30 July 1919, CO 418/177/44387, 65–9. Munro Ferguson approved tours by distinguished Britons on 29 May 1919, Novar papers, MS 696/1160, NL. Jellicoe: *DNB* 1931–40. 'Shrewd emissaries': *Australian Worker*, 15 April 1920. Imperial intentions of British government: letter from prince's private secretary to Munro Ferguson, Novar papers, MS 696/4891, NL. Prince of Wales tour: K. Fewster, 'Politics, pageantry and purpose', *Labour History*, no. 38, May 1980, 59–66. Trades Hall boycott, *SMH*, 19 March 1920. 'Nauseating drivel': *Australian Worker*, 3 June 1920.

p. 149   'Elimination as a constitutional factor': Munro Ferguson to Lord Liverpool, governor-general of New Zealand, 22 August 1918, Novar papers, MS 696/52333, NL. Long's response to wish to return, and report of Hughes' reaction: 26 August 1918, Novar papers, MS 696/1511, NL. Offer to Jellico: A.T. Patterson, *Jellicoe*, 212; also I. MacGibbon, 'The constitutional implications of Lord Jellicoe's influence on New Zealand naval policy 1919–1930', in *New Zealand Journal of History*, vol. 6, no. 1, (April 1972), 57–80. Avoidance of interregnum: Munro Ferguson to Long, 9 July 1920, Novar papers, MS 696/1289, NL. Oriel's verse is in *Argus*, 14 August 1920, reproduced in the *Presbyterian Messenger* (Melbourne), 20 August 1920. I am grateful to Mrs Mary Mohan and Mr R. Lucy for this reference. 'Good riddance': *Labor Call*, 26 August 1920. Later political career: Baldwin papers, vol. 35, 35–6, and vol. 79, 80, Cambridge University Library. Obituary: *The Times*, 31 March 1934.

p. 150   'Survival of the process': Amery to Munro Ferguson, 3 May 1920, Novar papers, MS 696/5258–60, NL.

p. 151   'Juvenile noblemen': see above, p. 4. For Barton's 1902 suggestion and CO minutes see Tennyson's cable, 26 October 1902, CO 418/19/44392, 361–2. Hughes' memorandum, 2 July 1919, and Lambert's minute: CO 418/185/42086, 198–204. Watt's cable, 29 January 1919: CRS A 1606, A21/1, 'Appointment of governor-general', AA.

p. 152   'Blowing off steam': CO 418/185/42086, 198. *Herald* (Melbourne) report was on 13 May 1920. Hughes' response is in Munro Ferguson's cable. 18 May 1920, CO 418/202/31221, 386. Milner's cabled reply, also 18 May 1920, is in Novar papers, MS 696/5040, NL. Hughes asked who Milner had in mind in Munro Ferguson's cable, received 24 May 1920, CO 418/202/31221, 385. Offer to

Baldwin: K. Middlemas and J. Barnes, *Baldwin: a biography*, 75. Milner's cable submitting the three names, 1 June 1920, is in Novar papers, MS 696/5045, NL. Appointment of Jellicoe: secret minutes of Imperial Conference, 12 July 1921, in Hughes papers, MS 1538, box 109, NL. Hughes and 1921 Conference: [Cmd. 1474], 17. Irish and South African dissatisfaction: D.W. Harkness, *The restless Dominion*, 24, and H. Duncan Hall, *Commonwealth: a history of the British Commonwealth of Nations*, 310.

p. 153   Seely and Donoughmore: *DNB* 1941–50. Forster: *ADB*, vol. 8. For a brief note of the cabinet meeting of 7 June 1920 which chose Forster see Hughes papers, MS 1538, box 155, folder 2, NL. 'A reference to his cricket': H.C. T[hornton] to W. Scott, 14 June 1920, CO 418/202/31221, 394.

p. 154   Copy of June 1920 correspondence over expense and special allowance: Forster to Churchill, 11 January 1922, CO 418/218/20927, 89–114. I am grateful to Lord Forster's daughter, Lady Wardington, for information about her mother and father's period in Australia. Met Munro Ferguson: Forster's dispatch, 20 October 1920, CO 418/190/57716, 676. Yachting: *Argus*, 20 February 1922, and Forster to Stonehaven, 19 May 1925, Stonehaven papers, MS 2127, series 3, NL. *Argus*, 14 January 1921 and 11 March 1922 reports tennis and polo attendance. Presence at rowing: *Daily Telegraph*, 3 May 1923. Stonehaven's letter to Harding, 4 November 1929, mentions compulsory race-going, Stonehaven papers, MS 2127, series 1, folder 6, NL.

p. 155   *Argus*, 3 November 1921, reported 'brilliant function' at Government House; *Bulletin* cartoon criticising the ball is 4 November 1921. Complaint of expense: Forster to Churchill, 25 September 1921, CO 418/219/7960, 384–91. Agricultural show: E. Page, *Truant surgeon*, 74–5. Chermside: *ADB*, vol. 7.

p. 156   Hopetoun's avoidance of church: Tennyson papers, MS 479/2, 33, NL. Barnardo's home: *SMH*, 12 April 1921. Lady Forster's G.B.E.: *Argus*, 1 January 1926. 'Incessant speechmaking': Forster to Stonehaven, 19 May 1925, Stonehaven papers, MS 2127, series 3, NL. Labor objection to incautious speech: *Argus*, 27 October 1923. Blakeley: *ADB*, vol. 7. Speech on courage: *Brisbane Courier*, 6 August 1921. 'Draw closer the interstate ties': *Argus*, 25 September 1920. Travelling: *Argus*, 7 October 1921. Papua visit: *Argus*, 28 August 1924.

p. 157   Acquisition Kirribilli House: CRS A461, item Y7/1/1, AA. The King's qualities: H. Nicolson, *King George the fifth*.

p. 158   Attempt to appoint Forrest governor: minute by J. Scaddan, premier, 17 August 1915, enclosure in dispatch of 31 August 1915, CO 418/139/45033, 535–40. Hughes' eagerness to be rid of Forrest and Long's promise to offer no objection: Long to Munro Ferguson, 23 January 1917, CO 418/166/4412, 207–9. McPherson: *DAB*, vol. 2. His statement about governors: *Argus*, 11 July 1919. Victoria requests postponed appointment: 9 October 1919, CO 418/19/ 57976, 569–70. Stradbroke: obituary, *SMH*, 22 December 1947. Theodore: *DAB*, vol. 2. Nomination of Lennon: Theodore to Milner, 9 July 1920, CO 418/202/31257, 411. Lennon: Melbourne *Punch*, 22 January 1920. Nathan: *DNB* 1931–40. His selection accepted: CO 418/202/31257, 416. Munro Ferguson's support of change: dispatch, 22 October 1919, CO 418/177/71435, 445–52. Views of Stanley: dispatch, 21 August 1917, CO 418/160/56818, 383–92. Weigall: *Who was who* 1951–60; his attitude: dispatch, 2 April 1921, CO 418/210/22867, 37–43.

p. 159   'Local man': minute by J.F.N. Green on a Tasmanian dispatch, 30 October 1922, CO 418/223/53909, 230–33. Weigall resignation: telegram 1 December 1921, CO 418/210/59880, 190–3. For Allardyce see *ADB*, vol. 7; his resignation: *Argus*, 25 January 1922. O'Grady: *Who was who* 1929–40. His appointment, use of new Government House: *Mercury*, 22 July and 23 December 1924. Newdegate's estimate: dispatch, 16 June 1921, CO 418/210/36260, 634–41. Davidson: *ADB*, vol. 8; his complaint: 21 January 1919, CO 418/179/23970, 17–27. The 1925 premiers memorial is reproduced in [Cmd. 2683], 4–7. Allan: *ADB*, vol. 7. Eggleston: *ADB*, vol. 8; his memorandum: [Cmd. 2683], 11–19.

p. 160 Petitions and letters: ibid., 20–39.

p. 161 Amery had separated Dominion from other colonial affairs, but retained both portfolios: Cross, op. cit., 46–9. Amery's reply, 3 March 1926, copy in [Cmd. 2683]. A.N.A. resolution: forwarded 1 June 1918, CO 418/175/39384, 119. Labor Party's motion: *Report of conference ... 1919*, 80–1. Forster's dispatch about premature resignations: 11 January 1922, CO 418/218/20927, 98–102. Hughes' anxiety that Forster stay, and Churchill's minute: ibid., 103–4. Forster's aloofness: J. Smith, *My life story*, 249. Commonwealth insistence that Forster restrict expenditure: Forster's letter 21 September 1921, CRS A1606, item SC A21/1, AA.

p. 162 Direct communication with League: Cabinet Office to CO, 12 January 1921, CO 418/216/1941, 13–5. Washington conference: *Victorian Parliamentary Papers 1922*, II, 1953–2024. Trade representative in the east: *CPD* 1923, vol. 105, 3048. Foreign Office cabled reports cease: CP 78, series 30, AA. Hughes' receipt of Foreign Office prints: D.C.S. Sissons, Attitudes to Japan and defence, MA, University of Melbourne, 1956. 'Wretchedly': Forster to Churchill, 25 September 1921, CO 418/219/7960, 384–91. Forster's complaint to Hughes, 18 October 1921, is quoted in P.M. Sales, 'W.M. Hughes and the Chanak crisis of 1922', *Australian Journal of Politics and History*, XVII, no. 3, December 1971, 392–405. Chanak crisis: D. Walder, *The Chanak affair*. Hughes' complaint of delay: dispatch 30 September 1922, CP 78, series 32, AA.

p. 163 Dominion dissatisfaction over Lausanne conference, Hall, op. cit., 498–505. Bruce: *ADB*, vol. 7. His dissatisfaction: *CPD* 1923, vol. 104. Casey appointment: R.G. Casey, *Friends and neighbours*, 29–31, and *My dear P.M.*, W.J. Hudson and J. North eds. 'Torrent of documents': J. Eayrs, *In defence of Canada*, 91–3. Jellicoe: MacGibbon, loc. cit. 'Secret service type': see above, p. 148. R. Hall, *The secret state*, 14, 15, 213, for Pitt-Rivers' M.I. 6 connections and his memorandum. 'Big constituency': Forster to Stonehaven, 19 May 1925, Stonehaven papers, MS 2127, series 3, NL. Forster's departure: *Advertiser* and *Register*, 7 October 1925 and *SMH*, 10 October 1925.

p. 164 Submission of names to cabinet: *Argus*, 20 May 1925. List of candidates: Amery to Baldwin, 23 February 1925, Baldwin papers, vol. 96, 29–30, Cambridge University Library.

p. 165 Seely's 'distress': ibid., 59. Cecil, Ronaldshay and Sutherland: *Who's who*, 1925. Stonehaven: *Argus*, 19 May 1925 (25 November 1926 for 'fox-hunting'); *The Times*, 21 August 1941, and *DAB*, vol. 1. Duff: *ADB*, vol. 8. Air crash: *Argus*, 17 February 1926. Town-naming proposal: Department of Air to Prime Ministers Department, 18 August 1943, CRS A461, C7/1/2, AA.

p. 167 Opinion of Bruce: Stonehaven to Lord Irwin, 10 May 1926, and Stonehaven to Forster, 11 December 1925, Stonehaven papers, MS 2127, series 1, folder 2, and folder 1, NL. In ibid., folder 5, can be found letter of 27 May 1929, to an unidentified recipient, about the Labor opposition. Balfour report:[Cmd. 2768], 14. Smuts: *DNB* 1941–50. His arguments: Hall, op. cit., 310. The Smuts paper is quoted in full in H. Borden (ed.), *Robert Laird Borden: his memoirs*, II, 900–1. Ireland's attitude: Harkness, op. cit., 107–8. Byng: *DNB* 1931–40. The King-Byng crisis is discussed in Keith, *Responsible government*, 146–52, Forsey, op. cit., 131–249, and Evatt, op. cit., 55–64. King's determination to separate functions: H.B. Neatby, *William Lyon Mackenzie King 1924–1932*, 130–75,

180–1.

p. 168   Amery convinced of change: see his letter to Munro Ferguson 3 May 1920, quoted above, p. 150. Resolutions of 1926 conference about governors-general's functions: [Cmd. 2768], 16. Bruce's intention to institute government to government communication: memorandum, 21 May 1927, and draft telegram to secretary of state, 17 December 1927, CRS A461, item G334/1/2, AA. Starling: Melbourne *Punch*, 8 November 1906, and *Canberra Times*, 7 April 1966. His papers are in AA. Stonehaven's letter to Passfield, 18 December 1929, from which I quote extracts, is in DO 121/42/2.

p. 170   Ceremonies at Canberra: *SMH*, 10 May 1927. Renovations to Government House: *SMH*, 31 March 1927. Stonehaven's belief that he should 'live on a different footing' and his complaint about expenditure: letter to Harding, 4 November 1929, Stonehaven papers, MS 2127/1/6, NL.

p. 171   Crutchley reported 'stupid' expenditure in letter to Harding, 3 February 1935, DO 121/44. Wine consumption and entertainment details: Stonehaven's notes for his successor, 17 October 1929, DO 35/66/D15300, 247–72. Early enthusiasm: letters 12 October 1925, 8 March 1926, Baldwin papers, vol. 96, 31–2 and 174–7, Cambridge University Library. 'Strain': Stonehaven to Harding, 4 November 1929, Stonehaven papers, MS 2127/1/6, NL. 'Decent little fellow': Stonehaven to Baldwin, 25 November 1929, Baldwin papers, Cambridge University Library. Dissolution (1929): Evatt, op. cit., 234–5; *CPD*, vol. 121, 873–4. *Labor Daily* interview: 26 October 1925.

p. 172   Latham: Z. Cowen, *Sir John Latham and other papers*. 'I do hope the sound men': Stonehaven to Latham, 5 October 1930, Latham papers, MS 1009/1/2969–70, NL. Somers: *DNB* 1941–50. Criticism: *Labor Daily*, 26 April 1930. 'Irritating, costly and useless': *Smith's Weekly*, 16 August 1930. Chairman of Conservative Party: Baldwin papers, vol. 46, Cambridge University Library.

p. 173   Dominions Office correspondence with Stonehaven and Stamfordham and the Davis memorandum of 1928: DO 121/42. Scullin's correspondence with Casey is in Scullin papers, MS 356, NL. Stamfordham: *DNB* 1931–40.

p. 174   Stonehaven's telegram of 28 March is in DO 121/42/27. R.R. Garran, *Prosper the Commonwealth*, 322, reports cabinet's consideration of Monash and Isaacs. Knox: *ADB*, vol. 9. Isaacs: Z. Cowen, *Isaac Isaacs*, on which I rely generally in this chapter.

p. 175   Stamfordham conveyed the King's 'astonished' response to Passfield on 29 March 1930, DO 121/42/30. For MacDonald (*DNB* 1931–40) telegram of 8 April 1930 see DO 121/42/35. Jowitt's memorandum: DO 35/396/11042/11. Correspondence between Scullin and MacDonald: DO 121/42, and also in Scullin papers, MS 356, NL, which also has Stonehaven's letters. See *CPD*, vol. 123, 704–6, for rumoured Australian appointment and *Maitland Mercury*, 23 April 1930 for report of Isaacs' name. Latham's outburst is in *Argus*, 25 April 1930. 'Preposterous': ibid.

p. 176   For press reaction see *SMH*, *Age*, 28 April 1930 and *Mail* (Adelaide), 26 April 1930. Hughes' comment is in *Argus*, 24 April 1930.

p. 177   Dormant Commission discussion: DO 35/407/11516/1, in particular memo by Harding, 7 July 1930. For my account of Scullin's negotiations in London I draw on three main sources: Nicolson, op. cit., 477–82, ('but upon the principle': 479); Scullin papers, MS 356, NL (this is file cited by L.F. Crisp in his important *HS* article, April 1964, vol. 11, no. 42, 253–7); and Cowen, *Isaacs*, 191–216. King 'very adverse to approval': note by Sir E. Harding of a conversation with MacDonald, 15 April 1930, DO 121/42/54.

p. 178   Disputes over governors's nomination to Legislative Council: Evatt, op. cit., 121–36; A.S. Morrison, 'Dominions Office correspondence on the NSW

Constitutional Crisis 1930–32', *JRAHS*, vol. 61, pt 5, March 1976, 323–46, and H. Radi and P. Spearritt (eds.) *Jack Lang*, 99–118, 160–78. Scullin's account of Stamfordham interview: Scullin papers, MS 356, NL.

p. 179   Imperial conference resolution: [Cmd. 3717], 27. Stamfordham's letter to Crewe, 17 November 1930, is in Crewe papers, Box 558, Cambridge University Library. Macmillan: *DNB* 1951–60. Casey's letter to Scullin, 21 November 1930, is in Scullin papers, MS 356, NL.

p.181   I quote Scullin's account of the final interview from ibid. For Stamfordham's account and the King's diary entry see Nicolson, op. cit., 480–2. Details of the announcement: Cowen, *Isaacs*, 202. Copies of the Mitchell and Fullager opinions of 31 January 1931 were sent to London by Professor Harrison Moore and are in DO 35/444/20110/13.

p. 182   'Imported poo-bahs': *Labor Call*, 4 December 1930.

p. 183   Swearing in: *Argus* and *Canberra Times*, 23 January 1931. Cancellation of lease of federal Government House: *Argus*, 18 and 30 December 1930. *Argus*, 4 May 1931, reported opening of Canberra football season. Goodwin's letter to Stonehaven of 17 February 1931: Stonehaven papers, MS 2127/1/552, NL. Goodwin: *ADB*, vol. 9 (he was addressed as 'Sir John'). Hore-Ruthven's letter, 16 February 1931, is in Stonehaven papers, MS 2127/1/547, NL. I am grateful to Sir Zelman Cowen for his information, from General Finlay, of Game's opinion of Isaacs.

p. 184   Correspondence on British High Commissioner in Australia: DO 117/66/D763. Stonehaven's opposition is referred to in minute of cabinet committee, 22 June 1927, DO 117/65/D6731. He urges change in letter to Thomas, 30 June 1930, Stonehaven papers, MS 2127/1, folder 7, NL. Further correspondence upon representation of British government: DO 35/124/4378. Crutchley's instructions: 16 June 1931, DO 114/124, 197. Scullin's lack of enthusiasm: telegram from Crutchley, 22 January 1931, DO 35/124/4378/4. For Crutchley see *Argus*, 23 May 1931. Whiskard: *Who was who* 1951–60. Crutchley referred to the vigilante organization in a letter to Batterbee, 19 December 1932, DO 35/392/10980/4. 'Good sheep station': Crutchley memorandum, March 1932, DO 35/124/4378/104.

p. 185   Isaacs relinquishes part of salary: *SMH*, 15 July 1931. Lease of 'Stonnington', *Argus*, 6 November 1931. Hogan: *ADB*, vol. 9. Bracegirdle: *ADB*, vol. 7. 'Guarded speaker' and speech to Millions Club: *Argus*, 28 May 1931. 'Ringing inspiring': *Canberra Times*, 3 January 1936. My summary of the Transport Workers Act regulations relies heavily on Cowen, *Isaacs*, 212–4. See also Evatt, op. cit., 187–9.

p.186   Sound constitutional practice: Cowen, *Isaacs*, 214. Scullin's dissolution: Evatt, op. cit., 236–7. Dominions Office comment: DO 114/41 194–8. Speculation about possible snub: Cowen, *Isaacs*, 216. Lyons: P.R. Hart, J.A. Lyons: a political biography, PhD, ANU, 1968.

p. 187   Bruce's suggestion of royal replacement for Isaacs is in note of conversation, 23 October 1933, with Harding, DO 35/464/20538/24. Harding: *DNB* 1951–60. DO 121/44 contains correspondence on appointment of a successor to Isaacs. Huntingfield: *ADB*, vol. 9. Crutchley's report, 17 July 1934, of friction over visit of Duke of Gloucester: DO 35/464/20538/99. Argyle: *ADB*, vol. 7. Cup presented to Peter Pan, *Argus*, 7 November 1934. Early announcement of Hore-Ruthven's appointment: *SMH*, 15 August 1935. For official announcement see *The Times*, 19 August 1935. Correspondence about the announcement is in DO 35/444/20110/2.

p. 188   Retirement and death: Cowen, *Isaacs*, 217–57.

p. 189   'Connecting link': *Table Talk*, 3 January 1901. 'Visible link': *Argus* editorial on 'Links of Empire': 8 February 1930.
p. 190   'Had a very real influence': see above, p. 151. Dominions Office minute, 1936: DO 35/444/20110A/9. 'Personal discretion': W. Harrison Moore, *The Commonwealth of Australia: four lectures on the Constitution Bill*, 89–90.
p. 192   'No one ever consults': Forster to Stonehaven, 26 October 1929, Stonehaven papers, MS 2127/1/5, NL.

Bibliography

This bibliography includes only material mentioned in the text or notes. Newspapers and parliamentary papers and debates and reference works such as *ADB*, *DNB* and *Who's who* are not listed as they are cited in the notes when they have been used.

1. *Colonial and Dominions Office records, Public Record Office, London*
    (a) records microfilmed by the Australian Joint Copying project which were consulted in the NL:
         CO 201/611 to 629. New South Wales, correspondence, 1890–1900
         CO 309/135 to 150. Victoria, correspondence, 1890–1900.
         CO 323/451 to 481. Colonies (General), correspondence, 1900–1902.
         CO 418/1 to 226. Australia (General), correspondence, 1899–1922.
         DO 35. Dominions, correspondence.
    (b) records consulted in Public Record Office, London:
         DO 121/42. Correspondence leading up to the appointment of Sir Isaac Isaacs.
         DO 121/44. Governor-generalship of the Commonwealth of Australia.
         DO 117/65–6. Representations in the Dominions of His Majesty's Government in Great Britain, 1927.
         CO 881/10/172. Confidential Print *Australian No. 172*. Federation of Australian Colonies: Governors' salaries: correspondence.
         CO 881/11/189. Confidential Print *Australian No. 189*. Constitution questions: correspondence.
         CO 881/14/217. Confidential Print *Australasia No. 217*. Letters from Sir Rider Haggard.
         CO 881/15/231. Confidential Print *Australian No. 231*. Australian Constitution Questions: further correspondence.
         CO 886/1/3. Confidential Print *Dominions No. 3*. Treatment of Asiatics in the Dominions: correspondence.
         CO 886/1/4. Confidential Print *Dominions No. 4*. Australia. Reservation of Bills of the Commonwealth Parliament; memorandum by Mr Keith 29 June 1908.
         DO 114/41. Confidential Print *Dominions No. 133*. Constitutional Relations of the Empire, 1932.

2. *Australian Archives*
    CP 78. Records of the Office of Governor-General, 1901–1927.
    CP 290, series 12. Prime Minister's Department, papers relating to the conduct of Executive Council Meetings, 1903–1926.
    CP 451, series 1. Executive Council Minute Book, 1901–1902.
    CRS A1. Department of External Affairs, correspondence.
    CRS A2. Prime Minister's Department, correspondence, 1904–1920.
    CRS A461. Prime Minister's Department, correspondence, 1934–1950.
    CRS A571. Department of the Treasury, correspondence, 1901–1930.
    CRS A1606. Prime Minister's Department, correspondence, secret and confidential series, 1926–1939.

MP 84, series 1. Department of Defence, general correspondence, 1906–1913.
MP 1049, series 1. Department of Navy, classified general correspondence, 1911–1921.

3. *Private papers*
Baldwin papers, Cambridge University Library.
Balfour papers, British Library, Add. Mss. 49697.
Barton papers, MS 51, NL.
Birdwood papers, Australian War Memorial, Canberra.
Campbell-Bannerman papers, British Library, Add. Mss. 41225.
Chamberlain papers, University of Birmingham Library.
Chandos papers, Churchill College Archives, Cambridge.
Crewe papers, Cambridge University Library.
Deakin papers, MS 1540, NL.
Denman papers, MS 769, NL.
Fisher papers, MS 2919, NL.
Forrest papers, microfilm G660, NL.
Griffith papers, Mss. 363, ML.
Harcourt papers, Bodleian Library, Oxford.
Hughes papers, MS 950 and 1538, NL.
Latham papers, MS 1009, NL.
Northcote papers, C.O., Gifts and Deposits, P.R.O. 30/56/1.
Novar papers, MS 696, NL.
Pearce papers, MS 213, NL, and microfilm 10027, Australian War Memorial.
Ripon papers, Add. Mss. 43518 and 43552, British Library.
Rosebery papers, National Library of Scotland.
Scullin papers, MS 356, NL.
Selborne papers, Bodleian Library, Oxford.
Shepherd memoirs, unpublished mss, A1632, AA.
Stonehaven papers, MS 2127, NL.
Tennyson papers, MS 479 and 1963, NL, and A5011, ML.

4. *Books, articles and theses*
Ashton, J. *Now came still evening on*. Sydney, 1941.
Atkinson, L. Australian defence policy: a study of Empire and nation 1897–1910. PhD thesis, ANU, 1964.
Bagehot, W. *The English Constitution*, R.H.S.Crossman (ed). London, 1964.
Bean, C.E.W. *The official history of Australia in the war of 1914–1918*, vol. 1, *The story of Anzac: the first phase*. Sydney, 1940.
[Blouet, P.] *John Bull & Co., the great colonial branches of the firm: Canada, Australia, New Zealand and South Africa*. London, 1899.
Borden, H.(ed) *Robert Laird Borden: his memoirs*. London, 1938.
Brassey, T. *Papers and addresses: Imperial federation and colonisation from 1880–1894*, A.H. Loring and R.J. Beadon (eds). London, 1895.
Brett, M.V. *Journals and letters of Reginald, Viscount Esher*, vol. 2. London, 1934.
Broadhead, H.S. The Australian Federal Labour Party 1900–1905. MA thesis, ANU, 1959.
Browne, G. A biographical register of the Victorian parliament. MA thesis, Monash University, 1982.
Cannon, M. *That damned democrat: John Norton, an Australian populist 1858–1916*. Melbourne, 1981.
Casey, R.G. *Friends and neighbours: Australia and the world*. Melbourne, 1954.
—— *My dear P.M.: R.G. Casey's letters to S.M. Bruce, 1924–1929*, W.J. Hudson and J. North (eds). Canberra, 1980.

Child, A.C. *Cranbrook: the first fifty years 1918–1968*. Sydney, 1968.

Clifford, Sir B. *Proconsul: being incidents in the life and career of the Honourable Sir Bede Clifford, G.C.M.G., C.B., M.V.O.* London, 1964.

Cockburn, Sir J. *Australian federation*. London, 1901.

[Cockerill, G.] *Scribblers and statesmen*. Melbourne, 1944.

Collis, E.H. *Lost years: a backward glance at Australian life and manners*. Sydney, 1948.

Coulthard-Clark, C.D. *The citizen general staff: the Australian Intelligence Corps, 1907–1914*. Canberra, 1976.

Cowen, Sir Z. *Isaac Isaacs*. Melbourne, 1967.

—— *Sir John Latham and other papers*. Melbourne, 1965.

Creighton, D. *John A. Macdonald: the young politician*. Toronto, 1952.

Crewe, Lord, *Lord Rosebery*. 2 vols. London, 1931.

Crisp, L.F. *Ben Chifley*. Melbourne, 1961.

—— 'The appointment of Sir Isaac Isaacs as governor-general of Australia, 1930: J.H. Scullin's account of the Buckingham Palace interviews', *HS*, 11, no. 42, April 1964, 253–7.

—— *The parliamentary government of the Commonwealth of Australia*. 3rd edition, London, 1961.

Cross, J.A. *Whitehall and the Commonwealth: British departmental organisation for Commonwealth relations 1900–1966*. London, 1967.

Cunneen, C. The role of governor-general in Australia, 1901–1927. PhD thesis ANU, 1973.

Deakin, A. *Federated Australia: selections from letters to the 'Morning Post' 1900–1910*. J.A. La Nauze (ed). Melbourne, 1968.

de Kiewiet, C.W. and Underhill, F.H. *Dufferin-Carnarvon correspondence 1874–1878*. Toronto, 1955.

Eayrs, J. *In defence of Canada: from the great war to the great Depression*. Toronto, 1964.

Evatt, H.V. *The King and his Dominion governors*. London, 1936.

Fewster, K. 'Politics pageantry and purpose', *Labour History*, no. 38, May 1980, 59–66.

Fingleton, J.H. *The immortal Victor Trumper*. Sydney, 1978.

Fitzhardinge, L.F. 'Australia, Japan and Great Britain, 1914–18: a study in triangular diplomacy', *HS*, 14, no. 54, April 1970, 250–9.

—— *William Morris Hughes: a political biography*. 2 vols. Sydney, 1964 and 1979.

—— 'W.M. Hughes at the Paris Peace Conference 1919', *Journal of Commonwealth Political Studies*, V, July 1967, 130–42.

Forsey, E.A. *The royal power of dissolution of parliament in the British Commonwealth*. Toronto, 1943.

Garran, R.R. *Prosper the Commonwealth*. Sydney, 1958.

Garson, N.G. *Louis Botha or John X. Merriman: the choice of South Africa's first prime minister*. London, 1969.

Glendevon, J. *The viceroy at bay: Lord Linlithgow in India, 1936–43*. London, 1971.

Gordon, D.C. *The Dominion partnership in Imperial defense, 1870–1914*. Baltimore, 1965.

Graham, N.I. The role of the governor of New South Wales under responsible government, 1861–1890. PhD thesis, Macquarie University, 1972.

Grimshaw, C. Some aspects of Australian attitudes to the Imperial connection, 1900–19. MA thesis, University of Queensland, 1957.

Hall, H. Duncan. *Commonwealth: a history of the British Commonwealth of Nations*. London, 1971.

Hall, R. *The secret state: Australia's spy industry*. Stanmore, 1978.

Hancock, I.R. 'The 1911 Imperial Conference', *HS*, vol. 12, no. 47, October 1966, 356–72.

Hannan, A.J. *The life of Chief Justice Way*. Sydney, 1960.

Harkness, D.W. *The restless Dominion: the Irish Free State and the British Commonwealth of nations, 1921–31*. London, 1969.

Hart, P.R. J.A. Lyons: a political biography. PhD thesis, ANU, 1968.

Hasluck, Lady A. *Audrey Tennyson's vice-regal days*. Canberra, 1978.

Heydon, P. *Quiet decision: a study of George Foster Pearce*. Melbourne, 1965.

Holman, A. *Memoirs of a premier's wife*. Sydney, 1947.

Hooper, M. 'The Naval Defence Agreement 1887', *Australian Journal of Politics and History*, XIV, no. 1, April 1968, 52–74.

Hoyle A.R. *King O'Malley: the American bounder*. Melbourne, 1981.

Hughes, W.M. *The splendid adventure: a review of Empire relations within and without the Commonwealth of Brittanic nations*. London, 1929.

—— *Policies and potentates*. Sydney, 1950.

Huxley, G. *Lady Denman G.B.E. 1884–1954*. London, 1961.

James, R.R. *Rosebery*. London, 1963.

Jauncey, L.C. *The story of conscription in Australia*. London, 1935.

Jose, A.W. *The official history of Australia in the war of 1914–1918*, vol. IX, *The Royal Australian Navy*. Sydney, 1941.

Keith, A.B. 'Recent changes in Canada's constitutional status', *Canadian Historical Review*, IX, no. 2, June 1928, 102–16.

—— *Responsible government in the Dominions*. Oxford, 1912, and revised edition, 1928.

—— *Imperial unity and the Dominions*. Oxford, 1916.

Keenan, J.J. *The inaugural celebrations of the Commonwealth of Australia*. Sydney, 1904.

Kelly, P. *The unmaking of Gough*. Sydney, 1976.

Kendle, J.E. *The Colonial and Imperial Conferences 1887–1911: a study in Imperial organization*. London, 1967.

La Nauze, J.A. *Alfred Deakin: a biography*. 2 vols. Melbourne, 1965.

—— 'Alfred Deakin and the 'Morning Post', *HS*, vol. 6, no. 24, May 1955, 361–75.

—— *The Hopetoun blunder: the appointment of the first prime minister of the Commonwealth of Australia December 1900*. Melbourne, 1957.

—— *The making of the Australian constitution*. Melbourne, 1972.

Leslie, A. *Edwardians in love*. London, 1972.

MacGibbon, I. 'The constitutional implications of Lord Jellicoe's influence on New Zealand naval policy 1919–1930', *New Zealand Journal of History*, vol. 6, no. 1, April 1972, 57–80.

McKinlay, B. *The first royal tour, 1867–68*. Adelaide, 1970.

Mackintosh, J.P. 'The role of the Committee of Imperial Defence before 1914', *English Historical Review*, LXXVII, July 1962, 490–503.

Madden, A.F. 'Changing attitudes and widening responsibilities 1895–1914', *Cambridge History of the British Empire*, III. Cambridge, 1959, 337–405.

Magnus, P. *King Edward the sixth*. London, 1964.

Martin, A.W. *Henry Parkes: a biography*. Melbourne, 1980.

Matthew, H.C.G. *The Liberal Imperialists: the ideas and politics of a post Gladstonian elite*. London, 1973.

Mehrota, S.R. 'On the use of the term "Commonwealth"', *Journal of Commonwealth Political Studies*, II, 1963–64, 1–16.

Middlemas, R.K. *The master builders*. London, 1963.

Middlemas, K. and Barnes, J. *Baldwin: a biography*. London, 1969.

Moore, W. Harrison. *The Commonwealth of Australia: four lectures on the Constitution*

Bill. Melbourne, 1897.

Mordecai, J. *The West Indies: the federal negotiations.* London, 1968.

Morrison, A.S. 'Dominions Office correspondence on the NSW constitutional crisis 1930–32', *JRAHS*, March 1976, 323–46.

Murdoch, J.R.M. Joseph Cook: a political biography. PhD thesis, University of New South Wales, 1969.

Nairn, N.B. 'A new look at an old master', *ANU Historical Journal*, no. 4, October 1967, 13–7.

Neatby, H.B. *William Lyon Mackenzie King: 1924–1932: the lonely heights.* Toronto, 1963.

Neuendorff, G. *Studies in the evolution of Dominion status: the governor-generalship of Canada, and the development of Canadian nationalism.* London, 1942.

Nicolson, Sir H. *King George the fifth: his life and reign.* London, 1952.

Nielsen, H.L. *The voice of the people or the history of the Kyabram reform movement.* Melbourne, 1902.

Norris, R. The emergent commonwealth. PhD thesis, ANU, 1970.

O'Connor, T.P. (ed) *In the days of my youth.* London, 1901.

'O'Rell, Max', see Blouet, Paul.

Page, Sir E. *Truant surgeon: the inside story of forty years of Australian political life.* Sydney, 1963.

Paterson, A.B. *Happy dispatches.* Sydney, 1934.

Paterson, A.T. *The Thirty Ninth: the history of the 39th Battalion Australian Imperial Force.* Melbourne, 1934.

Patterson, A.T. *Jellicoe: a biography.* London, 1969.

Phillips, G. *The Diehards.* Harvard, 1979.

Ponsonby, Sir F. *Recollections of three reigns.* London, 1951.

Poore, Lady I.M. *Recollections of an admiral's wife.* London, 1916.

Priestley, J.B. *The Edwardians.* London, 1970.

Quick, Sir J. *Legislative powers of the Commonwealth and States of Australia.* Melbourne, 1919.

Quick, Sir J. and Garran, Sir R.R. *The annotated constitution of the Australian Commonwealth.* Sydney, 1901.

Radi, H. and Spearritt, P. (eds) *Jack Lang.* Sydney, 1977.

Reid, Sir G.H. *My reminiscences.* London, 1917.

Reynolds, J. *Edmund Barton.* Sydney, 1948.

Richardson, J. *The pre-eminent Victorian.* London, 1962.

Ricks, C. (ed) *The poems of Lord Tennyson.* London, 1969.

Robertson, J. *J.H. Scullin: a political biography.* Perth, 1974.

Robson, L.L. *The First A.I.F.: a study of its recruitment 1914–1918.* Melbourne, 1970.

Sackville West, V. *The Edwardians.* London, 1930.

Sales, P.M. 'W.M. Hughes and the Chanak crisis of 1922', *Australian Journal of Politics and History*, XVII, no. 3, December 1971, 392–405.

Sawer, G. *Australian federal politics and law, 1901–1929.* Melbourne, 1956.

Scott, E. *The official history of Australia in the war of 1914–1918*, XI, *Australia during the war.* Sydney, 1943.

Serle, G. *John Monash: a biography.* Melbourne, 1982.

Serle, P. *Dictionary of Australian Biography.* 2 vols. Sydney, 1949.

Simpson, H. *Boomerang.* London, 1932.

Sissons, D.C.S. Attitudes to Japan and defence, 1900–1914. MA thesis, University of Melbourne, 1956.

Smith, F.B. *The conscription plebiscites in Australia 1916–17.* Melbourne, 1969.

Smith, Sir J. *My life story.* Sydney, 1927.

Spence, W.G. *Australia's awakening: thirty years in the life of an Australian agitator.* Sydney, 1909.

Swinfen, D.B. *Imperial control of colonial legislation 1813–1865: a study of British policy towards colonial legislative powers.* Oxford, 1970.

Sydenham, Lord *My working life.* London, 1927.

Templeton, J.M. *The consolidation of the British Empire, the growth of citizen soldiership and the establishment of the Australian Commonwealth.* Melbourne, 1901.

Tennant, K. *Evatt: politics and justice.* Sydney, 1972.

Tennyson, Hallam, Lord. *Jack and the Beanstalk: English hexameters.* London, 1886.

_____ *Tennyson: a memoir by his son.* London, 1887.

Tennyson, Lionel, Lord. *From verse to worse.* London, 1933.

Thompson, J.R. The Australian High Commission in London: its origins and early history 1901–1916. MA thesis, ANU, 1972.

Todd, A. *Parliamentary government in the British colonies.* 2nd edition, London, 1894.

Tuchman, B. *The proud tower: a portrait of the world before the war 1890–1914.* London, 1966.

Walder, D. *The Chanak affair.* London, 1969

Watson, J. *The Queen's wish. How it was fulfiled by the Imperial tour of T.R.H. the Duke and Duchess of Cornwall and York.* London, 1902.

Wise, B.R. *The making of the Australian Commonwealth 1889–1900: a stage in the growth of Empire.* London, 1913.

Wright, D.I. Commonwealth and States 1901–1910: a study of the executive and administrative relations of the seven governments of Australia in the first decade of the federal system. PhD thesis, ANU, 1968.

_____ *Shadow of dispute.* Canberra, 1970.

Index

Books of related interest from
George Allen & Unwin Australia

Inventing Australia: *Images and Identity 1688–1980*
Richard White

Argues that popular images of the 'typical Australian' grow out of
assumptions about nature, class, democracy and sex and are
'invented' to serve the interests of particular groups.

The Wasted Years? *Australia's Great Depression*
Edited by Judy Mackinolty

Twelve historians, economists, and political scientists trace the
impact of the Great Depression and re-examine the causes and
the panaceas.

Gallipoli Correspondent: *The Frontline Diary of*
C.E.W. Bean
Selected and annotated by Kevin Fewster

C.E.W. Bean landed at Anzac Cove on that fateful first morning, 25
April 1915, and stayed until the evacuation; his diary is the single
most graphic first-hand account of Gallipoli that we have.

What Rough Beast? *The State and Social Order in*
Australian History
Sydney Labour History Group

Frontier essays in the 'new social history', this collection examines
the roles of the state in Australia during various political contests
from the 1840s to the 1940s.

Australia: **The First Twelve Years**
Peter Taylor

So often quickly passed over by historians, these first years of
European occupation were full of drama, turbulence and
excitement.